"Do you want to make love to me?" she asked.

"I would love to make love to you," Vic replied, gently touching her cheek. "But I promise you, Daphne, you'll never have to do anything you don't want to do. We can just lie here and talk, or stare at the ceiling, and then I'll take you home."

The little girl inside her healed under his warm and loving words, the woman in her slowly returned to life. She smiled at him. "Then my car would be in the wrong place again."

He grinned. "I could take you home in my car."

"Then how would you get back?"

"Maybe you'd invite me to stay."

She leaned forward and brushed her lips across his. "Maybe we should just make love and I'll drive myself home."

"Well," he said with theatrical uncertainty, "if you really think that's best."

Muriel Jensen is acknowledged as the author of this work.

ISBN-13: 978-0-373-82557-8
ISBN-10:   0-373-82557-9

UNDERCOVER MOM

www.eHarlequin.com

Printed in U.S.A.

MURIEL JENSEN

Undercover Mom

**He was the hunter.
She was the prey.**

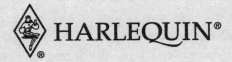

HARLEQUIN®

TORONTO • NEW YORK • LONDON
AMSTERDAM • PARIS • SYDNEY • HAMBURG
STOCKHOLM • ATHENS • TOKYO • MILAN • MADRID
PRAGUE • WARSAW • BUDAPEST • AUCKLAND

WELCOME TO A
HOMETOWN REUNION

Twelve books set in Tyler.
Twelve unique stories. Together they form a
colorful patchwork of triumphs and trials—
the fabric of America's favorite hometown.

Unexpected Son Marisa Carroll

The Reluctant Daddy Helen Conrad

Love and War Peg Sutherland

Hero in Disguise Vicki Lewis Thompson

Those Baby Blues Helen Conrad

Daddy Next Door Ginger Chambers

A Touch of Texas Kristine Rolofson

Fancy's Baby Pamela Bauer

Undercover Mom Muriel Jensen

Puppy Love Ginger Chambers

Hot Pursuit Muriel Jensen

Mission: Children Marisa Carroll

Around the quilting circle...

Annabelle Scanlon snapped off a length of white threat between her teeth with an efficiency born of long experience. "My son-in-law's new wife," she announced, "said that Yes! Yogurt wanted to use that pretty little blonde from the yogurt shop in an advertising campaign and she almost got hysterical. Ran out of the room."

"I think she and her little girl are hiding," Tessie said importantly.

Bea Ferguson inserted the needle to make a stitch, then left it there. Frowning, she asked, "From whom?"

"That, ladies—" Tessie paused for dramatic effect "—is the question."

"Daphne Sullivan's not hiding," said Martha Bauer from the opposite side of the quilt frame. "She's gone to Santa Barbara with that handsome beau of hers. My granddaughter, Britt, told me."

Tessie leaned forward. "And that's another thing. I don't think he is who he claims to be. He may have been a cop, but there's no way he's retired. You just have to look at those eyes of his."

PROLOGUE

VIC ESTEVEZ WATCHED in fascination as a uniformed maid served tea. He'd thought tea trolleys had gone out with the nineteenth century, but here was one in all its glory, complete with gilt-trimmed bone-china teapot and cups, and a plate of fancy breads. The trolley was wheeled in between his delicately carved rosewood chair and that of his hostess.

Celeste Huntington waited serenely, long slender fingers folded in her lap, the single gum-ball-size diamond winking on her left hand.

Silver-white hair clung to her head in a smooth, almost-masculine style. Her face was faintly lined, her aquamarine eyes sharp and cool and lightly enhanced with makeup. Her nose and chin were subtly pointed, and her very slender body, draped in a gray silk dress, was square-shouldered and rigid.

Vic supposed she might be considered attractive for a woman of sixty-plus. But where he came from, women of all ages tended to be full-figured and warm, bright with laughter and passion and come-hither glances. Celeste Huntington seemed almost genderless in comparison.

"Thank you, Carmella." She smiled perfunctorily at the pretty, dark-eyed maid.

"Carmella is probably one of your countrymen, Mr. Estevez," she said, when the pocket doors quietly closed, isolating them from the rest of the Palm Beach mansion. "She came here two years ago from Cuba. Old Havana. Her father was a pharmacist."

Vic shook his head as she poured tea. "My grandparents emigrated from Mexico."

She gave him an interested glance over the cup she handed him. "I apologize." She passed him a dainty linen napkin. "I just presumed because this is Florida—"

He interrupted her with a straight face, dismissing the need to explain. "It's all right," he said. "We all look alike."

She studied him uncertainly for one moment, then obviously decided he couldn't be mocking her. He guessed no one ever did.

"You come highly recommended by Cornelia Muggeridge," she commented.

Muggeridge? Right. The wayward husband in Beverly Hills. He nodded modestly. "Thank you."

"She said you were discreet, efficient and so thorough that Harv even gave her stock in Micro-Foods, which he'd put off-limits in their prenup."

Vic guessed that was probably thanks to the color print of the trapeze episode.

"That's why I'm also expensive," he said.

She shrugged in a way that suggested money had never been—would never be—a problem. "Of course."

"You were telling me about your daughter-in-law," Vic prompted.

"Yes." Her tone altered subtly, and Vic watched her become even stiffer, colder. She reminded him of a mobile icicle. She put her cup down on a small round table at her elbow and offered him the bread plate. "I knew she was trouble the day Trey brought her home, but they were already married and there was nothing I could do."

For an instant she warmed just enough to look injured, then frosted over again. "At first I thought his actions were simply what came of overindulgence and an Ivy League education." She picked up her cup again and sighed, her thin, stiff torso moving only slightly. "Then I began to see how unhappy he was and forced him to tell me what was going on."

She paused, took a sip of tea, then hesitated again after swallowing. "She was a prostitute, Mr. Estevez," she said finally, her chin angled as though that somehow held her above the unpleasant topic. "My son…went to her while on a spree in Vegas with some friends, and boasted about who he was. She saw her opportunity and threatened to reveal their…association to the press if he didn't marry her." She took another sip of tea. "You may or may not know that Huntington Industries dabbles in all kinds of things—oil, software, a few hotels. But Trey managed our Beach Boy Shops all along the West Coast, and several prominent film stars were doing endorsements for us. Sordid publicity at that point in time…" She left the sentence unfinished.

Vic got the point. "Trey lived in Los Angeles?"

"At our beach place in Malibu. I was wintering in Bel-Air. Unfortunately," she continued, "by the time I discovered all this, she was pregnant and, of course, Trey's and my first concern became the baby. When Jennifer was born, she was so beautiful." Her eyes softened and she was quiet for a moment. "Trey became determined to make the marriage work. I tried to talk him out of it, but I was only his mother."

She sounded more annoyed than aggrieved. "He

should have listened to me. Now he's gone, and so is my Jennifer.''

Vic sipped at his tea, tasted flowers and cinnamon and barely suppressed a sound of disgust. He set the cup aside. ''Are you suggesting your daughter-in-law had something to do with Trey's death?''

Celeste made a subtle movement with one shoulder. He couldn't decide what it meant.

''Only indirectly,'' she clarified. ''He was killed in an automobile accident on a rural road in southern California. Considering he'd competed in Monte Carlo in a Ferrari three years in a row, my guess is things were deteriorating between them again and he was distracted.''

''I understand your grief and your...disappointment,'' Vic said diplomatically, ''But it isn't illegal for a man to marry a prostitute. And it isn't illegal for a woman to take off with her own child.''

''Certainly her blackmailing him into marriage is illegal.''

''Possibly,'' he admitted. ''If you have proof.''

She took a white envelope from the table beside her. ''This contains the canceled check he wrote her for $200,000. Trey said that was the first demand she made of him. After he paid it and she saw how easy it was, I think she simply decided to go for a permanent attachment to the source.''

Vic put his cup aside, removed the check from the envelope and studied the six-digit figure. Then he turned the check over. It was endorsed in a delicate, even hand: ''Diane D. Majors.'' He slipped the check back in the envelope.

He had an uneasy feeling about this. There wasn't really anything here to warrant his involvement except a group of rich and selfish people using each other to advance their own agenda. And he made a point of never taking on hate or vengeance cases. They tended to become explosive, while stranding the investigator at ground zero.

"Mrs. Huntington," he said finally, "I don't think there's anything I can do for you. It would be very hard to prove guilt on her part, particularly with your son gone."

She turned to the small table at her elbow and picked up a double, oval-shaped, silver picture frame. She handed it to him. "Much as I would like to build a criminal case against Diane, that isn't the real reason I want you to find her. I want Jennifer back."

The portrait of a little girl about a year old grinned at him. Baby-fine blond curls framed cherubic cheeks and blue eyes the same shade as her grandmother's. But the child's seemed to be lit from inside.

The other half of the frame held a photo of an exceptionally beautiful young woman with short dark hair, expressive, pale blue eyes and a sweetly seductive smile.

"Is this Diane?" he asked.

"Yes," Celeste Huntington replied coolly. "A beautiful girl. Certainly well equipped for her chosen field."

It didn't look like the face of a grasping manipulator. The curve of cheek and chin was gentle, youthful, even innocent. But Vic had worked the dark side long enough to know that beauty was a coin many women used to get everything from fifty bucks for a night to a man's very soul. He handed the photos back.

His hostess replaced the frame, then let her eyes wander over the opulent room with its antique appointments, the Chagall and the Matisse, the crystal chandelier, and the rock on her ring finger that would probably feed Miami's homeless for a year. Then she looked into his eyes. For the briefest moment he thought he saw genuine feeling there.

"I'm sure you probably took one look around you when you arrived today," Celeste said, "and thought to yourself, what could she possibly want that she doesn't have?" She swept a hand toward the photos. "*That's* all I want. I want my granddaughter back. She was just a year old when my son was killed. And I had it from Trey's friends that Diane took up her old profession again from the comfort of our Malibu home. So I filed for custody. That's when Diane ran away with her."

Vic didn't want to take this case. It was trouble; he was sure of it.

But he'd left the DEA because he'd been worn-out and demoralized by large and ugly problems he couldn't fix. And by how close he'd come to blowing away Federico Santos and solving *that* problem himself.

Vic hadn't done it, but he'd come close enough to realize that next time he might not think twice.

So he'd gone into private detection with the thought that he could simply collect data for other people and let them do their own fixing.

He'd learned in the past five years that that had been a naive concept. Sometimes what he discovered destroyed things—relationships, marriages. But sometimes, because of his work, families were reunited, fortunes were bestowed, truths were revealed that allowed people to go on with their lives.

And in this case, a little girl could be saved from the clutches of a grasping, promiscuous mother and restored to a life of wealth and comfort.

He looked up at Celeste Huntington and tried to imagine her cuddling a child. He couldn't.

But the alternative, considering Jennifer's mother's life-style, was worse.

He didn't want to do it. But it was hard to turn away from the needs of the baby.

"All right, Mrs. Huntington," he said. "I'll find your granddaughter."

The icicle didn't crack, but there was that subtle movement of her torso. "Thank you, Mr. Estevez," she said.

CHAPTER ONE

TYLER, WISCONSIN, population ten thousand, was the last place Vic had expected to find Diane Huntington. As he sat under a maple tree in the park and observed the Labor Day revelers, he concluded that the town lacked an adequate consumer base for a successful call-girl operation. The women looked wholesome and the men happy. The children were loud and plentiful.

Still, the only long-distance call made from the telephone at Diane Huntington's last known address, in Manchester, New Hampshire, had led him here. It had been placed several weeks before she'd run from there, and it had been of only a minute's duration.

Either she'd reached an answering machine or she'd changed her mind about talking. But it was the only long-distance call she'd placed in three months' time. Finding the identity of the owner of the number had been an easy matter with a reverse directory.

She was here somewhere. And so was Diane Huntington.

Vic looked around and couldn't help smiling. It was all so Rockwellian.

Beyond a welcoming banner that announced Tyler's End-of-Summer Celebration, colorful booths lined both sides of a trail that meandered through the acres of green. They offered food, crafts, games of chance, palm readings and the opportunity to learn more about insurance, recycling, astrology, cemetery plots, the benefits of vegetarianism and a home water-purification system.

Beyond the booths was a bright patchwork of blankets, where families and friends had gathered into groups to picnic. Close by was a well-equipped playground where children shoved and screamed and hung upside down from monkey bars.

Across the park some older boys were tossing a football, and a group of teenage girls supervised the play of rambunctious toddlers. A sign leaning against a park bench advertised Junior Girls Baby-sitting.

In the middle of the park a quintet of musicians sporting suspenders and straw hats stood in a white, flower-bedecked bandstand and oom-pah-pahed through a considerable repertoire of polkas. Everyone seemed to be enjoying Labor Day.

Vic eyed one of the majestic maple trees that dotted the park, noting how its enormous leaves stirred in the late-afternoon breeze, how its limbs reached up into the clear blue sky. When it changed color in a few more weeks, the sight would be truly breathtaking.

Not that he'd ever longed for life in a small town. He was a big-city kid, born and bred in Los Angeles, until his family had moved to Santa Barbara when he was fifteen. He was used to concrete, traffic noise, crowds and the curious ambivalence of solitude coupled with a sense of belonging that metropolitan living inspired.

But he could like it here, he thought. At least for a while. Amid the shouts of children, the calls of friends, the barks of dogs and the lively tuba was a serenity he hadn't felt in a long, long time.

Before he could get too comfortable with it, he rose to his feet, dusted off the seat of his slacks and wandered down the trail. In a moment, he was part of the crowd of shoppers that stretched from one end of the lineup of booths to the other.

Diane Huntington was here somewhere. He knew it. He could feel it. He had naturally good instincts, and a career spent matching wits with insidiously clever criminals had honed them to an art form.

Hands in his pockets, he moved unhurriedly, stopping casually to inspect one booth, then another, turning slowly to peruse each face that passed him while doing his best to look friendly and nonthreatening.

In this town, settled and populated by fair-haired, blue-eyed German and Scandinavian families and freckle-faced Irish, his Latino appearance precluded anonymity. So he opted for cheerful interest instead. He returned curious second glances with a polite greeting, and usually earned a smile in return. And all the while, he studied female faces.

This wasn't the kind of town where you could flash a photograph and hope someone recognized it. It was too small; people were too close. Someone would recognize her, and she'd be gone before he could get to her.

So he had to do it the hard way—if looking women over could ever be thought of as "the hard way."

"Vic! Hey, Vic!"

The sound of his name in this crowd of strangers brought him to a stop. Then he saw a tall, scrawny teenage boy loping toward him along the trail and recognized him as the boy he'd picked up on the road to Tyler yesterday. The boy's car had blown a tire and Vic had driven him to the family farm.

"Hi, Matt!" Vic's hand was taken in a strong grip, and a bright, open smile beamed up at him. The boy held a football in the crook of his other arm. "God, I'm glad to see you. I need a cop. I know you said you're retired and all, but you gotta help me! I'm being followed!"

Vic looked beyond him, scanning the park, instantly alert, his reflexes humming.

"Girls," Matt replied without turning around. "Are they still there?"

Vic relaxed and chided himself for almost reacting with the very qualities he was trying to hide. He spotted two young girls about ten yards away whose whispers, giggles and glances marked them as Matt's predators.

"A tall one with yards of red hair and a little blonde in a black felt hat with a big flower?"

Matt groaned mournfully.

Vic put a hand on his shoulder. "You know, most guys consider being followed by girls a *good* thing."

Matt rolled his eyes. "Those are my sister's friends. Kate's supposed to have a crush on me, but she won't talk to me. All she does is follow me and report back to Christy that she thinks I'm awesome. It's creepy. Isn't the government supposed to be working on stalking laws to prevent this kind of thing? Are they *still* there?"

Vic looked up to find that they'd moved into the trees behind the booths. "I think they're circling us," he said, turning Matt around and falling into step beside him. "Which one's Kate?"

"The redhead."

Vic smiled. In another year, he guessed, judging by the length of her legs and the color of her hair, Matt would be pleading for Kate's attentions.

"Let's get something cold and we'll discuss strategy. You recommend any of these booths?"

"Sure. My mom's."

Vic had met Matt's parents yesterday when he'd taken him home, and remembered that they ran an ice-cream shop or something.

The boy led him to a red-and-white-striped awning under which about a dozen people stood three abreast, awaiting their turn at the counter. A hand-painted sign on the counter boasted that they'd won a blue ribbon at a national dairy-products competition that summer.

Six-inch-tall red letters behind the young woman working a lineup of frozen yogurt machines read Yes! Yogurt.

"My mom was on 'Oprah,'" Matt said as they took their place in line.

"No kidding."

"Yeah. A couple of years ago. She's pretty big stuff now. And we just won first place in the national yogurt taste-off."

Vic reached for his wallet, but Matt shook his head. "We don't have to pay. I'm family and you're my guest. But we do have to stand in line. Mom gets really upset if we try to get in front of a paying customer."

Vic nodded. "Good business sense. Have you tried turning around and approaching Kate?"

Matt looked horrified. "No. She might talk to me."

"Well, that's the point." The line moved forward and they followed. "Maybe if you make yourself less of a mystery, she'll leave you alone."

Matt gave him a pitying look. "It's been a long time since you were a teenager, hasn't it?"

Totally rebuffed, Vic followed the woman in front of him as she took her place at the counter.

"Girls never leave you alone," Matt explained. "Except the ones you *wish* would notice you, and it's like they're blind when you're around. But Christy's friends are like they're made of Velcro. And they're so young, it's embarrassing! All the guys are on me about it.''

Vic looked up and saw that the two girls had positioned themselves behind the *Tyler Citizen* booth next to the frozen-yogurt stand.

''How old are they?''

''Kate's not quite fifteen.''

''How old are you?''

''Almost seventeen,'' Matt replied with a superior air. ''I know at your age a year doesn't sound like much, but I'm a senior this year, and she's just a sophomore. I'm almost a man, and she's still a kid.''

And I, Vic thought, *am beginning to feel like Methuselah.*

The woman in front of him moved away, carrying a tall column of pink frozen yogurt teetering on a sugar cone, and Matt stepped up to the counter.

''Hi, Daph,'' he said to the young woman drying her hands on an apron printed with the words Just Say Yes! to Yogurt. ''Can you set 'em up for me and my friend Vic, here?''

The woman looked up, a polite smile in place, and it took all of Vic's control not to react. It was her. Diane Huntington. Maybe.

Her hair was blond and caught on top of her head in a casual knot, but that was reasonable. He'd expected she would have changed the color of her hair. And in the time since the photo had been taken, it had grown considerably.

The pale blue eyes were the same as those in the photograph—and probably like those of thirty or forty percent of the women in town.

The shape of her face was similar, although the angle

of cheekbones and jaw seemed more prominent. Also reasonable. Being on the run had to be hard on the body. Although that did look good—at least what he could see above the counter and under the apron top.

She was tall—five ten, according to Celeste's description. Her bosom was a little fuller than was typical of an athletic build, but her waist was small, her arms long and slender, her wrists fragile. Everything else he could only guess about.

He formed a mental ledger and named the file Diane Huntington—Is or Isn't.

She did look like the kind of woman who could build a fortune on a man's loneliness. That was a stroke on the Is side.

Although, judging by the look she was giving him now, she might have changed her mind about men. Or maybe it was just him in particular she didn't like.

"Your friend, huh?" Her terse question was fraught with suspicion.

Then he realized how his appearance with Matt might look to her. There had to be men who were bad news to kids, even in Tyler. And although Vic had worn his UC Santa Barbara sweatshirt and his most benign expression, he still had the look of an underworld kingpin. He couldn't help it. His friends maintained that he'd brought down the Rumorosa Cartel because he looked like a drug lord himself.

He extended his hand. "Vic Estevez," he said. "Retired cop. I came to Tyler to check out real estate and ran into Matt on the highway." He smiled. "Not literally, of course."

"I'd blown a tire," Matt said, and took the story from there of how Vic had driven him home and met his family. Vic was grateful. Although the woman had shaken his hand, he couldn't get her to crack a smile. And that was what would assure him that she was Diane Huntington. The smile. The sweetly seductive smile.

"Matt, you pea-brain barf bag!"

The gravelly voiced verbal assault was followed by the arrival of three boys about Matt's age in what appeared to be a uniform of long, baggy shorts and Tyler High T-shirts. One of the boys was tall and wore round, wire-rimmed glasses. Another was built like Mike Tyson, and the third was Matt's size but sported a blue Mohawk and an eagle tattoo on his right biceps. He snatched the football from Matt's arm, then turned to smile at the woman behind the counter.

"Hi, Daph," he said politely.

"Hi, Deke," she replied with a fractional smile.

It wasn't big enough for Vic to tell.

Deke turned back to Matt and punched him in the shoulder. "I know you're only the quarterback," he said with a theatrical show of patience, "but when we send you to chase after the ball, you don't run away with it, because it's the only ball we got. You can't stop for yogurt like some southern California culture clown. You gotta—"

Matt cleared his throat and indicated the large UC Santa Barbara emblem on the chest of Vic's blue-and-gold sweatshirt. Vic played the role and looked severe.

Deke looked at the shirt, then at up at Vic in awe. "You're on the soap 'Santa Barbara'? We got reruns of that on the nostal—"

Matt put a hand over his eyes. The other two boys groaned.

"UC Santa Barbara," the woman behind the counter said, "is a university in California, Deke. This gentleman is one of your 'culture clowns.'" She repeated

Deke's words with the same denigrating tone he'd used. "Maybe you should tell him you didn't mean to make snide remarks about him or Matt's mom's frozen yogurt."

Deke snorted a rapid series of embarrassed laughs and offered Vic his hand. "Course I didn't. How are ya? D.K. Bullard."

Vic shook it.

"He's a retired cop," Matt said. "Thinking of moving to Tyler." Then to Vic, he added, "Deke's dad is a realtor. Maybe he could show you around."

Vic nodded. "Good idea. Where do I find him?"

Deke pointed to the gazebo. "He's the tuba player. They're gonna break at four."

"Good. Thanks."

Deke and his friends dragged Matt away. "See you around, Vic!" Matt shouted.

Vic watched them shove each other across the grass and wondered with a private smile what it was like for a man who sold real estate and played polkas on the tuba to have a son with a blue Mohawk.

"Mighty Mocha, Very Vanilla or swirl?" the young woman asked. "Sassy Strawberry, Chunky Chocolate or swirl? Pretty Peach, White Almond Chocolate or swirl?"

Vic looked into the pale blue eyes that were assessing him without revealing anything, and chose to ignore the question. "Daph's short for Daphne?"

She looked surprised by the question, then suspicious of it.

Vic made a stroke on the positive side of his mental ledger. Then he erased it. No point in being too eager. She probably just suspected him of coming on to her.

She held up a sugar cone and repeated, "Mighty Mocha, Very Vanilla or swirl? Sassy—"

"White Almond Chocolate and Mighty Mocha swirl," he replied.

She lowered the cone. "Can't do that," she said. "Different machines."

He had to make her smile. He couldn't tell unless she smiled. "But that's what I want. Daffodil?"

She closed her eyes for a moment, as though summoning patience. "Can't. Sorry."

He shifted his weight and leaned a hip against the counter. The booth was momentarily devoid of customers. "Can't you put the cone under the chocolate part of one machine, then under the mocha part of the other?"

She sighed. "I guess I could. But then it's a stack, not a swirl."

"You could stir it with a spoon."

"It's not in my job description."

He shook his head. "I'd report you to your employer, but I don't know your name. Daph for…Daffy Duck?"

The muscles in her jaw tightened. She was trying not to smile.

"*Daph*initely not," she said, and turned to the machine that held the chocolate.

I DON'T LIKE HIS LOOKS, Daphne thought as she pressed on the chocolate spigot and partially filled the cone with the creamy frozen yogurt.

Even with her back to him she could still see his features—black eyes slightly slanted over the prominent angular cheekbones. A strong nose. The suggestion of softness in a full, smiling mouth negated by the sharp angle of jaw and chin.

And then there was the glossy black hair waving subtly from a precise side part.

A little shudder ran through her. He was dangerous. She'd learned to recognize danger in a man when she was fifteen, and the instinct had only heightened with age and experience.

The one time she'd been wrong about it had been when she'd fallen in love with Trey—and that had been because the danger was from his mother, not him.

The mocha was swirled perilously high atop the chocolate when the voice behind her said politely but urgently, "Ah, that'll do it. That's enough. Dafoe? You can stop now. DeForest?"

She turned with a wince and handed him his cone. It was a shame that danger was so gorgeous. "DeForest?" she asked.

"DeForest Kelley," he said, accepting the cone and passing her a bill. "The doctor on 'Star Trek.' Thank you."

She gave him a quarter change. "That's really reaching." Then, as though she had absolutely nothing to hide, she said politely but without a smile, "Daphne Sullivan. Welcome to Tyler."

"Thank you." He smiled in surprise at her capitulation.

Tyler had made her soft, she thought. Exhausted, desperate, she'd needed a place to hide, and although she hadn't forgotten what had brought her here, she'd slipped into the warm, relaxed atmosphere and found home.

Sometimes she flirted with the possibility of staying here forever. But every once in a while, a memory of the other life invaded and brought her back to reality.

Vic Estevez was just such a memory. He was an ex-cop, Matt had said. She looked into his eyes, trying to decide if the ex part was true. She'd dealt with a few cops early in the other life. She recognized that quick, once-over look, followed by the assessment and either arrest or dismissal.

Only this one seemed to be continuing his assessment and hadn't yet dismissed her.

Was that the look of a cop on her trail, she wondered, or the simple interest of a man trying to make time with a woman?

Tyler had made her soft, but it had also made her paranoid.

"Where were you a cop?" she asked conversationally.

"Palm Beach," he said.

The single word churned everything inside her. In the other life, she'd worked on Hollywood Boulevard, then in Las Vegas. But Trey's family was from Palm Beach. His mother lived there. His mother wanted Jenny.

Under the guise of smiling interest, Vic watched her for a reaction. Although he'd never worked as a cop in Palm Beach, he thought it might betray her into revealing something. But she concentrated on wiping off the counter and avoiding his eyes.

When she looked up at him again, he thought he saw a glimpse of fear under the facade of control. He felt a trace of professional excitement and a curious sensation of guilt. He was momentarily surprised by it.

She opened her mouth to say something, but was halted by the sudden, piercing shriek of a child.

Daphne hurried behind the frozen-yogurt machines to the playpen she'd set up for Jenny to nap in. Her daughter sat there screaming, blankets thrown aside, plump face purple with rage.

"I'm right here, baby," Daphne crooned, lifting the toddler to her shoulder. The little face, flushed with sleep, burrowed into her neck.

"Mommy!" Jennifer said in an accusing tone. "Gone!"

Jennifer was never afraid of anything, only angry when things didn't go as she expected. Daphne ducked her head around the yogurt machine to check for customers. There were none, but Vic Estevez remained there, peering in her direction.

"Everything okay?" he asked with a frown.

"Everything's fine," she replied in a clipped tone. She'd hoped he was gone. Then, feeling guilty that she'd barked at him when he hadn't done anything but look handsome and out of place here, she lowered her voice and pointed toward the gazebo. "The band's stopped. Mr. Bullard will be free."

Vic looked uncertainly in that direction. "You think he'll want to talk business on a holiday?"

Her mouth quirked wryly. It didn't qualify as a smile. "One day he'll probably talk Saint Peter into walking through a listing. Good luck, Mr. Estevez."

"Thank you, Mrs. Sullivan."

There was that wry quirk again. "Call me DeForest."

Daphne watched him walk away with a sense of relief. The man represented danger in more ways than one. Even if she was paranoid and he wasn't looking for her, he had the kind of eyes that reached inside a woman and made her want to know what mysteries lay beyond them. She'd seen women destroyed by that kind of attraction. Her own mother had been a helpless victim of it.

The man invariably turned out to be on some self-indulgent quest for personal profit or satisfaction, and she would be out of the picture when his search was over. High and dry. Lost and lonely.

Daphne settled Jenny in the playpen with a cup of milk, a cookie and half the toys she owned, and considered herself lucky that she didn't want or need another man. The brief time with Trey had been a glimpse of what life could be like, but that was over. This was her reality—alone and on the run with a two-year-old.

Leaving Jenny munching greedily on her cookie, Daphne went to the counter as a group of giggling teenage girls approached.

VIC WAS CAREFUL NOT TO look back as he headed for the gazebo, where the musicians were putting their instruments aside, taking off their straw hats.

He thought he'd hit pay dirt. Daphne Sullivan had a two-year-old girl—another stroke on the positive side of the ledger. Of course, there were a lot of little girls in this park with angelic faces and corn-silk hair, but clues were stacking up.

Still, the woman was a little skittish. He was going to have to do this carefully. That meant it would take time, and he had to have a good reason for hanging around. So he waited at the bottom of the gazebo's few steps for the tall, barrel-bellied man whom he'd seen playing the tuba.

CHAPTER TWO

"THERE'S A MAN for you." Britt Marshack elbowed Daphne. They sat side by side under a maple tree, backs leaning against its rough trunk. Before them on the blanket, Daphne's daughter played with Britt's two-year-old Jacob. Britt was Daphne's employer and friend.

Daphne looked over the children in the direction Britt indicated. To her chagrin, she saw Paul Bullard and Vic Estevez wandering slowly down the lane in earnest conversation.

Daphne closed her eyes and pretended she'd misunderstood. "Paul Bullard has a wife and three children. And fond as we all are of Deke, we know he must be the product of a mutation experiment."

She heard Britt's patient sigh. "The *other* one. Will you open your eyes and look? That's Vic Estevez. He's moving to Tyler. Used to be a cop. He picked up Matt yesterday when he had a blowout on the highway. We invited him in for coffee. Jake liked him."

"I know who he is." Daphne tipped her face up to catch the beam of sun shafting through a bare spot in the canopy of leaves. "Matt brought him by the booth."

"Oh." She felt Britt turn to her in interest. Daphne kept her eyes closed. "Did you talk to him?" her boss asked.

"Yes."

Britt waited for a moment. When Daphne didn't elaborate, she demanded, ''Well, what did you say? What did he say?''

''I said, Mighty Mocha, Very Vanilla or swirl? Sassy Straw—''

Britt elbowed her again. ''What did *he* say?''

Daphne answered without opening her eyes. ''He said Chunky Chocolate and Mighty Mocha swirl, but I said we couldn't do—''

''Did you,'' Britt interrupted, ''exchange words of any significance? And before you answer, bear in mind that I control your cost-of-living raise and your nighttime baby-sitter.''

Daphne opened her eyes and turned her head so that she looked into her friend's pale blue gaze. It was that look of authority, she guessed, that controlled four older children and the rambunctious Jacob.

''Don't threaten *me*, or I'll tell Christy you've been wearing her tights to our aerobics class.''

Britt made a face. ''She already knows. She complained about the baggy seat and I was forced to confess and buy her a new pair. So, what about Vic Estevez? Didn't you talk about anything but frozen yogurt?''

Daphne rolled her eyes. ''We were in a *frozen-yogurt* booth. I work for you selling *yogurt*. Did you want me to make time on company time?''

Britt shook her head slowly, pitifully. She was the picture of Tyler wholesomeness, Daphne thought, with her curly strawberry-blond hair, and her peaches-and-cream complexion. She wondered privately what Britt would think of her if she knew about her other life. Daphne didn't even want to speculate. The friendship they'd developed over the last eight months was something she treasured.

"He told us when he brought Matt home that he was coming to Tyler to start over," Britt said. "He's obviously looking for new people in his life."

"Well, I have just the right number of people in my life right now. If I invite in any new ones, the ecological balance will be upset."

Britt settled back beside her. "You do remind me of a healthy heap of compost. I'm going to invite the two of you to dinner."

"Me and my compost?"

"You," Britt said severely, "and Vic Estevez."

"Fine. Just do it on different nights."

"Invite who for dinner? When? Where? Am I invited?"

Daphne opened her eyes at the sound of her landlady's voice. "Hi, Judy," she said, sitting up to pat the area of blanket between her and Britt and the toddlers. "Park it right here. You're a single woman. Will you please talk sense into this love-struck lunatic?"

Britt shook her finger at the tall honey blonde in jeans and a dark blue T-shirt. "Judy Lowery, if you start your male-bashing rhetoric in her defense, I won't buy your book when it comes out. And I'll tell my friends not to buy your book—I don't care how you plead and carry on."

Judy patted both babies' heads and sat, Indian-style, facing Daphne and Britt. "I do *not* male bash," she corrected. "I just happen to know a lot of stories that prove men are not only unnecessary to a woman's life, but detrimental." She shrugged eloquently. "So, prove me wrong and I'll shut up."

"I have two words for you—" Britt began.

Judy put a hand up to cut her off midsentence. "And I know what they are: *Jake Marshack.* Well, might I remind you that there was a time when you wouldn't have him on a bet?''

Britt stiffened and folded her arms. ''That was before I let him into my life,'' she said, ''and before he invited me into his. See, the thing is, neither of you will let a man into *your* lives. You don't want to know that a man could make you happy.''

''Jenny,'' Daphne said firmly, ''makes me happy.''

Britt placed an arm around her as though she were a simple child who needed befriending. ''Daph. Listen to me. Mother love is wonderful and rewarding, but it doesn't replace romantic love.''

Daphne opened her mouth to speak, but Britt stopped her with a shake of her head. ''I know, I know. I was widowed once, too, and I thought my love life was over, that my children would be my life and I was no longer a sexual being.''

''Ooh, sex.'' Judy scooted closer. ''At last this is getting interesting. Men are useful in that regard—I just don't think we need to corrupt an entire life with them.'' She looked from one woman to the other. ''What prompted this discussion, anyway?''

Britt pointed to the realtor and the ex-cop, now wandering across the grass toward the duck pond.

Judy's eyes narrowed. ''Yeah. I spotted him from the Friends of the Library booth. Who is he?''

''Paul Bullard,'' Daphne replied.

''The *other* one!'' Britt and Judy said in unison.

Daphne laughed.

With a glower at her, Britt went on to tell Judy all they knew about Vic Estevez. Then she ended with, ''I thought he was very responsible and attentive to Matt—both fine qualities in a man. And you can't deny he's a very handsome specimen.''

Daphne watched his easy, long-legged stride in designer slacks, hands in his pockets, and thought he looked like a bandit dressed by Armani.

"He looks like he should be wearing a fedora and a trenchcoat over his shoulders," Judy said.

Britt smiled speculatively. "I see him on a horse. He's wearing a mask and a broad-brimmed hat, and there's a cape streaming out behind him." She elbowed Daphne. "And you're sitting in front of him in a swoon."

"All right. That's it." Judy pulled a book out of her large purse and dropped it on the blanket between them. "I've had it with this romantic nonsense. It's time to inject some blood and mystery into this do. Be the first to lay eyes on *Murder by Moonlight,* first novel of soon-to-be-acclaimed author, Judith Woodruff Lowery."

Judy and Britt shrieked together and examined the paperback cover with its wide swath of moonlight on a beach. In the bottom right-hand corner was the silhouette of a woman walking alone. In the upper left was the profile of a man, watching.

They examined Judy's portrait on the inside back cover. Her usually straight hair had been casually curled for it, and her pretty but plain features had been dramatized with makeup. She looked beautiful.

"You must have paid big for that," Daphne teased.

Judy swatted her arm. "Thanks a lot."

Britt read aloud from the teaser copy in the front, then turned the page and read the dedication. "'To my sister.'" She smiled up at Judy. "I thought you didn't know where she was?"

Judy hunched a shoulder. "But I love her anyway. And maybe she'll pick it off a shelf somewhere and read it."

Britt patted her knee and handed back the book. "So, when can we get copies?"

"At the Morgan and Main Bookstore. I have an autograph party scheduled for a week from Friday."

"This is *so* exciting!" Britt exclaimed. "I know how hard you've worked for this. I can't believe you're finally published."

Judy tucked the book into her purse. "Me, either. You know when our Lions' Club was neck and neck with Sugar Creek for most paper recycled in the state?" When Britt and Daphne nodded, she pointed a blunt fingernail at her chest. "My rejection slips put them over the top."

"Ladies. Good afternoon."

Rob Friedman, editor and publisher of the *Tyler Citizen,* appeared at the edge of their blanket. He wore khaki shorts, a short-sleeved green pullover and two cameras around his neck.

Daphne braced herself for flight. As nice as he seemed to be, his presence always meant two things to her. First, she and Jenny could not be photographed; Daphne couldn't take the chance that Celeste might see them. The woman was thousands of miles away, but her instincts were uncanny and her reach, long and powerful.

Second, if Judy was anywhere in the vicinity when Rob appeared, not only did sparks fly, but rockets were launched.

"Hi, Rob." Britt tried to wave him down to join them, but he lifted one of the cameras.

"Thanks, but I'm working." He smiled at Daphne, then turned his attention to Judy.

"How many times," Judy said in a cool, controlled

voice, "do I have to tell you how I feel about report-
ers?"

Daphne and Britt exchanged a glance.

"I understood you the first time." He fiddled with
the aperture setting. "It's hard to misinterpret 'self-
seeking, lying, sensational sycophants.' But I thought I
saw you with a copy of your book. An author is big
news in Tyler. I thought you could use a little publicity."

She subsided just a little. "I intend to buy an ad."

He smiled. "Good. Then I'll give you a big story."

She scorned him with a look. "I thought noble jour-
nalists were above pandering to their advertisers."

"Small-town publishers," he corrected, "appreciate
an advertiser's business and try to return the favor. Of
course, we can't keep you off the Public Record if you
or your kids get arrested, or out of the news if you do
something sensational, but we'll feature you in Business
News if we can, or, in your case, Art Around Town."

Daphne caught Britt's smile as Judy mulled over his
words. Judy finally opened her purse and handed the
copy of her book up to Rob. "Then, here," she said.
"Official review copy."

"Thank you." He inspected it for a moment, then
dropped his camera bag to the grass and put the book
inside. Straightening, he raised the camera to his eye to
focus on them.

"Gotta get back to the booth," Daphne said, scoop-
ing up her purse, her diaper bag and Jennifer.

"You can stay for one picture!" Britt shouted at her,
but Daphne was already headed for the trail, Jennifer
screaming in protest and reaching back toward Jacob
and the large plastic blocks they'd been sharing.

"Sorry!" Daphne called. "Promised I'd be back at three. Bye. Bye, Judy."

"See you at the chicken barbecue for dinner!"

Daphne waved her acquiescence.

A handful of Cheerios earned her Jennifer's forgiveness. Daphne put her in the playpen and took over from Barbara Blake, another Yes! Yogurt employee who'd agreed to cover for her breaks.

Daphne was frantically busy for the next hour, then was able to relax for a few minutes as the pace slowed down. She played with Jennifer and fed her some of the spaghetti she'd brought in a thermos.

Jennifer's eyes gleamed appreciatively over a small spoonful. She was a hedonistic eater with a good appetite. Generally, Daphne had none of the problems faced by mothers of children with finicky tastes.

Daphne kissed her forehead, weak with love for her daughter. *No one is ever going to take you from me,* she promised silently. *No one. Ever.*

"Hi, Daph!" a male voice called from the other side of the trail. It was Jake Marshack, Britt's husband. Walking beside him was Vic Estevez. He, too, waved.

Daphne felt a sensation like the thunder of cymbals right above her head. She wished Vic Estevez would go away. He made her nervous. She lifted Jennifer off the counter and put her back in the playpen with a book.

Another wave of customers kept Daphne busy for a considerable time afterward. She worked as quickly as possible, almost without looking up. She strained to hear orders in the hubbub of sound because the band was playing again. She filled cones, took money, handed out change and listened for the next order.

By the time she had a break again, the sun was lower and the crowds were beginning to thin. She leaned on the counter and looked up the trail, to see Vic Estevez walking away. His arms were wrapped around something big, obviously a recent purchase.

She was beginning to wonder seriously if he was watching her. Every time she'd looked up today, he'd been there. But then so had a good number of the Tyler population. Most people had spent the afternoon walking up and down the trail, checking out the booths, then retracing their steps. Many people had bought two or three frozen yogurts today.

Daphne had to be vigilant, but she had to guard against paranoia, too.

She went to the back of the booth to check on Jennifer—and felt panic ram her chest like a fist. The playpen was empty!

Daphne went over to it, unable to believe Jenny wasn't there. A book lay in a corner, the now empty cup of juice atop it. A scruffy stuffed clown lay on its face, and half-a-dozen other little toys were strewn around—but there was no Jenny!

Then Daphne remembered Vic Estevez walking away, his arms wrapped around something she'd mistaken for a purchase. She'd been right about him! He'd been after Jenny!

Red flared behind her eyes, filled her vision. Rage rose like a flame inside her as though she were a tinderbox.

She shoved so hard at the hinged section of counter that it flew back with a crash. She shot through the opening, hesitating only long enough to spot Vic Estevez near the bend in the trail, almost out of sight.

Then she began to run.

VIC WANDERED in the direction of his car, assessing the day's work. Not bad. He'd made contact with the woman he was ninety-five-percent certain was his quarry. He'd supported his cover story by talking with—

A scream intruded upon his thoughts, and he stopped. He isolated the sound from the bellowing tuba and the whining accordion, but couldn't quite decide where it was coming from. It wasn't children at play. It had a mature and desperate sound.

Then something struck him from behind and an arm closed around his neck.

Vic reacted automatically, from hard training and long experience. He went with the forward movement, gripped the arm and yanked as he doubled over.

It was only as his attacker began to fly over his shoulder with very little effort on his part that he realized he was dealing with an opponent much lighter than he was.

Oh, God, he thought, going down with his attacker in an attempt to ease his fall to the ground. Was it Matt playing a prank? One of his friends?

Vic realized in an instant that it was no prank as Daphne Sullivan scrambled to her feet. Her hair was loose, her color high, and her eyes glared at him with a determination that would have put him into killer mode, had she been a real opponent.

She attacked him again with that scream of rage, and he let her take him down, afraid the resistance necessary to stop her would have hurt her.

He didn't pause to think about why he was reluctant to do that. He'd come to take her back. That was his job.

He guessed it was because beneath that gleam of determined rage in her eyes was a horror he didn't understand…

Until she knelt astride him, took a handful of his sweatshirt in her left hand, then doubled up her right and drew it back as though she had every intention of letting him have it. "Where's my baby?" she screamed. "Where? Where is she?"

"I don't—" he began, and took her bony fist straight in his left eye. The blow glanced off his cheekbone and flung his head back to the dusty trail. He was grateful she was a small-boned woman, despite her height.

"Daphne—" he started to say, but she hit him again.

"Daph!" he heard a familiar voice shout. "Daphne, what are you *doing?*"

Britt Marshack knelt beside him and pulled at the arm Daphne had drawn back in order to hit him again.

"He took Jenny!" she shouted, trying to yank away from her. "He's got Jenny!"

"No, Daphne!"

Daphne grabbed Vic's shirtfront in both hands and tried to shake him. "Where is she?" she demanded, her nose inches from his. She reminded him of some beautiful-but-rabid she-cat. "Where's—my—daughter?"

"Daphne, here she is," a softer, younger voice said.

Vic turned, as Daphne did, to see a pretty blond teenager kneeling beside them, holding Jennifer. He recognized the girl he'd met yesterday. She was Christy Hansen, Britt's daughter.

For an instant, Daphne simply stared at her.

"I was supposed to take her at six," the girl explained quickly. "Remember? We talked about it this morning. So you could go to the barbecue with Mom and Dad after you closed the booth. I told you when I took her, but you were pretty busy and I guess you didn't hear me. I'm sorry."

Daphne grew pale and opened her arms for the toddler. Jennifer went into them and Daphne hugged her until she complained. Vic saw that the woman's hands were shaking.

He watched the scene propped up on his elbows because it was taking place astride his waist. Little plaid sneakers stood on his gut.

Jennifer finally pushed away from Daphne, pointed to something on the side of the trail and said excitedly, "Bear!" She scrambled off Vic's stomach and ran to retrieve a bright pink bear as big as she was. It was apparently none the worse for wear despite its role in the attack.

Jennifer dragged it back to Daphne. "Bear!" she said again with a delighted smile. "Jenny bear?"

Daphne, her face the same color as the bear from her throat to the roots of her hair, turned to look Vic in the eye. Hers were mortified.

"Is that what you were carrying?" she asked.

"Yes," he replied. It occurred to him that he should be enjoying this, but he couldn't quite. Her distress had been too genuine, too deep. "I won it at the Straight Shot booth."

She studied him guiltily for a moment, then turned to the child. "It's Mr. Estevez's bear, baby. You have to give it back. Mommy...made him drop it."

Jennifer looked stricken.

"You can have the bear, Jenny," he said, pushing it back to her when she tried to give it to him.

She needed little encouragement and hugged it tightly. "Jenny bear?"

He nodded. "Jenny's bear."

"Mr. Estevez, you needn't—" Daphne began.

"I insist," he said, then added with a fractional smile,

"I hate to point it out, but I think you owe me this one. Let it be Jenny's bear."

She studied him for a long moment, and he thought she looked as though she were barely under control. She nodded at her daughter. "Okay. That's Jenny's bear. You go with Christy and be good. I'll come for you later, okay?" She looked up at the teenager. "Thanks, Chris."

Jennifer walked off with Christy, and the crowd began to disperse.

"I'm taking both of you to the first-aid booth," Britt said firmly, helping Daphne to her feet. "You to get your head examined, and Vic to get something for that eye."

Vic stood and brushed dust and gravel from his slacks and sweatshirt. "I'm fine," he said. "Really. And I understand how she felt. Her child was missing and I'm a stranger...."

"A stranger," Daphne added quietly, her arms wrapped around herself, "whom I saw walking away with something in his arms."

Britt chided her gently with a look. "I'd have thought a mother of two years would recognize that children do not have pink fur."

Daphne returned her look. "I only saw his back, and I could tell he was carrying something in his arms. I thought... I panicked...I jumped to conclusions. I'm sorry."

"It's all right," Vic said. "I understand."

"Mom? Mom!" A young boy ran toward them, the high, limp crown of a chef's hat falling into his face. "Dad says we need another hand serving barbecue. Can you come and help? People are already coming through the line."

Britt looked uncertainly at Daphne.

"I'll take her to the first-aid booth," Vic said. "Go with David." He'd met Matt's brother, too, yesterday.

"I'm fine," Daphne insisted. He could hear the trembling in her voice. "I do not need first-aid."

"You look a little shocky to me," Britt said. She turned to Vic. "You promise you'll take her?"

"I promise."

She smiled. "All right. I leave her in your capable hands. And I'd like you to join our table for the barbecue. Daph'll show you. See you then."

The moment Britt was out of earshot, Daphne faced Vic, her expression a paradox of apology and aggression.

"I can't tell you how sorry I am for accusing you of kidnapping, and for hitting you." She drew a deep breath as though that had been a difficult admission. Then she squared her shoulders. Her bottom lip trembled. "But you are *not* taking me to the first-aid booth. I am fine."

"You're trembling."

"I'm fine."

"I promised Britt."

She doubled her puny-but-powerful fist. "And I'm warning *you* that I'll use this again."

He grinned. She didn't seem to like that. Now this he could enjoy.

"When you used it before," he said quietly, "you were sitting on my waist, and I chose not to react because I didn't understand what your problem was. This time—" he rested his hands lightly on his hips, ready for action "—we're on even terms, and I know you're just being stubborn."

She folded her arms. "I'll bet you don't even know where the first-aid booth is. And I won't tell you."

In a movement too quick to provide an opportunity for struggle, he swept her into his arms. She huffed indignantly and looked around to see if anyone was watching. A few stragglers on the trail were looking on with interest.

"I'll bet," he said, heading off across the grass toward the small brick building on the other side of the playground equipment, "that I stopped at the park building this morning, looking for a map of Tyler, and saw a first-aid center set up in one of their offices."

She was going to smile. He saw it form in the cool depths of her light blue eyes, watched it billow like a puff of smoke. He watched her lips, knowing he would recognize her as the woman in the picture when the smile reached them.

But she was distracted, wondering what to do with her arms. She started to put one around him, then folded it over her chest. When she obviously found the posture uncomfortable, she finally looped it around his neck.

In the process, her smile was diverted and never reached her lips. But he was aware of the slight weight of her arm resting across his shoulders, her hand curled near his chin, and considered it a satisfactory, if not definitive, trade-off.

"You're kind of a smarty, aren't you?" she asked.

"Yes," he agreed amiably. "And you wear iron underwear, don't you?"

CHAPTER THREE

SHE DIDN'T WANT to like him. In fact, she tried not to, but he was difficult to resist. It was almost as though he'd picked up her determination to remain distant just as he'd picked up her body, and had taken it where he'd wanted to take it.

Cece Baron, who'd been manning the first-aid station, took one look at her and forced her down onto a cot, covering her with a blanket.

Then she'd looked at Vic's purpling eye. "What on earth is going on at this one-big-happy-family get-together? One of you is in mild shock and the other looks as though he's gone a few rounds with Mike Tyson." She sat Vic down in a chair near Daphne's cot.

Vic shrugged broad shoulders as Cece dabbed at his eye with ointment. "She came on to me big time," he said. "I tried to resist, and she chased me down and worked me over until I agreed to stay for the dance tonight."

Cece smiled. Daphne didn't.

"She's not from here," Cece said, dipping the Q-Tip again and working on his bottom lid. "I imagine people from L.A. are less subtle than we are in a small town." Then she winked at Daphne. "But good going, girl."

Daphne groaned. "He's lying through his teeth. I did hit him, but it was all a misunderstanding. Can I get up now? What are you doing here, anyway? I thought you'd given up nursing, at least for now, to take care of the twins.''

"I have," Cece replied, pushing Daphne back down as she tried to rise. "This is my contribution to community service. No, you may not get up. Just lie still for a few minutes. It won't kill you. I thought I told you the last time I saw you to try to put a little meat on those bones. A woman your height should weigh at least ten pounds more than you do. Then your body wouldn't react so adversely to the pressures placed on it.''

Daphne closed her eyes and shuddered again as she remembered the shock of that empty playpen and her resultant panic. She couldn't imagine any physical conditioning easing the stress of that moment.

She opened her eyes and glared at Cece. "Honestly," she said, "a body faints once, and you bring it up every time you see me.''

Cece leaned over her. "And I'll continue to until you take better care of yourself. Now, you have to rest there for a full half hour.''

Vic Estevez stayed with her, making small talk about his family in Santa Barbara. He was the third of six children, whom his parents couldn't seem to get out of their hacienda-style house outside the city.

His two older siblings were married and in business together, so their children were always staying with his parents when their parents were out of town. The three younger ones remained unmarried and came and went with friends, girlfriends, boyfriends, and, in the case of the youngest, most of the Santa Barbara College football team.

Daphne listened avidly. She'd always envisioned a family like that when she'd been a child. In the quiet late-night hours after…after Gordon… She had curled onto her side and blotted out reality with fictional images of what life might have been like if her father had lived. Or if she'd had a different mother. Or if her mother had picked the men in her life more carefully.

And later, during the other life, she'd wondered what kinds of families the johns went home to. They couldn't have been like Vic's or they wouldn't have come to her in the first place. But they were probably better than hers.

It was nice to know someone had experienced the warm sense of belonging she'd dreamed about. Sometimes still dreamed about.

Daphne did feel better after thirty minutes of lying still and listening to Vic's stories. Cece admonished her one more time to try to eat better, then shooed her out of the first-aid station.

They stopped at the frozen-yogurt booth to pick up the purse Daphne had left tucked away in a box. Christy had apparently come for the playpen.

Vic walked beside Daphne across the grass to the far side of the park, where dozens of tables were set up under a shelter. The aroma of barbecue wafted toward them from an enormous grill set up beyond the shelter. Around it, eight men in chef's aprons and hats turned steaks, pieces of chicken, hamburgers and hot dogs.

Vic put a hand to his flat stomach. ''Smells like home. We ate outdoors every night during the summer.''

''On a patio?'' Daphne asked.

He shook his head. ''Just a big backyard hedged by gardenias.''

Daphne let the image and the fragrance form in her

mind and felt herself begin to relax for the first time since she'd thought she'd lost Jennifer.

She spotted Judy, standing head and shoulders above the crowd and beckoning her with a broad wave of her hand. Daphne caught Vic's arm and pulled him with her through the crowd in that direction. Judy stepped down from the picnic table bench as they arrived.

Britt's younger children, David and Renee, were already sitting at the table in front of plates piled high with food.

"Vic, this is my landlady, Judy Lowery," Daphne said as Judy looked the stranger up and down. "Judy, meet Vic Estevez. He's thinking about moving to Tyler."

"Landlady?" he asked, shaking Judy's hand. This was the woman Daphne had called from Manchester. "Do you have apartments?"

"No," she replied. "Daphne rents an old farmhouse I own near Britt's place. I moved into town just for a change of scene. Why? Are you looking for an apartment?"

"I'm looking for a house, but I'm staying at Timberlake Lodge in the meantime. If it takes a while to find something, though, I'll need a place bigger than my room. I feel claustrophobic already."

Daphne imagined he did. He was big, and she could feel the energy that emanated from him. She could also remember what it had felt like to be carried by him. For those few minutes, it had been as though she had abdicated responsibility for her life, and all she had to do was hold on to him. But even the memory of that fantasy was too dangerous to contemplate.

She reacquainted him with David, who had to lift the chef's hat out of his face to look up at him.

Vic leaned across the table to shake his hand.

"And this is Renee."

The little girl smiled up at him, said a polite, "Hello," then went back to her food with sincere enthusiasm.

"We'd better get in line if we hope to get anything," Judy said, indicating the long ribbon of people now stretching halfway back to the park office.

It took more than thirty minutes to reach the grill and the buffet tables, but Daphne didn't notice the wait. Judy was engaged in conversation with the postmistress, Annabelle Scanlon, who stood in line ahead of her, and Daphne was free to talk to Vic.

"So, what do you do," he asked, "when you're not manning a frozen-yogurt booth at an end-of-summer celebration?"

"I work for the Marshacks. I manage their frozen-yogurt shop near Gates Department Store."

When he looked blank, she added, "That big sort of Art Deco building on the north side of the town square."

"Okay. I know where that is. I had breakfast this morning in a coffee shop near the square."

"Marge's."

"How long ago did you leave L.A.?"

Daphne felt herself tense. "A long time ago," she answered simply.

"Matt told me you're a widow."

She gave him a wry smirk. It was close to a smile, but not close enough for him to read Diane Huntington in it. "Matt's mother is always trying to fix me up with eligible men. Now I think she's put her children on the case."

He laughed softly. "Must be related to *my* mother.

You'd think with four grandchildren and the potential of more from all my other siblings, she'd leave me alone.''

''I think it's impossible for happily married people to leave single people alone.'' Daphne rubbed her arms. The sun was going down, and the evening breeze was picking up. It brought with it the fresh scents of grass and woods and mingled them with the aroma from the barbecue.

''Cold?'' Vic asked. He put a hand to her bare upper arm and found it cool to the touch.

She nodded and looked uncertainly toward the park entrance. ''I brought a sweater, but I left it in the car.'' She gave him that funny, wry twist of her lips again—still not enough of a smile for him to identify her. ''Unfortunately, I had to park about four blocks away.''

''I have a better solution,'' Vic said, pulling his sweatshirt off. He was dropping it over her head before she could protest.

Then she abandoned all attempt to protest when the warmth it carried from his body slid over her torso and along her arms as he helped her tug the sweatshirt into place. Considering her height, it was just a little too long, but the raglan seam hung almost to her elbows, and folds of fleece hung over her chest.

''Now you'll freeze,'' she said, rubbing her hand over the warm fabric, feeling the coziness of it penetrate her bones. He was down to a simple white T-shirt.

He pulled her long hair out of the neck of the shirt with a gentle gesture that reached almost as deeply inside her as the warmth. Then he put his hands on her shoulders and pushed her forward as the line moved.

''Not as long as we get to the food,'' he said.

Daphne kept her back to him as they drew closer to

the grill and the buffet tables. She felt almost debilitated by his touch, and that confounded her.

In the other life she'd been touched often and by many men. And before that, there'd been Gordon. So she'd closed a door inside herself to protect the real Diane. But it had been closed for so long, she suspected Diane had suffocated.

And she was Daphne now, a woman composed of deceit and illusion. Nothing in this life was real, except Jennifer. So this couldn't be real, either. Daphne just wanted it to be.

Vic could still feel her hair against his fingertips. It had been like cool silk. And now, as she stood with her back to him, he watched the pale blond color become like soft lamplight as dusk darkened the sky and folded the shadows in around them.

He was beginning to hope she *wouldn't* smile.

Britt and Jake took their break to join them for dinner just as David went back to help at the grill, and Renee disappeared to help Christy and her friends with baby-sitting.

Matt and Deke arrived with heaped plates and sat opposite Judy.

Britt studied the amount of food on her son's plate and shook her head.

"What?" Matt asked in genuine perplexity.

Jake patted Britt's hand. "It's all very motion efficient," he said. "It eliminates the need to go back for seconds. We studied time and motion at the plant, remember?"

Matt elbowed him. "Thanks, Jake. I wouldn't have thought of that."

Vic smiled over the exchange. A stepfather and teenage stepson getting along. That was unusual. He wondered at the courage of a man willing to marry a woman with four young children.

Then he saw Britt smile into Jake's eyes and realized there was nothing to wonder about. Love radiated between them, almost palpably. Nothing in the world could stand against that. He'd seen it between his parents.

He turned to Daphne and saw her watching them greedily. She had blackmailed her husband into marriage, Celeste had said. He found himself wondering why a woman who would marry for money would look at the Marshacks' love as though she were starved for it.

But because he couldn't ask about that at the moment, he chose to deal with starvation of another kind.

"I've been counting," he said quietly to her as the Marshacks and Judy got into a discussion about books. "You've eaten three bites of lettuce and two bites of chicken and you've pushed your plate away."

She seemed surprised by his interest. "I have a lot of trouble with indigestion."

"Probably because your stomach's empty," he guessed. "Remember what Cece said."

She studied him for a moment, and he was certain she was about to smile. But she didn't. She sipped at her paper cup of coffee instead. "I suppose when you were a cop," she said, "you were a food cop."

He acknowledged the gibe with a scolding frown. "I was DEA," he said.

Her brow furrowed. "Drug enforcement?"

"Yes."

"That must have been ugly."

"And frustrating and demoralizing."

"What are you going to do now?"

He'd known someone would ask him that question and had fabricated an answer. Curiously, he found it hard to lie to her. But in the interests of getting the job done, he'd done a lot of things over the years that had been hard.

"I have some investments that'll keep me going for a while. But I've been thinking about a sporting-goods store."

"Good idea," she said after a moment's thought. "I think everyone goes to Sugar Creek for that stuff. The drugstore carries fishing line, and the market has bait, but I think that's about it."

Jake, who had overheard, also endorsed the idea. "And there are a couple of storefronts downtown in prime locations. One between the Lutheran church and the bank, and another one near the video-rental place on Main Street."

Britt leaned forward enthusiastically. "You could have Deke's father show you through them while you're house hunting."

Vic nodded, feeling a small stab of guilt at their interest and eagerness to help. But that meant his cover was working. He should have been pleased.

"Do you have experience in sporting goods?" Judy asked. She was suspicious of him, and she didn't seem to mind that everyone knew.

He smiled amiably into her penetrating gaze. "None at all. Unless you count experience with guns from my cop days, and with basketballs from my weekends."

"You play basketball?" Jake asked. "We play pickup games at the Y on Thursday nights. Seven o'clock. Come and join us."

Vic grinned and warned, "They don't call me Magic or anything."

"It's all right," Jake said with a teasing glance at his son and his son's friend. "Matt and Deke can't play, either, but we let them come anyway."

"Mr. Marshack!" Deke pretended hurt feelings.

"Ha!" Matt said. "Who ran into the drugstore to buy your linament when you couldn't even get out of the car that first time you let us play?"

"You're grounded," Jake said offhandedly as he reached for his coffee. "You promised to be quiet about that."

"You might want to think twice about that." Matt smiled blandly at his stepfather. "There are a few other things you've asked me to be quiet about that Mom would probably like to know."

Britt leaned around her husband to look at her son. "Like what?" she demanded.

Jake whipped a ten-dollar bill out of his pocket. "Why don't you take Deke for one of those Belgian-waffle things for dessert?"

Matt leaned a forearm on Jake's shoulder. "Do you really think," he asked with exaggerated gravity, "that I could be bought so easily when a principle is at stake?"

"Yeah," Jake replied.

Matt snatched the bill out of his hand and stood. "You're right. Come on, Deke."

Britt turned her attention to her husband and repeated, "Like what?"

At that moment, the band that had played rousing polka music all afternoon began the first few bars of the moody and nostalgic, "It Had to Be You."

"Listen," Jake said, pushing his plate away. "Dancing music." And he caught Britt's arm and pulled her to her feet.

All around them, couples were leaving the shelter and streaming across the grass toward a dancing area near the gazebo roped off with Chinese paper lanterns.

Vic was reminded of home again, except that there his mother lined the yard with *luminarias,* candles placed in bags weighted with sand. The warm effect of lighting the darkness outdoors was the same.

And that was the impulse he followed when he drew Daphne to her feet. He wasn't the hunter and she wasn't his quarry—at least for that moment. They were simply two strangers at a festival dance.

Daphne glanced at Judy as Vic turned to her to excuse their departure, and caught her frown of disapproval. She ignored it. She hadn't danced since before Jennifer was born, and something eager inside her was already responding to the music. She hadn't known she had any eagerness left.

In the midst of the small crowd gathered on the grass, Daphne went into Vic's arms. She didn't expect the experience to be shocking. After all, just an hour ago he'd picked her up and carried her to the first-aid station, his arms wrapped firmly around her back and her thighs.

But it was shocking in the very literal sense of the word. She felt a rippling current move over her where his hands touched her upper back, then slid gently down, barely making contact with the fabric of his sweatshirt before settling confidently at the back of her waist.

She had little choice but to loop her own arms around his neck. And with that the current encircled them, flashing around them like the moving lights on the marquee at Times Square.

Vic looked into her now moonlit face and could see

none of the greed and careless cruelty he'd expected to find. Then he dismissed the thought. That wasn't for tonight. Tonight—this moment—was outside the reality of why he was here.

He pulled her closer. "Warm enough?" he asked, almost losing his voice on the last syllable as he felt the softness of her breasts against his chest.

"Yes," she said. At least, he presumed she did. He saw her form the word, but couldn't hear it over the music and the rustle of the evening breeze.

Although he still topped her by three or four inches, he was used to women who were much shorter than she was. He was accustomed to looking down onto the top of a head, the fans of eyelashes, the tip of a nose.

Being almost eye-to-eye with a woman was an unexpected pleasure. He saw deep into the blue pools to…secrets. That would be something to put on the plus side of the ledger, if he were doing that tonight. But he wasn't.

He lifted one hand to lean her head against his and closed his eyes.

Daphne felt his nearness like a balm. And she didn't understand that, because she had a long-standing rule about touching. Diane was not supposed to feel. She'd closed her off.

But this feeling ran deep—deeper than the fictitious surface that was Daphne. This went all the way to who she really was—the young woman she'd already been at twelve.

He would be horrified if he knew. Everyone would be. But she wouldn't think about that tonight. It lay under her awareness every minute of every day, but she would not think about it tonight. Tonight it didn't matter.

Tonight there was heartbreaking music, colorful lights strung in the trees and no past to haunt and bedevil her. Tonight could be hers.

They danced until midnight, long after the Marshacks and all the other parents with children going back to school tomorrow had left. Jennifer, wrapped tightly against the cool evening, lay in Daphne's arms, the pink bear in a death grip in hers. Vic's arms held all of them.

They pulled apart reluctantly when the music finally stopped.

Daphne looked into Vic's eyes, saw kindness and the beginnings of sexual interest there, and knew that it had to be over. That it *was* over.

Pain as intense as her pleasure had been all evening unmercifully swept away every impossible dream.

For the first time since Trey's funeral, she wanted to cry.

Vic saw the door close in her eyes. That didn't bother him. He'd picked locks during his illustrious career, shot them off and kicked in doors. He wouldn't be kept from where he wanted to go.

But the sadness in her eyes ripped into him—and with that came the spotlight of reality. If she was who he thought she was, he was going to hurt her even more.

This would be a good time to turn around and walk away, he thought. He would tell Celeste Huntington that he'd run up against a dead end and would give her her money back.

But in one brief afternoon and evening he'd gone too far to turn back. Daphne could be what his employer said she was, but he didn't think so. And if she wasn't, there was something at work here that she probably couldn't handle on her own. He had to find out what it was.

"Well." She took a step back from him and held out her hand. "Thank you for your charming company. I hope you find what you want in Tyler."

He took the playpen from her as she tried to struggle with it one-handedly. He found the hinge and folded it. He picked up the diaper bag and tucked it under his other arm.

"I'll let you know if I do," he said, heading off in the direction she'd pointed when she'd talked about leaving her sweater in the car. When she didn't follow, he stopped and raised an eyebrow. The only way to win with this woman, he knew, was to leave her no options. A chauvinistic attitude, certainly, but his father would have been proud. "You coming?"

She came just close enough to try to take the playpen from him. "I can manage," she said.

He shook his head. "I'm not about to let you walk four blocks in the dark. Even if you weren't carrying furniture and a baby."

She growled softly and led the way.

The night was quiet and fragrant, and he found it hard to believe that the excitement and gaiety of the end-of-summer celebration had simply dissolved into history.

Time seemed to have a different quality here. The present was so vivid, it seemed eternal.

She drove a small red Ford Escort whose trunk barely held the folded playpen. He tucked it away for her while she put Jennifer into the car seat in the back. He heard one single whine of complaint, then silence. When he looked in, the child was asleep, the pink bear sitting beside her, one of its ears clutched in her little hand.

Daphne had put the driver's-side door between them. Her manner was now cool, dismissing.

"Thanks again," she said. "And thank you for the

bear. You can see she loves it.'' She tossed her head, and her moonlit hair rippled in the shadows. ''I apologize again for knocking you down. I... Jenny's everything to me.''

He'd seen that in her eyes. A stroke for the negative side of the ledger. This was reality now. He was doing that again.

''I understand,'' he said. ''I'll let you know how my house hunting goes.''

She looked into his eyes, hers wide and mournful despite her pose of uninterest. ''No, don't,'' she said briskly. ''It was a nice evening, Vic. But it's over, and I have a life that isn't conducive to relationships.''

''Some relationships,'' he insisted, holding the door when she slipped in behind the wheel and tried to pull it closed, ''flourish whether conditions are conducive or not.''

She looked up at him, her expression no-nonsense. ''This one is over.'' She yanked the door closed.

In self-defense, he had to let it go, but he rapped on the window.

With a forbearing roll of her eyes, she turned on the motor and hit the electric window control.

He smiled, leaning inside. ''So, if you think it's over, you're admitting that it's begun.''

She stared at him in utter frustration for a moment, then turned the key in the ignition with an exasperated shake of her head.

''Goodbye, Vic,'' she said firmly. Then she smiled at him over her shoulder and drove away.

The smile imprinted itself on his brain—and confirmed what he'd probably known all along but had been reluctant to admit because he was already in trouble here, big time.

It was her. Diane Huntington.

CHAPTER FOUR

"WAS IT HER?"

Celeste Huntington's voice was quiet but avid.

Vic stood at the window of his room and looked out on the gently rolling countryside beyond the lodge. The morning was golden, with evaporating mist steaming up from the grass like some ethereal stage effect.

"I'm not sure," he said into the telephone receiver. He pushed the lace curtain aside and opened the window. Fresh air wafted in, cool and fragrant, to surround him. The last thing he wanted to do at the moment was talk to his employer. But he had to remember what this was all about. "The woman I've traced here is physically very different."

"You had anticipated that possibility," she reminded him. "But she can't have done anything about her height."

"This is a region that was settled by Scandinavians, Mrs. Huntington. Tall women are not an oddity around here."

"Does she have a little girl?"

"I don't know that yet," he hedged. "I'm working on it. Try to be patient. This could take some time."

"I'm not a patient woman, Mr. Estevez. And I've already been too long without my granddaughter."

Vic could imagine her pouring tea from the trolley as they spoke. Could picture her glacierlike stillness.

"I'm afraid you'll have to learn to be, Mrs. Huntington," he said. "If I ask too many questions of the wrong people and she suspects me, she'll be gone and we'll be back where we started."

He heard a sigh on the other end of the line. "All right. But I'd like you to check in every day."

"I'll check in when I know something, Mrs. Huntington."

"Can you at least tell me where you are?"

"When I'm certain I have the right woman."

Her voice rose a notch in annoyance. "May I remind you that I'm paying you handsomely for—"

"That's precisely," he interrupted, "why I'm being thorough. And I work best without interference."

Silence. Then she said stiffly, "Very well. I'll hope to hear from you soon. Goodbye, Mr. Estevez."

"Goodbye, Mrs. Huntington."

Vic hung up the phone, grateful to be able to put his employer out of his mind, at least for a while. She *was* the reason he'd come here, but he suspected things were not precisely the way she'd presented them, and he was determined to find out why.

But that could wait an hour. Right now, he intended to take a walk, find a newspaper and read it over breakfast.

He reached into a dresser drawer for a blue cotton sweater. As he pulled it on over khaki cotton pants, he smiled at the thought that Daphne Sullivan still had his UC Santa Barbara sweatshirt.

He stood quietly in the middle of the room for a minute, remembering the night before. Had she really been that beautiful? Had there really been dark mystery in her eyes, or had it all been the moody result of dancing under the stars surrounded by Chinese lanterns and a town that seemed to exist out of time? Like Brigadoon.

He rolled his eyes and patted his pockets, checking for wallet and keys. If his old DEA buddies could see him looking lovestruck and speculating over a romantic fantasy, they would have him committed. That was not Victor Guadalupe Estevez.

But what was? he wondered, pulling the door open and heading for the stairs to the lobby. Suddenly he wasn't sure.

Paul Bullard, however, seemed to be. He stood at the desk, conferring with the pretty blonde who managed the lodge.

"There he is now," she said, smiling at him over Bullard's head. "Sleep well, Mr. Estevez?"

"Very well, thank you," he replied. That was a lie. He'd tossed and turned most of the night. But it had nothing to do with the lodge's comfortable accommodations. He extended his hand to the realtor. "Good morning," he said.

Bullard, his blazer with the realty-company logo on the pocket straining at the buttons over his stomach, smiled cheerfully and pumped his hand. Then he patted the black vinyl portfolio under his free arm.

"I'll bet you're French," he said.

Vic eyed him narrowly. "With a name like Estevez?"

Bullard caught his arm and tugged him toward the dining room. "No, no. French *Provincial.* I have one where Main Street meets the highway. Four bedrooms, three-car garage, curved window heads, angular bays, brick quoins at all corners, a diamond-paned picture bay over the recessed entrance *and* a circular staircase with a wrought-iron railing. I can see you in it."

"Really." Vic abandoned his plan for a quiet walk and allowed himself to be led to breakfast, trying to imagine what in the hell a quoin was.

"HOW COULD HE HAVE painted the television screen without any of us noticing?" Glenna Nielsen turned to Daphne, her gentle expression bewildered.

Daphne knelt down beside her on the carpet before the masterpiece and considered. Putting in her time at TylerTots two days a week was always an adventure, but today had been almost legendary, thanks to Jacob Marshack. Mercifully, it was nap time, and he and his companions were asleep.

"It probably happened when you were supervising the playground. Billy and Barbie Morrison were disemboweling the ottoman, and I was trying to get the stuffing away from them because you know how Billy is about flushing things down the toilet. I'm sorry. It's my fault."

Glenna shook her head, still staring at the television screen. It was a strange shade of melon and had texture, almost as though Jacob had been trying to create a relief.

"It's not your fault. We're overbalanced on the side of two-year-olds." She turned to grin at Daphne. "Do you know that the State Accident Insurance Fund rate is higher for day-care workers than for fighter pilots?"

Daphne elbowed her and laughed. "Well, I'll clean it up, starting with a rubber spatula."

Glenna turned back for a closer look at the concoction. "What on earth do you think it is? It smells like...apples."

Daphne nodded, getting to her feet. "We had applesauce for morning break. My guess is he added his to a pail of sand from the sandbox.''

Glenna stood beside her. ''You know, Barbara Blake's boys told me their applesauce was missing. I just thought they were angling for seconds and gave it to them. Jakie must have taken theirs, too.''

''That would account for the solid texture.''

Daphne had most of the screen cleaned, and was working valiantly to have it done by the time the children woke up from their naps. She couldn't imagine what would happen if it were time for ''Queenie's Cartoons'' and they were unable to watch it. The notion was too ugly to contemplate.

''Oh, no.'' The words were quietly but desperately spoken.

Daphne turned to find Britt standing behind her in a teal-and-black leotard and black tights, a coordinating sweatband tied under her bangs. Car keys dangled from her fingers as she stared in mortification at what remained of Jacob's creation on one corner of the screen.

''Jakie did that,'' she said.

''And very well, too,'' Daphne replied, scraping carefully but firmly at a stubborn corner. ''If you ever decide to mortar anything, you might ask him for his recipe. This stuff could coat the space shuttle and survive reentry.''

Britt came forward, a hand to her mouth. ''He did the same thing at home with oatmeal and egg yolk. I'm so sorry!''

''Please.'' Daphne put the job aside for a moment and stood to smile at her friend. ''Maybe there's a sculpting career in his future. Or maybe he'll be a chef once he distinguishes between what's edible and what isn't.''

"Want me to finish that?"

"No. I've almost got it. How was aerobics?"

Britt fell into an overstuffed chair that occupied one corner of this carpeted common room in the basement of the church. Glenna and another aide sat with the sleeping children in the basement's other two rooms. "It used to be easier before I had Jacob. Now there seems to be more stomach to prevent my fingertips reaching my toes."

Daphne laughed and sat on the arm of the old sofa at a right angle to Britt's chair. "I hear ya."

Britt gave her a disparaging look. "Yeah, right. You're such a stringbean. And all of twenty-six. That's disgusting."

"Oh, motherhood makes you creaky no matter how old you are."

"Well, before you rust into immobility," Britt said, "tell me about Vic Estevez. Have you seen him since Labor Day?"

The sound of his name reminded Daphne of obsidian-black eyes, glossy dark hair, a smile that had been bright in the lantern-lit darkness.

But for Britt's benefit, she pretended uninterest. "No. He was a nice dinner companion, but I came to Tyler to get over a man, not to dally with another one." It did surprise her that she hadn't seen him. Tyler was a small town. She'd thought she might bump into him downtown or at the grocery store. But in three days, she hadn't seen a sign of him. And she had convinced herself that that was good.

Britt crossed long, slim legs in the black tights. "He also made a handsome dance partner. And Cece tells me he carried you into the first-aid station. I love a physical man, don't you?"

Daphne looked heavenward in supplication. "He was kind and attentive, but I get the impression he's also stubborn, probably autocratic and single-minded. What woman in her right mind would want to deal with that?"

Britt shrugged a shoulder. "Depends on what balances that out. So far, all you've done is describe practically every man that ever walked. If he has redeemable qualities, he'd be worth all that."

"I don't want to know."

"Why not?"

"Because…" *Because he would lose interest in an instant if he knew my past. Because I can't afford to be distracted by a man now—and Vic Estevez could be distracting.* She had to be vigilant. Celeste would never give up. "Because two part-time jobs and Jennifer fill up my life."

Britt smiled agreeably. "I'll give you a day off."

"No, thank you."

Britt rested her elbows on her knees and leaned toward Daphne, her expression serious. "You've been in Tyler almost a year and you've put off every man who's tried to take you out. You never go anywhere. You don't do anything but work. Take it from me—a year is long enough to grieve. Now it's time to plan a future. If you don't think you want a husband, then think about Jenny needing a father."

"Jenny is fine," Daphne said stiffly. Way back in memories she'd locked away, she could recall her mother's friends saying those words when her mother had married Gordon. *Diane needs a father.* The incident surged forward into her awareness and she had to stand and walk away.

She went to the refrigerator across the room for a box

of apple juice while she struggled for equilibrium. She'd thought she'd dealt with all that a long time ago. What was this?

"Want a juice?" she asked Britt.

"No, thanks."

She closed the door to find her friend right behind her. Britt enclosed her in a quick hug as noise began to blossom from the nap room. When one child awoke, they all did.

"I apologize for being so pushy," Britt said. "Of course, it's your business. I just hate to see you being so reclusive." She studied her earnestly. "Are you all right?"

Daphne smiled and did her best to look surprised by the question. "Of course. Except for the fact that nap time's over, I'm fine."

Children streamed into the common room, energized by their rest, and moved in all directions, watchful aides following.

Britt snatched Jacob as he ran to her, and swept the little dark-haired bundle into her arms. His hazel eyes were bright.

"I'll speak to him about painting the television screen," Britt promised as Daphne turned to stop a three-year-old girl from feeding another child a crayon.

"Do that!" Daphne laughed. "See you Monday."

DAPHNE HAD ONE HAND on the waistband of Jennifer's cotton pants while the child strained to get away from her. With the other, she tried futilely to tie the laces of a pristine white athletic shoe on her own right foot.

Across the bank of chairs, the young salesclerk was helping a nice-looking man with a pair of loafers he appeared perfectly competent to deal with himself.

Daphne pulled Jenny back and sat her down in the chair beside her, where the pink bear sat. She looked firmly into her daughter's determined little face.

"You *have* to wait for Mommy," she said.

Daphne had a rule about shopping with Jenny: she never did it. But there'd been too many errands to fit into a lunch hour, and her exercise shoes were completely broken down. She had to have them for tomorrow night's class.

She'd told herself bracingly that Jenny was now twenty-six months old and learning new things all the time. How difficult could it be for her to stop after work and have Jenny sit still for five minutes while she tried on shoes?

But the clerk had been busy. Five minutes had turned into ten, then fifteen, and now that they'd been there almost half an hour, Jenny was about to blow.

Her daughter pointed tearfully at a pair of shiny white Mary Janes worn by a teddy bear on display.

"Bear shoes!" she demanded, as she'd been doing ever since she noticed them. "Bear shoes, Mommy!"

"Bear does not need shoes," Daphne said, letting go of the child long enough to pull on the laces of the new shoe.

It was a mistake. Jenny was away in a flash, and seeing her mother rising in pursuit, she ran around a high display and headed, Daphne was sure, for the door to the street.

"Jenny, *stop* at the door!" she shouted, hobbling after her, one shoe on, the other foot covered only in a plain white sock. "Jenny!"

She rounded the display, stepped on the trailing laces of the shoe and pitched forward with a little scream of alarm.

A long arm shot out from the other side of the display and caught her at the waist with sufficient force to drive the breath from her.

She looked up into a pair of black eyes she'd seen in her mind's eye often over the past few days. In his other arm, Vic held her daughter, who looked perfectly happy to be there.

"You know, if you continue to have this problem," he said with a smile, "you might put a homing device on Jennifer."

For an instant Daphne indulged herself with a sensory inventory. He looked wonderful. He wore blue athletic shorts, a simple white T-shirt and a pair of Nike sandals. His arms and legs were lean but muscular, and lightly covered with dark hair.

His hair was damp, a tight curl at his left temple fighting the slicked-back order he'd apparently recently imposed on it. He smelled of something herbal and masculine that mingled enticingly with the shoe-store smell of leather.

The black eye seemed only to add to his dangerously handsome good looks.

And Daphne felt as though she stood within a vise of muscle as he continued to support her—his chest against hers, his arm around the back of her waist, his thigh against the side of her hip. It reminded her sharply of what it had felt like to dance with him the other night. And that she could never do so again.

She pushed against him with an apologetic smile. He freed her instantly.

"At least I didn't blame you for Jenny's disappearance this time," she said, taking her daughter from him. "How's the eye?"

"Fine. I'm telling everyone I was resisting a seduction."

Jenny pointed to the display bear wearing the white Mary Janes. "Bear shoes!" she exclaimed, obviously sensing a new ally in Vic.

He raised an eyebrow in puzzlement.

"She thinks her bear should have new shoes," Daphne explained. "Which is making mincemeat of my efforts to buy shoes for myself."

He followed her back to the lineup of chairs and saw the woolly pink bear occupying one. Daphne put Jenny down, and the child immediately grabbed the bear and held it up to Vic. "Jenny bear," she said.

"Would you like me to keep her busy?" he asked, taking the chair on the other side of the one the bear had occupied. Jenny immediately put the bear in his lap.

"Thank you," Daphne said, quickly pushing the other shoe on while Jenny was busy chattering. "But I'm sure you have other things to do."

"Actually, I came to buy shoes," he said, moving the bear to his left knee as Jenny decided to climb into his lap. He hooked an arm around her to help her.

Daphne looked up from pulling the laces tight. "Really?"

"Really. Basketball shoes. I'm meeting Jake and Matt at the Y tonight."

She tied a bow and stood to test the fit.

Jenny scrambled off Vic's lap, holding Bear by the throat in her left arm, and headed for the purses. "Bear purse!" she cried.

Daphne took a step in pursuit, but Vic stopped her with a hand on her arm. "I'm on it. Finish with your shoes."

The salesclerk who'd been attending the nice-looking

young man with the loafers now turned her attention to Vic as he followed Jenny around the store, lifting her up to look at everything she exclaimed over, but gently pulling her tiny hand back when she reached out to touch.

Daphne, glancing their way occasionally to make sure Vic was still in control, stuffed the running shoes back in the box and without help from the clerk, quickly found a three-pack of socks and a spray can of cleaner. She hurried to the counter with her purchases.

"*He's* a woman's dream come true," the clerk said, indicating Vic with a jut of her chin while stuffing Daphne's receipt into the bag. She handed the bag across the counter. "Some people have all the luck."

Daphne enjoyed the irony of that remark as she went to relieve Vic of her daughter.

"Thank you," she said sincerely. "I don't think I could have accomplished this if you hadn't happened along."

"My pleasure. What did you buy?" He passed the toddler to her, but Jenny retained a grip on the front of his T-shirt.

"Aerobics shoes." Daphne pried gently at the little hand. "Sweetie, you have to let Vic go."

Jenny didn't seem to think so. She clutched firmly at her handful of T-shirt, forcing him to remain very close. She looked into his eyes with obvious fascination.

"Vic home," Jenny said clearly.

Daphne continued to work at the little hand, keeping her eyes on the job. He was so close she could feel the warmth of his body, could almost feel his heartbeat. Or was that hers?

"Uh...no," she said. "We can't take Vic home. But

Bear wants to go home. Vic's going to go play basketball with Uncle Jake and Matt.''

''You can take me home,'' Vic corrected softly. ''If you want to.''

Daphne felt shy. Nervous. She didn't understand it. ''You're on your way…'' she said breathlessly. ''To play basketball.''

His eyes were wandering over her hair, their velvety darkness feeling like a touch. ''I'll leave a message. Tell them I had a better offer.''

''I, uh… Jenny has to eat.''

''We'll pick up something.''

Daphne finally wedged her index finger into Jenny's little fist and pried it open, freeing Vic's shirt. Jenny screamed her objection.

''Vic home!'' she demanded.

Daphne forced herself to look into his eyes. Under their dark interest, she felt a deep blush rise up her throat and inch across her cheeks. Good grief.

She began to back away. ''I'm sure your basketball game—'' she collided with a table of summer sandals, then moved around it ''—will be more fun than spaghetti with a cranky two-year-old. It can get pretty disgusting.''

Vic advanced on her slowly as she continued to back toward the door. ''I like spaghetti,'' he said. ''And I like two-year-olds.''

She felt the breeze of the street at her back and knew enormous relief. She was almost out of the store.

''I—I'm usually asleep by nine.''

His smile turned slightly wicked. ''I like to sleep.''

She felt the metal threshold of the door under her feet, heard the overhead bell signal her departure.

She looked at Vic, who'd come to within a foot of her. She was at a complete loss for words.

"Vic home!" Jenny said forcefully, reaching out toward him.

He caught her hand and she grasped his index finger and tried to pull him toward them.

He resisted, but met Daphne's unsettled expression. "You need help getting into the car with Jenny and all that stuff?"

Yes. She did. But she made an instant decision. She closed her hand over Jenny's wrist, gave a gentle but firm tug, and Vic was free.

She stepped out of the store, felt the breeze in her hair, heard the quiet traffic noise of downtown Tyler. She was free.

"No, thank you," she said with a polite smile. "Enjoy your game. Goodbye."

Daphne put a highly disgruntled Jenny into her car seat and kissed her cheek as she buckled her in.

"I know men are intriguing," she said, reaching into the pouch on the back of the front seat to find the plastic bag of graham crackers. She handed one to Jenny. "But they all turn out to be trouble. Even the good ones. Your daddy was a good one, but he was used to being rich so we couldn't get him away from your grandma, who is a five-star witch."

Jenny snapped off a corner of cracker and ate it with great concentration, bored by her mother's monologue.

"And we have to watch ourselves, anyway. Vic seems very nice, but he comes from Palm Beach where the witch lives. I don't like that."

With one knee on the back seat, the other foot braced on the ground, Daphne reached for the other packages and tossed them into the car.

"It probably isn't likely that she sent him, but she's powerful and tricky. On the other hand, even if everything he says about himself is true, he could just be entertaining himself with us while he's getting settled. Men do that, you know. We're just somebody to keep them warm."

Daphne set Bear on the seat beside Jenny, and it was only then that she noticed. Bear wore the white Mary Janes her daughter had admired in the shoe store.

VIC LAY ON HIS BACK on a bench in the Y's locker room, every muscle in his body feeling the way his eye looked. After three hours on the basketball court, holding off Matt and Deke and three of their buddies with Jake and a friend of his, his last reserves of energy were gone. He felt as though the Maple Leafs and the Canadiens had used him for a hockey puck.

"That was a really good idea, Jake," Vic said as he waited for his pulse to settle down. "'The three of us,'" he quoted in a phony bass voice, "'will take on the five of you.'"

Jake, lying on his stomach on the bench across the narrow aisle from Vic, raised a limp hand off the floor. "We won, didn't we? They owe us pizza. What are you complaining about?"

"Death," Vic said without moving, "is hardly a satisfactory trade-off for winning."

"Jeez." Michael Kenton, the third party on their team, stood in the aisle between them and frowned at each one in turn. "You sound like a couple of old ladies. I feel great."

"You're younger than us," Vic said.

"And you're married to a minister," Jake added. "You probably had divine assistance."

Michael went to the mirror to comb his hair. "I don't need prayer on the court, thank you. Just some good teammates who can guard or score or rebound. But I managed anyway. Where was Brick tonight?"

"Britt's cousin," Jake explained to Vic. "He and Karen took a vacation. He'll be back next week. Oh, God." He uttered a long and mournful groan as he pushed himself to a sitting position. "I guess we'd better get moving if we're going to collect on that pizza."

Vic, too, sat up, everything on him from hair to toes protesting painfully.

Across the locker room there was a loud commotion as Matt and his friends, changed into street clothes, came to join them. Deke dribbled the basketball, then shot it into Michael's open locker.

"Good form," Matt praised dryly. "You should have shown some of that on the court."

Deke frowned at his friend's criticism. "Hey. These guys have *decades* of experience on us. If you put it together, it might even be a *century*."

Vic exchanged a wince with Jake.

"They're old and slow," Deke continued, "but they're really good."

"There were only three of them," one of the other boys reminded.

Deke shrugged the shoulders of his leather jacket. "So, what does that prove?"

Vic got to his feet and patted Deke's Mohawk. "That we're twice as good." He was careful not to hobble as he turned to the locker. "Accept it, Deke, and pay up gracefully."

There was a moment's silence. All three men turned to the boys.

"About the pizza..." Matt said with a glance at his

friends. They seemed to find interest in the ceiling, the floor, an empty locker.

He smiled winningly at his stepfather. "We're a little short. Can you lend me the money to pay you off with?"

CHAPTER FIVE

FROM A BENCH ACROSS the street, Vic watched a group of women emerge from the basement of the Lutheran church dressed in various degrees of athletic fashion, from color-coordinated exercise wear to tattered sweats splotched with paint. Some of them carried or led children, some peeled off singly to run to their cars. Loud, bouncy music still thrummed from the open windows of the church basement.

He'd watched Daphne go in dressed in a deliciously form-fitting black leotard with a wraparound skirt tied at her waist. Her hair was caught in a slightly mussy knot. On her feet were the new aerobics shoes. She led Jenny by the hand. Jenny held Bear in her right arm.

He'd learned a lot about Daphne's schedule this week. She worked Yes! Yogurt's shop Monday, Tuesday and Wednesday, where she started at eleven and got off at six. She picked Jenny up at TylerTots at six-fifteen. Labor Day, of course, had been an exception to the schedule.

On Thursday and Friday, she worked at TylerTots from seven-thirty until half past four. Tuesday and Thursday evenings and Saturday morning she took this aerobics class, then usually stopped with Jenny at a drive-in.

She spent evenings and the weekend in a little white farmhouse on the edge of town.

He'd seen no evidence of child neglect. In fact, he'd witnessed the opposite. When Daphne wasn't working at Yes! Yogurt, Jenny was always with her, and seemed to have the happy, confident princess-in-charge attitude of a little girl well loved.

And he hadn't seen one sign of a man in Daphne's life, much less a stream steady enough to constitute a business.

She also seemed to have too many friends for a woman purported to be selfish and manipulative.

He was beginning to believe that Celeste Huntington had an ax to grind that had nothing to do with the reasons she'd given him for tracking down her daughter-in-law.

He watched Daphne stop to talk to another young woman and thought he saw an uncharacteristic slump to her shoulders.

"Evening." An unfamiliar male voice brought him out of his speculations. He hid annoyance as he turned to face the stranger. If Vic had been this lax in the old days he'd have been dead. It was all Daphne's fault. He found it increasingly difficult to watch her and not be totally absorbed by her.

The man who sat down beside him was tall and muscular. And he was a cop. Vic knew that without being told. He looked into a pair of quiet blue eyes and understood that he'd been pegged. Hell. He'd counted on comfortable, lazy law-enforcement. And here he was on a park bench watching enticingly clad women and little children. Great. He probably looked like a perverted Forrest Gump.

"Victor Estevez," the man said. He was telling Vic he had his number.

Vic tried to look amenable without going overboard. "Right. You have me at a disadvantage."

"Brick Bauer. Sheriff's Department. Was just driving home and saw you sitting here."

"Brick," Vic repeated. Where had he heard that name before? Then it came to him. Britt's cousin. "The other man on Jake Marshack's Thursday-night basketball team?"

Brick looked surprised. "Yes."

Vic extended his hand. "I stood in for you last week. You picked a good time to be away. Jake's son brought his friends."

Brick's demeanor softened only fractionally, but he shook Vic's hand. "How do you know Jake?"

Vic gave him his cover story—retired cop looking to start over. Then he told him about finding Matt on the side of the road. "I took him home, spent some time with the Marshacks at the Labor Day celebration at the park last Monday, and he invited me to the game."

Brick studied him for a moment, his manner polite but less than warm. "So, you're planning to stay?"

"Paul Bullard's helping me find a place," Vic replied.

Brick nodded. "So, what are you doing here? On this bench?" He gestured toward the women and children still milling around in front of the church. It was clear the man was not convinced his motives were innocent.

"I was checking out storefronts," Vic replied with careful ease. "Jake told me about one between the Lutheran church and the bank." He pointed to it, a splotch of red brick between the cheerful commotion at the church and the neoclassical bank front. "I came to sit here and examine it from this perspective. The women leaving the church drew my attention. That's all."

Brick studied him for an extra moment. He didn't look convinced. *A first-rate cop,* Vic thought.

"Well, that's good," Brick finally said, "because it would upset me to think you were watching the women and children. And when I'm upset, somebody pays."

Vic smiled to himself and thought he would damn well bet somebody paid. "I'm not a threat to society, I promise you."

"Good. Good." Brick stood and gave him a polite nod. "Welcome to Tyler. I guess I'll see you at the game next Thursday night."

"I guess you will."

When Brick walked away, Vic felt as though he'd just survived a back-room interrogation.

The late-afternoon sun was low and the street had grown quiet. The music had stopped and the women had dispersed. The narrow street was now empty of cars, and Vic noticed Daphne, with Jenny in tow, walking down the street to the next block, where she'd parked the Escort just a minute or two before class time.

She stopped at the corner, making a production of looking left and then right, probably for Jenny's benefit. He noted her weary posture again. With her hair caught atop her head, her neck looked too slender to support it, the line of her shoulders too fragile.

He'd intended to keep his distance for a few days because the intensity of his involvement in this case was beginning to worry him. And he'd seen in her eyes in the shoe store that she was attracted to him.

Generally, he would have considered that a good thing. But he'd been hired to find her and transport her back to Palm Beach so that her mother-in-law could take her to court and get Jenny away from her.

He couldn't be honest with Daphne until he understood what was going on and could offer a solution. He couldn't find out what was going on without getting to know her side of the story. And he was already feeling too much to listen objectively.

When he made a mess, he did a fine job of it.

He saw her put a hand to her eyes, shake her head as though to clear it, then lower her hand and start across the street.

Then he saw her dissolve into the landscape. What? As he loped across the street, he heard Jenny's panicky cry, "Mommy!"

He looked down the straight stretch of sidewalk and saw Daphne crumpled in the middle of the street, with Jenny screaming and pulling on her hand.

He took off at a run and was there in an instant. "Daphne!" he said, leaning over her.

Her eyelids fluttered open, and he experienced a relief that felt too big for his body. She tried to push herself up, but fell back again.

"Mommy!" Jenny wailed.

Vic reached across Daphne for the purse and diaper bag that had fallen beside her.

"Mommy's okay, Jenny," he said. "Come on with me. We're going to take her to the car."

"Want Mommy!" she sobbed pitifully.

Vic took her by the shoulders and gave her a small shake. "Bring Bear," he said firmly, "and come with me. I'm going to carry Mommy to the car."

He shouldered the diaper bag and purse and lifted Daphne into his arms. Her eyelids fluttered open again, but her head lolled against his shoulder.

"Okay, Jenny," he said. "Here we go." He started back across the street, since not a soul was visible in either direction. He was relieved to see that Jenny, still crying, held tightly to her bear and followed.

"Good girl," he praised.

She stayed with him until he reached the blue Corolla he'd rented. But once there, she pointed down the street to Daphne's Escort. "Mommy car," she said.

He set Daphne on her feet and leaned her body against his as he unlocked the car door. "I know, but we're taking my car home. Can you get in the back?"

Daphne came to with startling suddenness. "What happened? Jenny? Jenny!"

"Right here." Vic held Daphne still as she tried to push him away in her concern for her daughter. "She's here. In the back seat."

"Mommy!" At the sound of her mother's voice, Jenny leaned out of the back seat, beaming. "Mommy fall!"

Daphne put a hand to her head and sagged against him. "Dizzy," she complained weakly.

"Okay, we're going to sit you down." He eased her into the passenger seat and laid her head back against the rest. Then he brought the seat belt across her and snapped it in place. He locked and closed her door.

Then he leaned into the back to belt Jenny in, knowing he wasn't in compliance with child-restraint laws, but seeing no way around it at the moment.

Daphne appeared fairly lucid when he climbed in behind the wheel. "Did I...faint?" she asked.

"Yes. Just sit still and we'll find out what's wrong."

She tried to turn in his direction. "Vic..."

He slid his key into the ignition, then put a hand out to her to still her movements. "Just relax. Jenny's okay, and we're going to get you—"

"If you take me to the hospital," she warned with a

weak smile, "I will personally see that Matt and his friends rematch you next Thursday night."

Vic turned the key. "I don't think it's protocol," he said over the sound of the motor, "to threaten your rescuer. How do you feel?"

"Weak. Dizzy," she admitted. "But I know what it is. I forgot to eat lunch, and the instructor was out to get us tonight, I'm convinced she was. It's only a sugar low. *Please* don't take me to the hospital. I just need food." She gave him a warm smile. "Okay?"

But Daphne was not entirely surprised five minutes later to find herself being carried into the emergency room of Tyler General Hospital. She'd been through this with Vic before, on Labor Day. He was apparently not susceptible to pleas and promises.

Jenny, directed to hold on to his pant leg, ran to keep up with them.

An hour later Daphne was carried out again after having been tested and lectured. "You need food and rest," a stern middle-aged doctor told her. "You women and your diets and your exercise classes. The Special Forces probably train less rigorously than you do. There's no evidence of ulcers or diverticulitis or gallstones. Your stomach juices are working on your stomach lining because you aren't giving them any food! Eat something and you'll feel better."

"May I ask," Daphne inquired quietly as Vic headed for the car, "where I'm being taken?" The sky was dark blue now, and the North Star was clearly visible. The evening was cool, and there was something very nice about being carried. She held on and suppressed all the cautions that tried to claim her attention.

Vic stopped at the car, put her on her feet, but kept an arm around her as he opened the door.

"The way I see it," he said, pushing the back seat forward to let Jenny in, "you have two choices."

Daphne raised an eyebrow in exaggerated surprise. "My, my. You're slipping. *Two* choices when I'm not usually allowed even one."

At her sarcasm, his lips twisted. "You want to hear them, or shall I just do what I want to do?"

"Oh, let's hear them, by all means." She held on to his forearms for support as she leaned down to sit. "Thank you."

He belted Jenny into her seat, belted Bear in beside her per her instructions, then slipped in behind the wheel. He turned in his seat to face Daphne. She felt the full impact of a very displeased glare.

"I can take you to Britt's, tell her that you collapsed in the street, endangering yourself and Jenny because you skipped lunch, then went to an aerobics class. She could keep an eye on you tonight."

And wouldn't that be fun. Daphne would be scolded, force-fed, and harassed unmercifully for days.

"Or we can pick up some groceries," he offered, "I can take you home, fix something to eat and hang around for a while to make sure you're okay."

Oh, God. That was infinitely the better personal choice—but the one that held the most potential for long-range trouble. She was in so much trouble, anyway, Daphne finally decided, what was a little more?

She tried to look as though she were reluctant to make the concession. She folded her arms. "You don't have all the advantages here, you know. I could make a citizen's arrest."

He grinned skeptically. "Of me? For what?"

"You have a two-year-old in the back of your car in

a simple seat belt," she said with a judicious air. "She's supposed to be in a car seat."

He shook his head at the suggestion of guilt. "Considering the circumstances, I'm sure any police officer would excuse me. And anyway, I think it's just a fining offense, not cause for arrest." He grinned. "Unless we're talking handcuffs. Then I might let you do it."

She laughed. She couldn't help it. "Jenny and I both love eggs," she conceded. "That would be easy to fix."

"It doesn't have to be easy. I'm pretty good in the kitchen."

"Thank you, but it's getting late and Jenny's probably starving."

"All right. Eggs, it is."

A short while later Daphne set the small oblong table in her roomy kitchen and glanced toward the stove, where Vic was preparing omelets. Jenny hadn't left his side. With Bear in his Mary Janes held in her arms, she followed Vic from the stove to the coffeepot to the toaster, the outlets widely spaced due to the farmhouse's old wiring.

"Whoa." Almost tripping over her on his way back to the stove, he lifted her onto his hip.

Daphne laughed softly as he was confronted with the problem of cooking with the stuffed animal in his face.

"Can we sit Bear on the counter?" he asked.

"No," Jenny answered without considering the matter. "Jenny Bear."

"Okay." He put the spatula down and moved the fuzzy toy in her arms so that she held him by the neck rather than around the waist. "How's that?"

"Good," she said, her other arm wrapped around Vic's formidable triceps.

"Good." He smiled at her. "A reasonable woman is

a rare thing, you know. You'll be in great demand when you grow up.''

She smiled back at him, obviously having no idea what he was talking about, but liking the sound of his voice. ''Yeah,'' she said.

''Yeah,'' he replied, and bumped his forehead against hers.

She giggled delightedly.

Daphne watched in amazement as Jenny packed away a good half of the small omelet Vic had given her, and half of an English muffin. But Daphne had to stop her from playing with the cheese in the omelet.

''Killjoy.'' Vic laughed, topping up her coffee. ''Half the fun of mozzarella is being able to tie bows with it and wrap it around your neck.''

''You're right, of course,'' Daphne agreed with a scolding glance at him, ''but if I don't stop her from doing it now, she'll play with her mozzarella one day at the country club in front of her prospective in-laws. Come on, Jen. Let's wash your hands and you can ride your trike for a little while.''

Vic cleared off the table and noticed that Daphne had eaten little more than her daughter had. But she wasn't getting around him. He'd bought strawberries and cream—good, nutritious, tasty stuff.

He set a small bowl of it at her place and put the dishes in the dishwasher.

She came through a moment later, carrying a baby-size tricycle. Jenny skipped along beside her.

Daphne moved the coffee table in the living room away from the sofa, creating a track of sorts for her little racer. Jenny hopped on the trike and pedaled as though the living room were the Tour de France.

Daphne came back to the table and frowned at the

bowl at her place. "I can't eat another thing," she protested.

"Yes, you can," he insisted. "Or the threat to call Britt still holds."

Her expression was half amused, half accusatory. "The deal was dinner. You didn't say anything about dessert."

"Dinner includes dessert. And anyway, you ate less than half your dinner, so your part of the deal isn't met."

He noticed the moment she decided to change tactics. Her eyes softened and took on a slightly helpless look that belied the black eye he still sported.

"I'll get sick if I eat it, Vic," she said, her voice climbing a little. It was a cajoling tone she might have used on Jenny.

Much as he would have enjoyed indulging her to see where it led, he held firm. "Try. When you turn green, I'll let you stop."

She measured him with a look. "The doctor told me I should eat lightly for a few days until my appetite returns."

"Sorry." He rewarded her effort with a grin. "Good try, but he mistook me for your husband, and while you were getting dressed, he told me your problem is that you aren't eating enough. So, before you make yourself seriously ill and collapse in the street again—" he pointed to the bowl "—eat it."

She gave him a glare related to the one she'd worn when she'd punched him. "Look," she said. "I appreciate your concern and your eagerness to help, but you have no right to tell me what—"

"You didn't hear Jenny screaming and sobbing when you fell," he retorted. "You didn't see the terror on her face when she couldn't wake you up. What would have happened to her if there'd been traffic on that street and I hadn't come by?''

Common sense warred with pride and finally won, though not graciously. Daphne grabbed her fork and stabbed a strawberry, looking very much as though in her mind it represented some part of his anatomy.

He folded his arms on the table and leaned toward her. ''When did you start having trouble eating?''

She gave him a fulsome glare. ''I'm not talking to you. I'm busy eating. You may as well go away.'' She put the berry in her mouth and chewed.

An angry shriek came from the living room. Daphne tried to stand, but he pushed her down again and went to investigate.

As Jenny kicked at a pedal, Vic saw that the trike's right rear wheel was caught against the leg of the coffee table. He released it and pushed her off. She sped away, making motor noises, her anger abandoned now that she was free.

At the table, Daphne chewed as though she were eating year-old jerky. Vic resumed his chair, took a sip of coffee and rolled his eyes at her dramatics.

''Give me a break. They're ripe and succulent. I had a few when you were washing Jenny's hands. Are you bulimic, too?''

''No!'' she snapped. ''Nor anorexic. I just get indigestion.''

''Why?''

She pushed the bowl away, daring him with a look to give her grief over it. ''I thought the doctor mistook you for my husband and told you everything.''

Satisfied that there were only two berries left, Vic pushed the bowl back toward her and handed her the spoon he'd used to stir sugar into his coffee. "He told me what the problem is with your stomach. I want to know what the problem is with *you*. Eat the cream. It's good food value."

"It'll clog my arteries."

"If you die of malnutrition, nothing's going to flow through them anyway."

"You are such a smart a—!"

"And you're mule-headed. We've been through this. The sooner you eat the cream, the sooner I'll go."

With a growl of barely contained exasperation, she spooned up the cream. "There!" she said at last, slapping the utensil on the table. "Goodbye."

He didn't move. "When did the indigestion start?"

She huffed impatiently. "You promised you'd go!"

"I will. This is just personal interest. When?"

She fell back against her chair, clearly at the end of her rope. He felt guilty for pushing her, but he could still remember her crumpled in the middle of the street, her child terrified. He had to know what lay at the bottom of this convoluted mystery.

"Why does it matter?" she asked reasonably.

He looked into her eyes and said just as reasonably, "I'm not sure. Why do *I* matter to *you*?"

A loud silence filled the kitchen, except for the tick of the clock, the hum of the refrigerator and the nonsensical sounds Jenny produced as she made her hundredth trip around the coffee table.

Vic waited, heart thumping a little hard. If she was going to draw back from him, she would do it now. A simple denial of his question would say everything.

He accepted that this had nothing to do with the case, but everything to do with him—with what he wanted.

He'd never worked that way—indulging his personal

interests in the middle of a case. It horrified him a little that he was doing it now. Or it would have if he'd had a choice.

She looked steadily into his eyes, then answered his original question. "Because the world is a tricky and sadistic place." She pushed away from the table and stood.

When he didn't follow, she sat back down on the edge of her chair and said quietly, flatly, "My father died when I was twelve, and my mother married a man I hated. Every time we sat around the table to eat, my— my stomach hurt." She put a hand to it now, and her fingers trembled at the memories. She pushed them away to concentrate on getting Vic Estevez out of her house, out of her life.

"I've had indigestion ever since." She folded her arms and said resolutely, "Now, I appreciate all you've done for us tonight. And thank you for the bear, and for the shoes." Her voice and her manner softened. "Jenny was thrilled with them." She stiffened again and looked him straight in the eye. "Listen to me carefully. I hope you enjoy Tyler, and that you find happiness here, but I never want to see you again, do you understand? Whatever it is you think you want from me, you're not going to get it—not friendship, not sex, not anything. I don't know how to make it any plainer than that."

He smiled at her. "Why not?"

She brought both hands up to cover her face, then, when he thought she was about to scream, she lowered them to her lap and said with strained patience, "Because I still love my husband. I always will."

He looked into her eyes and shook his head. "No. Maybe you loved him when he was alive. Maybe a part of him will always be with you." He pushed himself to his feet and she did the same. He pinned her with his gaze from across the table. "But right now, you're very interested in me."

Jenny, seeing him walk toward the door, abandoned her trike and ran to him. "Vic go bye-bye?" she asked, obviously displeased.

He lifted her into his arms, ignoring Daphne's look of helpless frustration. "I have to go home, Jenny. But I'll see you in the morning, okay?"

"Didn't you hear anything I said?" Daphne demanded.

Vic nodded innocently, hugging Jenny. "Everything. But how are you going to get to your car in the morning?"

As she pondered that, he continued, "I'll pick you up. And I'll make it an hour early so we can have breakfast first."

"No, I—you…"

Vic handed Jenny to her. "See you at ten."

"But—"

"Bye."

Daphne, still in a mystified daze, bathed Jenny and put her to bed.

She tried to re-create their conversation in her mind and couldn't figure out where she'd gone wrong. Unless simply listening to him had done it.

CHAPTER SIX

DAPHNE STARED AT the spreading mound of cookie-crumb topping she'd dropped on the floor behind the counter and wondered what on earth had happened to her. She'd been on the run for a year, and she'd known some very desperate moments, but she'd pretty much kept it together. Her body and her mind had worked in tandem. Her brain made decisions and her hands carried them out.

Then Vic Estevez had arrived in town.

Britt, who'd come to the shop to pick up the bank deposit, moved up behind her to look down on the mess.

"Well," she said, "I'd never have thought of putting the crumb topping *there,* but I told you to run this place as though it were your own."

Daphne walked around her as if she weren't there and went for the broom. "I'm sorry," she said crossly. "You can take it out of my check."

Britt folded her arms and leaned against the juice case. "Right. Like I would do that."

Broom and dustpan in hand, Daphne bent to sweep up the pile. "You should. This morning I caught my smock on the coffee spigot and dumped half the butter-toffee crumbs into the sink."

Britt laughed. "I think it's kind of neat to see you a little out of control."

Daphne cast her a dark glance. "Some business manager you are. This is waste. You're not supposed to smile over waste.''

Britt bent down to hold the trash can steady as Daphne dropped in the contents of the dustpan. "I can smile because I'll always be a woman before I'm a business manager. And that's what's wrong with you.''

Daphne scooped in the last of the crumbs and straightened to frown at her. "That I'm *not* a business manager?''

"That you *are* a woman.'' Britt followed her into the back as she replaced the broom and dustpan. "You always think of yourself as Jenny's mother, as my employee, as a care provider at TylerTots. But there's more to you than that, and now that you're beginning to see it, I think your system's just a little out of whack. You simply have to adjust to it.''

Daphne glanced toward the front of the shop and, seeing that it remained empty, patted Britt's arm and asked candidly, "What *are* you talking about?''

"You know what I'm talking about. Or who. Vic Estevez.''

"I told you—''

"Yes, but you had breakfast with him this morning, with Jenny climbing all over him. And that was after he carried you into the hospital last night when you collapsed after aerobics class. How were the omelets he made for dinner?''

Daphne spread both hands in frustration over the lack of privacy in small-town life. "How could you have found all this out in under twenty-four hours?''

Britt looked pleased with herself. "Jake met Michael Kenton for breakfast this morning at Marge's and saw you. A friend of mine at the ER desk saw you carried in and carried out, and her daughter Sandy is on the

Christmas-in-Tyler committee with me. We met this morning.''

Daphne absorbed all this information with a disbelieving shake of her head. ''And how, pray tell, did you know he made omelets for dinner last night?''

''Ingrid Norgaard checked out his groceries last night while you waited in the car. She's on the committee, too.''

''But you could do anything with a dozen eggs.''

''Yeah, but he also bought cheese and sausage. I thought omelets were a pretty safe bet. Were they good?''

Daphne breathed out, feeling as though she had to open a safety valve or explode. ''Delicious.''

''That was a thoughtful thing for him to do. But I'm a little surprised you let him go home with you.'' Britt looked into her eyes. Daphne tried desperately to keep them shuttered.

''That was only because the alternative he gave me to letting him come home with Jenny and me and fix dinner was taking me to your house and having you nurse me.'' She smiled blandly at Britt. ''I had to choose between his bullying or your nagging.''

Britt hugged her effusively. ''And you chose him! Maybe there's hope for you, after all.''

''But I'm not seeing him again. Ever.''

Britt hugged her once more. ''That's what I said about Jake. You'll come to your senses.''

Daphne hung limply in her friend's fervent embrace. She was still stuffed from the fruit and the bran muffin Vic had insisted she eat at Marge's. She asked Britt in a strangled voice, ''Shouldn't you go to the bank before it closes?''

"A MESSAGE FOR YOU, Mr. Estevez," Sheila Wagner called to him from behind the counter. She handed him a folded sheet of paper as he approached.

He opened it and found a note on Tyler Realty letterhead. He smiled. He found something comforting in Paul Bullard's enthusiasm.

"How's the house hunting going?" Sheila asked.

"I don't think French Provincial is my style," he replied, then waved the note at her as he headed for the stairs. "But it looks like Mr. Bullard has another idea."

He did.

"A Tudor adaptation," the note read. "Half-timber, stucco, master bedroom *suite,* three other bedrooms, stone fireplace, patio. I can take you by this afternoon."

Vic went to the window in his room to look out on the softly rolling landscape. It was overcast this morning, the green grass and trees looking somber rather than vibrant.

Something ached a little in his gut and he put a hand to it, although he knew he couldn't rub it away. It was loneliness.

That surprised him. In all his years of dangerous work, some of it out of the country, he'd always felt very self-contained, self-sufficient. When he was gone for long periods, he sometimes missed his parents, his siblings, but their love for each other, their interconnectedness, was as much a part of him as his skin, so he never really felt without them.

This was something else. This was like a longing for something new, something born out of this pretty little town: a smiling little two-year-old who'd stood on his knees in the restaurant booth this morning and fed him pieces of toast, and a beautiful woman with sad secrets in her smile.

He fell onto the edge of the bed and contemplated the phone. He should call Celeste Huntington and report in, tell her he was still investigating, ask her to be patient.

When he got close enough to Daphne to hear her side of the story and figure out what the hell was going on, he could assess the situation and decide how to react.

Right now, he couldn't tell Celeste any more than he'd told her that last time.

So he picked up the phone and dialed Bullard.

"MOMMY HOME!" Jenny leaned backward out of Daphne's arms and whined, bored with the wait in line.

Daphne braced herself and struggled not to drop everything—purse, book and child. Mercifully, she'd talked Jenny into leaving Bear in the car.

Britt, standing behind her in line in the bookstore and holding Jacob by the hand, quickly tucked her own book under her arm and took Daphne's from her.

Daphne used her free hand to right her child. "Jenny, please be patient," she cajoled. "It's almost our turn."

Daphne turned to reclaim her book. "Thanks, Britt. I'll buy you a cup of coffee after we have our books—"

Without warning, Jenny strained out of Daphne's arms again, this time leaning toward something at the head of the line.

"Jenny, what are you…?"

"Vic!" Jenny shouted.

He turned while Judy Lowery, seated at a table decorated with flowers at the head of the line, signed his copy of *Murder by Moonlight*. He waved at Jenny.

Jenny pushed at Daphne's chest. "Go, Mommy!"

"No!" Daphne said firmly. "You have to stay right here. Vic is busy."

Vic turned away from the table at that moment, his book in hand, and the line moved forward.

Daphne smiled politely as he approached them. It had been three days since her fainting incident, and she hadn't seen or heard from him. Not that she'd wanted to. She just wondered where he disappeared to when he left her. Where he came from when he suddenly reappeared. Britt often mentioned seeing him, but she, Daphne, never did. It was almost as though she had a blind spot somewhere, and he remained aligned with it.

"Hi," he said warmly. His eyes went over her face as though he could read her thoughts.

She felt herself stiffen just a little. She did not want to admit, particularly to herself, that she'd been piqued by his absence. And she certainly didn't want him to see that in her.

She intended to keep her distance, but Jenny reached out of her arms to grab a fistful of his shirt and he had no choice but to lean closer or risk getting a hole in the blue-and-black flannel when she ripped a button off.

"May I?" he asked, circling Jenny's little body with his large hands.

Considering Jenny was already halfway out of her arms and reaching for his neck, Daphne simply smiled in reply. "Sure. But be on guard. She's really squirmy today."

His brow furrowed. "Literally?"

Before Daphne could reply, Jenny leaned backward out of his arms and squealed delightedly as he shifted his hand to strengthen his hold on her.

"Ah. I see what you mean." He scooped Jenny upright and lifted her onto his shoulders. "Hi, Britt."

"Hi, Vic. Deke told me his father showed you that Tudor place at the west end of Morgan Avenue."

He nodded, wincing as Jenny played drums on his head. "It was very elegant. But I'm looking for something less formal, more…just comfortable."

"A farmhouse?"

"Yeah. With a raggy garden and room for a big dog."

"Do you have a big dog?"

"No. But I want one."

Vic remained in step with the women as they moved ahead in line. In his area of work he'd always been fast on his feet with a good fabrication, and he seemed to be maintaining the skill.

Only this wasn't precisely a lie, he discovered, as he moved slightly sideways to prevent Jenny from yanking at a bright red cardboard apple dangling from the ceiling as part of the store's back-to-school promotion.

This wasn't a story he'd agreed upon with his superiors, as he'd done in his DEA days. And it wasn't one of the out-and-out lies he'd often told as a private detective to get where he wanted to get or learn what he needed to know.

He was tapping into his own fantasies, and he found it just a little unsettling.

After a week and a half in Tyler, he was seriously considering the town as a place to settle when he felt comfortable enough to do so. That was providing people here were still speaking to him, depending upon the eventual outcome of this case.

He would love to have a place here with a big, unstructured garden, and children and dogs running around.

He would like a wife.

That admission confounded him. As attached as he was to his family, he'd always thought that falling in love would compromise his freedom to move, his spontaneity.

But he'd felt inexplicably more stationary lately. The thought of being secure in one place had a sudden appeal it hadn't had before.

"Hi, Daph!" Judy Lowery greeted her as it was finally Daphne's turn to have her book autographed.

"I'm so thrilled for you!" Daphne said, handing her book across the table. "I can't wait to read it. I'll bet it's brilliant."

Judy, in a subtle gray power suit worn with a pink blouse, leaned gravely over the book as she wrote. Then she handed it back with a smile. "I did my best to be clever," she said. "If you don't like it, please keep it to yourself. If you love it, please call me and gush!"

Daphne nodded. "You've got it. Thanks."

"Have you had lunch?" Vic asked as Daphne joined him and Jenny, who now seemed to be steering him by the ears.

"Yep. Bowl of soup," she replied, reaching up for Jenny.

"What kind?" he asked as Jenny slapped her hands away.

Daphne blinked and focused on him. "What do you mean, what kind?"

"What kind?" he repeated, lifting Jenny off his shoulders and into his arms as they approached the low overhang of the shop's doorway. "You know, tomato-rice? Beef-vegetable? Broccoli-cheddar?"

"What possible difference could it make?" she asked.

He stopped in the doorway and looked into her eyes. "You're lying, aren't you? You haven't eaten. Did you at least have breakfast? Have you had anything since I left you the other morning?''

Daphne intended to ignore the question as presumptuous and claim her daughter. But Jenny said, ''No!'' in her best two-year-old manner and turned her face away from Daphne and into Vic's neck.

Vic patted Jenny's back. ''Lying's not a good example for her, you know,'' he said.

''I am not lying,'' Daphne said, feeling enormous exasperation coupled with a curious exhilaration. She didn't understand it and didn't want to. She wanted to take her daughter and go home. Only her daughter seemed to have completely shifted allegiance to the man who'd bought patent-leather shoes for her bear.

He disputed her claim with a scolding tilt of his head.

She sighed. ''I was thinking about having soup. I just haven't had a chance yet. I came here first.''

''So you'll have to eat now.''

She shook her head. ''I spent too long in line and now I'm out of time. Someone covered for me this morning because I had to take Jenny for a checkup. But now I have to go to work.''

''All right, Daph,'' a male voice said from the sidewalk. ''Flash your book and smile!''

Daphne turned to find Rob Friedman focusing on her with his camera. Before she could react, she heard the shutter click. No! Not a photo of her *and* Jenny!

This couldn't happen, she thought, trying not to panic. Not after all the trouble she'd gone to to keep Jenny out of Glenna's videos, all the pains she'd taken to avoid Rob Friedman at every Tyler occasion.

How could she object, she wondered frantically, without making everyone within view suspicious?

''Rob, I never take a good—'' she began, but fate

intervened in the shape of her energetic daughter. Jenny reached out of Vic's arms, grabbed the dangling strap of Rob's camera and pulled.

Vic watched with considerable satisfaction as the camera fell to the ground. Good move on Jenny's part. Good timing on his own.

He'd seen the panic in Daphne's eyes and thought he understood what it was all about. Any photo that ended up in a newspaper, even in a small, out-of-the-way place like Tyler, could be picked up by a larger metropolitan chain. Particularly when it accompanied a story of broader-than-local interest, like the publication of a book.

He'd also sensed Jenny's curiosity, the outward movement of her little arm; one small step on his part had placed her close enough to allow her to pull the camera out of the unsuspecting reporter's hands.

It landed lens-down on the concrete with considerable force, and the back flipped open, exposing the film.

Daphne put a hand over her mouth in horror, but Vic saw the disbelieving relief in her eyes.

He reached back to his hip pocket for his checkbook. "God, Friedman, I'm sorry," he said, injecting as much sincere contrition into his voice as he could. "I had no idea she was going to do that. Let me—"

He stopped when he saw that the reporter wasn't buying his story. The man didn't say anything, simply looked into his eyes with an expression that condemned him for taking him for a fool.

"It's all right," Friedman said after a moment, reaching down to pick up what was left of his camera. He rested his dark eyes on Vic and said significantly, "I know it wasn't the baby's fault."

Daphne frowned. "You two know each other?"

"Paul Bullard introduced us," Rob said, examining the pieces of camera he held in his hand. "When I went to pick up an ad at his office." His mouth quirked as he glanced darkly at Vic. "He told me he was a nice guy."

"Oh, Rob," Daphne said. "I'll replace it for you."

He sighed. "Naw. It was just an old camera. Too new to be an antique, and too old to fit any of the new refinements. Forget it. How's the party going?"

"It's crowded in there," Britt replied as she stepped out of the store, carrying Jacob. "Daphne and I waited half an hour in line." She frowned down at the camera he held in one hand and the broken lens in the other. "What happened?"

"Jenny," Daphne said guiltily.

"Not a problem," Rob said, "I always have a spare in the Jeep. Pleasant afternoon, ladies. Estevez."

Vic thought he detected a trace of hostility in the sound of his name, and didn't blame Friedman.

But he himself had saved Daphne from the risk of discovery. Great. Now he was clearly working for the other side.

"Well." Daphne tried to take Jenny from him again. "I have to get to work."

Jenny turned away from her again and clutched Vic's neck.

"Aren't you going to have some lunch?" Britt asked.

"I invited her," Vic said, then he grinned. "She said she didn't have time."

Daphne pointed to her watch. "It's almost one-thirty."

"You can have the afternoon off," Britt said.

Daphne glared at her, obviously trying to send a message with her eyes. "I don't think so. Barbara came in to sub for me just this morning. I promised—"

Britt smiled blithely. "I do think so. And as your employer, it's my opinion that counts. Barb's been wanting more hours." She reached up to Jenny. "Want to come home with Jakie and me and watch *Pocahontas* and have ice cream?"

Jenny clapped her hands, affection for Vic abandoned in a heartbeat.

"Okay. Daph, want to get me your car seat?"

"No, I do not want—" Daphne stopped when she realized she was talking to thin air. With Jenny in his arms, Vic was following Britt and Jacob to the Marshack van.

Feeling completely thwarted and still oddly exhilarated, Daphne went to get Jenny's car seat.

STUFFED ON A CUP of beef-barley soup and half a roll, Daphne stopped just outside Marge's and jammed her hands into the pockets of the red blazer she wore over her jeans.

Vic stopped beside her, car keys in his hand. It was beginning to drizzle.

She smiled companionably, deciding she was out of here now. He was trouble today. More trouble than usual. She couldn't quite define it, but there was a subtle difference in the way he looked at her.

At first she'd attributed the observation to years of paranoia. She'd once thought in the other life that her profession was written on her face. She'd been sure every decent person she met saw inside her and was repulsed.

But what she read in his eyes wasn't revulsion. She thought it was seduction.

Not that she hadn't seen that in men's eyes before, but seducing a woman bought and paid for left mystery out of the equation.

But that was what she saw in Vic's eyes—an invitation to follow him toward undefined promises.

A vigorous sense of self-preservation, finely honed over the past year, screamed for her to run.

"Thank you for lunch, Vic," she said briskly. "I can walk back to work from here."

"Britt gave you the afternoon off." He took her elbow and tried to lead her across the parking lot toward his car.

She held firm. "Then I'll take advantage of the time to run some errands."

He took several steps backward toward the car, a small smile curving his lips. "Come on," he said, enticing her with a beckoning gesture. "You know you'd rather spend the time with me."

She rolled her eyes and tried hard not to smile back. "Is this that Latino macho we hear so much about? You think you're irresistible to me?"

"Yes," he said, his smile growing wider. He held his hand out to her. "Come with me."

She felt herself sway in his direction, not only emotionally but physically. But she couldn't. She couldn't.

He was a nice guy ready to put a stressful past behind him and start over in beautiful Tyler. He saw renewal here, romance.

But her role as a romantic figure was over; had been over since she was twelve. All she had to offer him was heartbreak.

"I..." She shook her head.

He dropped his hand, closed the distance between

them in two long strides and silenced her with an index finger on her lips.

"If you tell me you can't," he warned with a further widening of that smile that was generating heat all the way to the dark and icy depths of her, "I'll carry you to the car and kidnap you. Have you noticed the windows?"

"What windows?"

"Marge's windows."

She turned to look over her shoulder. All the diners seated at the window booths were watching them. Marge herself stood at the door, peering shamelessly through the blinds.

"It's possible," he said, "that those are people who watched me carry you to the first-aid station at the park. Maybe even saw me carry you into the hospital. If they see me carry you to the car, they might pitch in together and buy you a wheelchair."

She folded her arms and considered him. "Did you really retire from police work?" she asked. "Or were you given insanity leave?"

"It's called administrative leave," he corrected. "And I might have been close to that if I'd stayed any longer. Now, please. Won't you accept my invitation?"

It was growing increasingly hard to hold back the smile. "I don't think 'Come with me or I'll kidnap you' constitutes an invitation."

He offered her his hand again. "Last chance."

And it was those two words that decided her. She'd been so sure there were no more chances.

This wasn't a real one, of course. This couldn't go anywhere; she wouldn't let it. But it was a chance for today—just for today—to be the woman she might have been, had things been different. Had there been no Gordon in her life and everything that resulted from his presence there.

Resolved to have this afternoon and to stop it there, she stretched out her hand and placed it in his.

She saw the flash of male arrogance in his eyes and might have been annoyed, except that he brought her hand to his lips and kissed it.

"Where are we going?" she asked, as he looked left, then right before pulling out of the parking lot.

"The House of Three Gables," he replied, executing the turn.

She frowned at his profile. "Pardon me?"

"The House of Three Gables," he repeated, casting her a glance as he eased into the quiet traffic. "Aren't you intrigued?"

She relaxed in her seat, determined to enjoy the afternoon. She leaned her head back and closed her eyes. "The House of Clark Gable might intrigue me. What's the House of Three Gables?"

She heard his soft laughter. "Paul Bullard's idea of a joke, I think. I'm supposed to meet him at two-thirty at a listing on the west end of town. He referred to it as the House of Three Gables."

Daphne's eyes snapped open. That was *her* house. Not the house she rented, but the house she'd chosen as the one she would buy if some miraculous intervention took place and she was able to stay in Tyler.

It was just outside of town, a rambling, country-gentry sort of farmhouse with a deep front porch that ran the length of it, add-ons that meandered beside and behind it, and three gables. It had flowers, trees, and bushes that had grown wild over the summer during the owner's absence.

She closed her eyes again, a little stab of pain marring

her "last chance" afternoon. She could see him barbecuing in the yard. But she couldn't see herself there.

It WAS BEGINNING to rain in earnest as Vic turned into the driveway. Paul Bullard waited for them in the shelter of the porch, his burgundy Le Baron pulled up to the garage.

"Daphne. Hi," he said in mild surprise. "Good thinking, Vic. A woman's opinion in these matters is invaluable."

Bullard cast one quick speculative look from Vic to her, then led the way inside.

Vic tried to keep a level head, but it wasn't working. The house was wonderful; he'd thought so the moment he'd pulled up. And he'd heard Daphne's little gasp of pleasure as they walked inside.

A short hallway with a hardwood floor led them to a huge, open room with long windows and a marble fireplace. The walls were painted a soft white that seemed to glow with comfort while rain drummed against the roof.

The room flowed into another that held a built-in buffet, then on into a wide country kitchen painted yellow. It had tall, glass-fronted cupboards, the traditional window over the sink and a windowed back door that led outside to a second, large porch.

Leaving the kitchen through another exit, they walked into a long room that took up that entire side of the house. It boasted a deep bay window with a window seat, another fireplace and built-in shelves on all the walls.

"A library," Daphne breathed in amazement. "Just like you read about in novels. A library!"

Bullard then led the way upstairs. A very large bedroom opened off the upstairs hall.

"Master bedroom," Bullard said. "Very spacious. Notice the fireplace. Nice touch in a bedroom. French doors that open onto a balcony big enough for picnicking or sunbathing."

Vic stepped out onto the balcony to look at the view—rolling pastureland with a woodlot in the distance. Bullard quickly followed him to shield him with an umbrella.

Daphne leaned a shoulder in the doorway. She smelled autumn in the rain. And the full-blown, last-rose-of-summer quality of her dreams.

"How much of this land belongs to the property?" Vic asked.

"Three acres. New roof last year. Whole place was rewired four years ago."

"Furnace?"

"Oil."

Daphne stepped back as the men turned to come inside. The fragrance of the outdoors clung to them, and as Vic wrapped a casual arm around her shoulders, she caught another whiff of her dreams.

Three smaller bedrooms, identical to one another except for the angle of the slope of the ceiling, comprised the other half of the upstairs.

Bullard smiled. "Bedrooms for your children and your mother-in-law." Here, too, there were built-in shelves and drawers, and a window seat in each dormer.

A loud electronic sound brought Bullard to attention. He reached into his pocket for a beeper and read the display.

He smiled apologetically. "You folks look around.

I'm going down to my car to call the office. I'll try not to be too long, then I'll answer all your questions.''

His heavy footsteps could be heard on the stairs as Vic went to the window in the middle room and bent a knee on the seat to look out.

''What's it like here in the winter?'' he asked.

She came up beside him and had to crouch on both knees to see anything. He braced an arm on the wall indenture beside her, and she felt the sudden tension of close confinement. Her pulse quickened, her skin prickled and she was sure he must hear the sound as she tried to drag in a breath. ''Cold,'' she replied. ''Lots of…snow.''

He turned his head to look at her, his arm a barrier right beside her cheek. On her other side, steady rain rapped against the window.

''Do you have a mother?'' he asked.

The question seemed like a non sequitur for a moment, until she remembered Paul Bullard's remark, ''Bedrooms for your children and your mother-in-law.''

Mother-in-law. Her heart ticked wildly at the notion.

''Uh…technically,'' she replied.

Her reply perplexed him. ''Technically?'' he repeated.

She nodded, reminding herself to be careful. ''Yes, well, I had a female parent. But she wasn't very maternal.''

His free hand came up to touch her cheek. ''I'm sorry.''

She hunched a shoulder. ''It was a long time ago.''

''No.'' He rubbed a thumb gently along her cheekbone. ''Childhood stays with us forever.''

She gave him a fatalistic smile that made him feel her pain. ''Those of us who didn't have barbecues in a big yard with loving parents and happy, noisy siblings just…make childhood go away.''

He nodded, remembering that she'd said her father had died. ''Was your father ill a long time?'' he asked.

She fidgeted in the small space in which he'd confined her—physically and emotionally.

''No,'' she replied after a moment. ''He was murdered.''

He stared at her in disbelief, then sat on the window seat and pulled her down with him. ''What happened?''

She sat stiffly on her side of the narrow space and thought back. This running and hiding, and the other life, had all seemed so interminable that she'd almost forgotten how it had all started.

It was hard to think about, but he was holding her hand.

''My mother,'' she said flatly, letting the memories spin out in her head, ''was a spoiled young heiress who loved money and dangerous men. Her first husband killed himself, so she married my father—a very sweet, loving man with a good head for business. Trouble was, his business wasn't legal.''

''Drugs?''

''Mob.''

''God, Daphne.''

''Somebody saw him with the police commissioner,'' she continued. So much had happened in the meantime, she felt as though she'd lost the personal connection. It was as if she'd watched it on television. ''Thought he was cutting some kind of deal for himself—and I came home from school one day to learn that he'd been shot five times over lunch in this little Chinese restaurant.''

Vic wished he hadn't asked. It hadn't been an entirely innocent question. He had to know about her in order to decide his role in this case—but she was so private, so secretive. He'd probed deliberately.

He pulled her close with the hand he held and wrapped the other arm around her. "I'm sorry," he said, rubbing gently between her shoulder blades. "I can't imagine how awful that must have been."

He'd seen horrible things, but he'd been a man trained to deal with them. Not an innocent, adolescent girl.

For one brief moment, he felt her wrap her arms around him and hold on. This had none of the electricity of their usual contact, he noted, but seemed to be powered by a need that went deeper than the charge of sexual attraction.

This was attraction of another sort. Soul for soul. Heart for heart.

Then she pushed out of his embrace, clearly determined to go no further—either in his arms or with her story. Her eyes were dry, but profoundly sad.

"You know, if you buy this place," she said, pointing out the window at the acres of grass, "you won't have time to picnic or barbecue or sunbathe. You're going to spend all your time pushing a lawnmower."

"I'll buy a ride-on mower," he said, getting to his feet and catching her hand to pull her along with him. "And one of those face-to-face swings."

"I love those, too," she said, with something faintly melancholy in her voice.

He stopped at the top of the stairs to put an arm around her shoulder. "Then you'll have to come and swing with me on balmy summer evenings."

"I'd love that," she whispered. Her easy agreement was negated by that fatalism in her eyes.

"Then it's a date," he said resolutely, retaining his grip on her as they started down the stairs.

CHAPTER SEVEN

"ARE YOU GOING TO BUY IT?" Daphne asked Vic as he took a last tour of the kitchen. Paul Bullard had just peered around the front door to say he had one more brief phone call to make.

Daphne went to the window over the sink while Vic examined appliance outlets. "I like it," he said absently, squatting down to pluck at a loose tile in a corner. Then he straightened and came up behind her, dusting off his hands. "Do you?"

She nodded, pointing out the window. "I'd build a gazebo under that maple tree and put a hot tub in it. Then I'd put a playground set right in the middle of the yard so I could watch the children."

"Children?" he questioned, turning to lean a hip against the edge of the counter and look into her eyes. "You have only one."

"I was talking," she said pointedly, "about you."

"But I don't have *any*."

She smiled casually. It was difficult. "You will some day. And in the meantime, your two older brothers will be visiting you with their children, won't they?"

Somehow, when he pictured her here with him, it all seemed so real, so possible. But when he pictured his family, it shook his fantasies, made him remember that he was playing a dangerous game here.

"And when you come to sit with me in the swing," he reminded her, "you'll be bringing Jenny."

She smiled, but her eyes brimmed with sadness. She lowered them. "Well," she said, "there won't be balmy summer days for a good eight or nine months now."

He caught her chin between his thumb and forefinger. Her eyelashes flew up. "I'd swing in the snow," he said softly, "if you were here with me."

She caught his wrist in one hand and put the other to his chest in a defensive gesture. "Vic, I—"

"Shh," he interrupted, and without stopping to examine his motives or the possible repercussions, he lowered his head to kiss her.

Her mouth was as warm and soft as he'd imagined, and her response as eager as he could have hoped.

Their lips explored each other's, touching, slanting, nipping. Then her lips parted and he delved gently inside. That is, he intended to.

But the tip of her tongue against the underside of his lip loosed a hunger he'd kept under tight control. He wound his fingers into her hair and held her still while he plundered her mouth with greedy abandon.

Daphne forgot everything but the tender passion of his lips and the possessive touch of the hand that cupped her hip to hold her to him. She knew they had no future, but the curious thing was that he made her feel as though she had no past.

All that existed was now. Her precious afternoon. This kiss.

She wrapped her arms around his neck and prayed that the moment could go on forever. It was everything she'd imagined in the darkest hours of the other life.

It wasn't real, of course, because he was loving a

woman who didn't exist. His kiss paid homage to the woman he thought she was, not the one she truly was.

She closed her heart to that knowledge for the moment and simply let it be hers. If she could ever have a man's love again, this was precisely how she would want it to be—that mystical melding of reverence and desire that every woman dreamed of.

Vic felt the urgency in her—a wild response that surprised and gratified him. She leaned her weight against him and ran gentle fingertips over his face, his shoulders, into his hair. He heard his own moan as sensations bumped along his spinal column.

Then the front door burst open, and Bullard's voice called apologetically from the living room, "Sorry, sorry. There's always one more detail somebody needs, one more phone call that can't wait till I get to the office."

Daphne wedged a space between her and Vic, her hands pushing against his chest. But he retained his hold on her, suddenly finding it critical that someone see them in each other's arms; that someone validate what he'd known almost immediately but seemed to be having difficulty reconciling with the professional he'd always been: that he'd fallen in love with the woman he'd been hired to find.

Bullard appeared more pleased than horrified. He probably presumed that a woman on his client's horizon made him more serious about buying a home.

But he applied no pressure. He handed Vic a folder he'd prepared for him that contained the specs on all the houses they'd seen so far, and several he intended to show him in the future.

He smiled companionably as he walked them out to Vic's car. "If you're free tomorrow morning," he said,

"I'll show you a great split-level across from the elementary school, and an old Victorian on Gunther Street near Kelsey's Boarding House. That's just a few blocks from the high school." He winked from Vic to Daphne. "Proximity to school can be noisy, but if you're going to have kids, that's the place to be. And living in town might be a consideration if you're thinking about opening a store."

Daphne ignored the realtor's comment, except for a quick glance in Vic's direction that seemed to blame him for the man's assumptions.

Vic shook the hand Bullard extended. "Thanks, Paul," he said. "I appreciate your efforts. What time in the morning?"

Daphne climbed into the car as Vic settled the details of the meeting. She folded her arms and tried to affect an air of calm, while inside, her emotions rioted in the wake of Vic's kiss.

You cannot have him, she told herself firmly. *And all you have to think about to convince yourself is how he would feel about you if he knew about the other life. This house and this man cannot be yours. Your last-chance afternoon is over.*

Vic sensed the change in her on the drive home and speculated over the reason. It wasn't that difficult to figure out.

On the run from her mother-in-law, she couldn't seriously entertain thoughts of permanence, of settling somewhere. Although he would have sworn there was a covetous look in her eyes when she'd surveyed the kitchen, the library, the children's rooms.

And there was covetousness in her eyes when she looked at him. He had no intention of letting her retreat from him.

"Where have you gone?" he asked her quietly. It was late afternoon now, and downtown was busy with Tyler's own little "rush hour." He pulled up at one of the town's few stoplights and turned to study Daphne's profile.

She looked out the windshield, her eyes unfocused. After a moment of silence, she blinked and turned to him. "I'm sorry. Did you say something?"

He frowned at her teasingly. "You have a lot to learn about dating. You're supposed to be hanging on my every word."

"Do forgive me." Her smile was both sad and sweet. "I didn't realize this was a date. I thought it was a kidnap and house-hunting expedition."

The light changed and he accelerated. "No, it was a date. And you have to admit it was more imaginative than the theater or a symphony."

"Yes, definitely."

Vic pulled up at a stop sign. Two young women hurried by, deep in conversation, their arms burdened with shopping bags emblazoned with the Gates logo. Businessmen strode to their cars, appearing preoccupied with the day's concerns.

A carful of teenage boys shouted and whistled at a group of teenage girls passing by. The girls waved back but kept walking.

"What's your favorite date?" Vic asked.

Daphne realized in some surprise that she'd never dated. Her father had died, then there'd been Gordon, and she'd run away to the other life before any boy at school could show interest in her, before other girls went to the mall to look for boys or dreamed about proms. By that time her dreams were already dead.

She'd chosen a long time ago not to remember that.

And when she'd met Trey, he'd listened; then he'd told her to put it all away again because she was starting fresh with him.

But it seemed suddenly like such a loss. The question brought the memory of those tender years flooding back to her, and she bit back a gasp at the sudden, vivid pain.

Her favorite date, she thought, would be sitting on Vic's swing.

But that couldn't be, so she chose her next-best fantasy. "A hayride," she replied with a smile. "You know. The smell of wood smoke, love songs sung under a harvest moon, the exciting promise of fall and the coziness of approaching winter."

The light turned green and he moved forward slowly with the traffic. "Mmm," he said. "And cider and doughnuts. But that surprises me."

She arched an eyebrow. "Why?"

The fingers of his hand on the steering wheel opened to express uncertainty, then closed again. "I guess I thought a young woman from L.A. would be thinking in terms of theater or opera."

She met his smiling glance with her own. "I guess I'm just a country girl at heart."

That wasn't a lie, she told herself, to assuage the guilt of being false with him. She'd come to love Tyler and the life she led here. She could even be happy, if only the specter of Celeste Huntington could be removed from her life.

But that wasn't likely, so she simply had to live with the small comforts she could claim.

Vic hated himself for trying to catch her off guard, to trick her into slipping and revealing the truth. But if she didn't betray something soon, he was going to have to admit to Celeste that he didn't believe what she'd told him about her daughter-in-law. And that would develop into a passel of trouble on its own.

Daphne would hate *him* for having deceived her, and Celeste would simply hire someone else to find Jennifer. Then where would Daphne be? Where would he be? He didn't want to think about it.

"All right, country girl," he said, accelerating as the traffic thinned. "We'll pick up a bucket of chicken at the Dairy King, get your daughter at Britt's and picnic in the car."

"No," she said.

He glanced in the rearview mirror to change lanes, then picked up speed as he headed for the highway that led to Britt's farm.

He did not ask, "Why not?" He offered no argument to the contrary. He simply continued to drive.

"Would you pull over," she asked, "so we can talk about this?"

"No," he replied.

Now she was the one who asked, "Why not?"

"Because you won't give me a reasonable answer," he said. "You'll offer some nebulous argument about not being able to love again or something like that, when I know you want to be with me. It's right there in your eyes. So why pull over to talk about it, if you're not going to be honest?"

"All right," she said after a moment. "I'll be honest. Please pull over."

His quick glance at her was doubtful.

"I will," she promised. "Please."

He tried to appear reluctant, tried not to betray the eagerness to know that had long ago broken the boundaries of professional interest and was now very personal.

"All right," he said coolly, and turned off the road, pulling up under a stand of red-tipped oaks. Beyond them, the lights of the Heidelberg Restaurant went on.

He unbuckled his seat belt, pushed the steering wheel to its farthest adjustment and turned to face her. He waited.

She remained confined in her belt and faced forward. She drew a deep breath and closed her eyes. "This is such a trite line," she said, "but I'm not who you think I am, Vic."

He felt his own breath catch somewhere in his chest. "Who are you?" he asked.

She shook her head. "I can't tell you."

Impatiently, he shifted back in his seat and turned the key in the ignition.

"No, wait!" Daphne shouted over the sound of the motor. "Vic, please!"

"That's not honesty," he accused, "that's secrecy."

"Vic." She put a hand to his shoulder. "It's not secrecy, it's...desperation."

He turned the motor off and faced her in angry exasperation that was only partly feigned. He guessed he was as angry with himself as he was at her for having created this situation, but that didn't help at the moment.

"Desperation," he asked with strained calm, "about what?"

She removed her seat belt and turned toward him. Her eyes were grim, and there was something firm about her mouth that told him he was going to get far less from this interview than he wanted.

"I can't tell you. I can't tell *anyone*," she said. "Because a seemingly harmless remark could be traced back to me."

"Trace who back to you?"

"The person I'm...hiding from."

He felt himself relax a little. He hadn't realized how important it had become that she trust him enough to share even that little bit. But he had to push for more.

"And I suppose you're not going to tell me who that is."

She considered a moment, then, apparently feeling that detail made little difference, admitted quietly, "My husband's mother."

"Why are you hiding?" he asked.

"Because she wants to take Jenny away from me." She said the words calmly, but the horror of losing her daughter was there in her eyes. "She even got a court order after Trey died, though she must have *bought* the judge, because no representative of the court ever spoke to me or questioned me. She's hired detectives. I just barely evaded one in New Hampshire."

Her voice rose a decibel as she spoke, and she fidgeted nervously.

Vic maintained a look of interest without betraying guilt at her innocent remark. But it raged inside him like something with claws.

"Why," he asked gently, reaching a hand out to touch her hair, to soothe her, "does she want to take her away?"

She put a hand to her head. Her fingers shook. He caught them in his and held them.

"Because Trey died, and she has to *own* some-one. She's scary, Vic. She always hated me because she felt I took her son away from her. We met when I was...working in Las Vegas. He was there with a few friends, we went to a show and...found it so easy to talk to each other. He decided to stay for a couple of weeks. We got married." She kept her eyes averted.

Vic said nothing, only listened.

"Celeste even offered me $200,000 to leave Trey," she added.

He remembered the check his employer had shown him. He guessed she'd forged it—both Trey's signature and Diane's endorsement.

"Of course, I didn't take it. Trey tried to stay between his mother and me, but she managed to get her licks in. And he could never quite distance himself from her. Then when he died driving *my* car, I think she considered *me* responsible."

"Why was he driving your car?"

"His was out of gas." She smiled tolerantly. "That happens when you grow up in a limo. You forget to put gas in your car. He was CEO of the Beach Boy Shops, one of Celeste's many companies, and he was supposed to be at the Coronado store that afternoon. So I canceled my lunch date so he could use my car." She wound her fingers together nervously. "Now she gets to kill two birds with one stone. If she gets Jenny, she can own someone again, while taking *my* child away from me."

Vic remembered the icicle woman in the beautiful parlor and found it a little difficult to believe that there was enough passion in her to support such an obsession. But he didn't doubt Daphne's word.

"Wouldn't it have been easier," he asked, "to simply figure it out in court?"

She gave him a pitying look. "She claimed I was an unfit mother." Her eyes darted away from his for a moment, but not before he saw the poignancy there. "Then, even before the court order was issued, she sent her 'butler' and her 'chauffeur' to pick Jenny up at day care. Fortunately, I'd finished my errands early and arrived to collect her myself just as they were pulling up.

When Trey was alive, he told me they'd often done strong-arm work for his mother.''

She drew a steadying breath and continued. ''I managed to get Jenny out the back door, and I've been running ever since.''

Vic imagined her running with a little child while being pursued by goons hired by a woman with unlimited resources, and felt a killing rage—part of it aimed at himself.

Daphne's shoulders stiffened visibly, and she swallowed. ''So please understand,'' she said, her voice quiet and firm, ''I cannot have a—a relationship. Right now, Celeste doesn't know where I am, but that could change at any moment. She found me in Manchester. She found me in Allentown, and she found me in Lexington. I have to be watching every minute. Nothing will ever be more important to me than keeping Jenny safe.''

Daphne looked touchingly heroic with her hair disheveled from the rain, her eyes wide with emotion.

''Don't you think two of us watching,'' he asked, ''would be better than one?''

She shook her head. ''You left all that, remember? You're starting over, with a new and quiet life.''

Way behind the brave smile in her eyes, he saw pain. She didn't want to lose him, but she thought she had to.

If he told her she didn't, he would have to explain, and he had no idea how to do that without making her hate him. He had to bide his time.

It wasn't difficult to look rejected and disappointed. He might really have felt both those things if he didn't have the blood of generations of bullheaded and indomitably cheerful Mexicans in his veins. He knew he could make this work out. He just couldn't tell her that.

So he had to watch tears pool in her eyes and just listen while she told him she'd had more fun with him than she'd had in years.

"If I ever could have another husband," she said softly, looping her arms around his neck, "I'd come and find you."

"Maybe you will one day," he said, unable to resist the impulse to kiss her. He would live on that assurance until he could have things his way.

She kissed him back—but briefly—then pulled away with stubborn resolution. "Maybe," she replied, but he heard the disbelief in her voice. "For now, would you please take me to Britt's to get Jenny, then take us home?"

"Your car's downtown," he reminded her. "I'll pick you up in the morning."

She shook her head and fixed him with a stern gaze. "It's Saturday. I'll ride in to my aerobics class with Britt. And you and I will have nothing more to do with each other except as members of the same community. You will find another woman for that swing, and leave me to concentrate on what I have to do."

She turned in her seat and buckled her belt.

"You think that you can tell me what to do with my life?" he asked as he turned the key in the ignition.

"Yes," she said with a little smile. "And don't give me that look of male indignation. You've taken control of events in my life several times since we met. The only difference is that I can't pick you up and put you where I want you."

He grinned at her as he pulled back onto the now

empty road. "Tell me where that is," he said, "and I'll get there under my own power."

"Vic," she said darkly, but her eyes were like velvet, "haven't you been listening to me?"

"Heard every word," he assured her.

"See that you remember them," she said.

After they'd picked up Jenny, he pulled into Daphne's driveway and turned off the motor.

"Vic..." she warned, reaching into the back to pull Jenny out of the car.

But her daughter scrambled out the other side and into Vic's arms.

He ignored Daphne's threatening glare and took several steps toward the porch. Then he stopped and waited for her to catch up. "My father taught me to walk a lady to her door and see her safely inside," he said.

"You're not coming in," she told him resolutely, chin angled up as she walked past him, then led the way.

"No," he agreed.

"Vic play!" Jenny said excitedly.

"And you're not kissing me good-night." They topped the porch steps and she delved into her purse for her key.

"But this is goodbye, isn't it?" he asked quietly, standing just behind her with her daughter in his arms. "You're not going to kiss me goodbye?"

"No," she said feebly, turning to take Jenny from him. She felt weak with anguish. "You're going and that's—"

The front door was yanked open suddenly, causing her to start and scream.

Vic shoved her and Jenny aside and had the front of

the intruder's shirt in one fist almost before Daphne understood what had happened.

He was completely surprised to find himself looking into a vaguely familiar pair of blue eyes set in a taut but pretty face.

"Judy!" Daphne gasped.

Judy wrapped her hand around Vic's wrist and yanked it away. She gave him one long, lethal look, then turned to Daphne. "Where in the hell have you been?" she demanded. "I have been out of my mind!"

"Judy," Daphne said mildly, casting Vic an uncomfortable glance and trying to push her landlady into the house. "You're always out of your mind."

Judy flung Daphne's hand away, too. Then she shook a finger at her. "We were supposed to go to the hardware store when you got off work, remember? But are you anywhere to be found? No-o-o-o. You take off with…"

Judy pointed a finger at Vic, then stopped abruptly. Color drained from her face, then suddenly reappeared in a bright pink flush. She tossed her hair as though she were making some inner mental adjustment, then she looked at Daphne.

Jenny spread her little arms toward the woman and cried happily, "Judy!"

Vic saw something there that prodded his professional awareness. He considered it for a moment, then decided he was right. It was the first real clue he'd found since he'd come to Tyler.

"I'm sorry," Judy said quickly, her voice strained. She took the toddler as Jenny wriggled out of Daphne's arms. She seemed embarrassed, Vic thought, and found that more than interesting. "You've been nagging me for months to repaint your kitchen and I finally set aside the time to do it and…you aren't here.''

Daphne put her free arm around Judy's shoulders and turned a smile on Vic that he recognized instantly was completely phony.

''Judy's a very devoted landlady and a nice person. Even Jenny likes her. But sometimes she takes herself just a little too seriously.'' She focused the phony smile on Judy. ''Britt knew where I was. Why didn't you call her?''

''I did,'' Judy replied, also sporting a smile that appeared painted on. ''She wasn't home.''

''Well.'' Daphne patted her shoulder. ''We can go to the hardware store tomorrow. Why don't you come in for a cup of coffee since you're here?''

''Thank you,'' Judy said with a vaguely sheepish glance in Vic's direction. ''Nice to see you, Mr. Estevez.''

He inclined his head. ''Miss Lowery.''

Judy, carrying Jenny, walked into the house and closed the door quietly behind her.

Vic turned to Daphne, hands in his pockets. ''So…you're sure you don't want to kiss me goodbye?'' he asked.

She looked into his eyes as though searching for something. He couldn't decide what it was. Was she wondering if he'd read anything into Judy Lowery's little display of temper? Or was Daphne simply wondering what it would be like to kiss him again?

''It would serve no purpose,'' she said softly.

The slipping sun was now a sparkle through the tops of the trees surrounding the property. The breeze had grown cooler, more fragrant.

On the chance that it *was* the kiss she wondered

about, he gave the issue a little push by placing his hands on her upper arms.

"Kissing isn't intended to serve a purpose," he said, "apart from communication. And you'll have to admit that a goodbye can be pretty cold when all you do is say the words."

She didn't move away from him. In fact, she turned her hands so that she could grasp his forearms. He did see a farewell in her eyes, but the melancholy there told him it was a farewell she didn't want.

He caught that knowledge to him and let it fuel him as he opened his mouth on hers. He didn't pull her close. He didn't move his hands. But in the silence of the kiss, he let his lips convey all the tenderness, all the admiration, all the love he felt for her.

Then he drew away, hurt by the pain he saw in the fragile smile she forced for him. But he could do nothing at the moment but appear to accede to her wishes.

He pulled away and went to his car without looking back.

Daphne watched him go, a little sob rising in her throat. She'd never been one to indulge in self-pity, to consider herself a victim—even in the other life. But at this moment, she desperately wished she were someone else.

CHAPTER EIGHT

DAPHNE SLAMMED THE FRONT door behind her and confronted Judy, who was studying the contents of the open cupboards. Jenny was already in front of the television, watching dinnertime cartoons.

"Remind me never to send *you* behind the Iron Curtain on a secret mission," she grumped, annoyed and miserable and feeling sorry for herself.

Judy turned to her with a look of shocked indignation. "*You* disappear for hours with Jenny, leaving me to think maybe the witch has found you, maybe all our efforts to hide you over the last eight months have come to nothing, maybe the sister I found after *years* of not even knowing if she was alive or dead is lost to me again, only to appear on the porch with a man and a lovesick look on your face...." She had to pause for breath, but lost none of her anger. "And *you're* mad at *me* because I let our cover slip?"

When Daphne just stared at her for a moment, she added, "And there no longer is an Iron Curtain! Or a Berlin Wall!"

Daphne stepped forward to wrap her arms around her. "I'm sorry, Judy. I completely forgot about getting paint this afternoon. After your autograph party, I was going to go to work, but Vic invited me out to lunch, and Britt, being the little matchmaker that she is, gave me the afternoon off." She drew back and smiled into her sister's still-thunderous expression. "Then he took me with him to look at a house. The one out on Morgan Avenue."

Judy's glower softened slightly. "The one you've picked out for when you win the lottery and Celeste ends up under Jimmy Hoffa in some ball field in New Jersey?"

"That's the one. You won't believe how beautiful it is inside."

Judy assumed a worried frown. "Do you think he suspected anything when I...you know...?"

"Started screaming like a maniac?" Daphne asked with a bland smile. "I don't think so." She pushed Judy aside and slapped the cupboards closed. "I have left-over chicken-and-noodle casserole. Can you stay? It'll just take a minute to microwave."

"Sure. I'll set the table." Judy went to the silverware drawer and pulled out knives and forks while Daphne took the casserole dish from the refrigerator.

"You think seeing Mr. Ebony Eyes is a good idea?" Judy asked as she worked.

Daphne divided the leftovers onto two dinner plates and Jenny's little bowl with a Winnie the Pooh pattern on it. She didn't look up. "No, I don't. That's why we just said goodbye."

Judy made a scornful sound.

Daphne reached for the plastic wrap and frowned at her. "What?"

Judy went to the counter for salt and pepper. "That kiss did not look like goodbye to me. Unless you were saying it in Hawaiian, where the word for hello and goodbye is the same."

The wrap made a vicious ripping sound as Daphne tore off a length. "You snooped?"

Judy thought that over for a moment, then admitted, "Yes. That's what big sisters do."

"No," Daphne corrected, fitting the plastic wrap over Jenny's bowl. "They accept your desperate collect call, they send you a plane ticket to join them, they agree to put you up in their fortunately vacant rental house and pretend they've never seen you before when you come to town, so that you can't be traced through them. They even chase all over the county to find you Moonbeam Blond hair color to help you maintain your disguise. But they stay the heck out of your love life."

Judy placed the salt and pepper on the table and looked up, stricken. "*Has* it become a love life?"

"No," Daphne said with a disappointed sigh. "I know better than that. There's no point in getting him entangled in this, too." She put the bowl in the microwave and set the timer, then stood by while the appliance whirred noisily. "But I *do* wish things were different." She let her head fall back for a moment and closed her eyes with profound regret. "Of course, considering my past, they'd have to be really different."

"Stop it," Judy said, moving the high chair up to the table. "You did what you had to do to survive, because our mother was a jerk. No one would blame you for that."

The microwave bell rang. Daphne removed the bowl, stirred the contents, then took a small bite out of the center to check the temperature.

Satisfied that it wasn't too hot, she put the bowl on the high-chair tray and scooped Jenny up from in front of the television.

The toddler protested until she saw the food. Daphne grinned at Judy. "There are distinct advantages to having a child who's a munch mouth."

Judy laughed and tied a bib around Jenny's neck.

"Noo-dals!" Jenny cried delightedly, and dug right in.

"Anyone who's been in that position would understand," Daphne said, resuming their earlier conversation as she covered the second plate in wrap. "But he has a Beaver Cleaver family, Mexican-style. He was taught to walk a woman to her door after a date, and judging by the way he treats me, to respect and care for her at all times." She sighed dispiritedly. "I think he'd have trouble with it. You want coffee or iced tea?"

"Tea sounds good. I'll get it." Judy pulled down glasses and went to the refrigerator. "Something about him bothers me. I don't believe his story."

Daphne carried the plates to the microwave. "What story? That he was a cop?"

"No, I believe that. He looks like he's seen a lot. But I can't imagine a man like that wanting to settle down in Tyler, Wisconsin. And didn't you say he's from Palm Beach?"

Daphne microwaved one of the dishes. "I know. I was suspicious of him at first. But he's had several opportunities to take Jenny since he's been here. She flies into his arms at every opportunity. But he hasn't done it."

"Because he knows you'd kill him. Maybe he's softening you up so that when he finally does it, you'll be so shocked, he'll have time to escape."

Daphne shuddered at the notion, while personally dismissing it as a possibility. "No. He's just an ex-cop thinking about settling down and opening a sporting-goods store."

After pouring two glasses of tea, Judy replaced the

pitcher in the refrigerator and carried the glasses to the table. "I think he's trouble."

Daphne smiled at her as she pulled one plate out of the microwave and put the other in. "You think every man is trouble."

"No, I don't," she countered, pouring milk into a training cup for Jenny. "I'd like to find one who owns a publishing company and a large estate in Scotland."

Daphne raised an eyebrow. "Why Scotland?"

"Because I have an idea for a period mystery series set there, and that would allow me to do on-the-spot research. And study men's knees."

"Ah. The kilts. You like knees? I'm a tush woman, myself."

Judy took the chair opposite Jenny and leaned back as Daphne placed a steaming plate in front of her. "Well, Mr. Ebony Eyes does have a lovely backside. Athletic, but not *too* lean."

Daphne sat down beside Jenny with her own plate. She made a threatening gesture at Judy with her fork. "You've been looking?"

Judy laughed. "I told you. That's what big sisters do."

VIC RECORDED SEVERAL notes to himself in a folder he kept in a briefcase under the bed. Then he dialed David Heath, a private-detective friend in Los Angeles, and asked him to investigate Celeste Huntington and Judy Lowery.

"Looking for what?" Heath asked.

"In Judy Lowery's case," Vic told him, "I'm looking for a family connection to Diane Huntington, née Majors. In Celeste Huntington's case, anything you can find."

"Urgent?"

"Mildly."

"A couple of days?"

"Good."

"And you're paying me for this in cash, not in caviar like the last time. I wouldn't eat that stuff if I was another fish."

"I explained about that," Vic replied. "The client was a restaurateur down on his luck. That's how he paid me."

"You stupid. You don't work for people down on their luck. You work for wealthy women looking to make lots of money on their husbands' infidelity."

"That's right. I keep forgetting."

"Straighten up. Call you soon as I know anything."

Vic hung up the phone and went down to the lodge's lounge to have a drink. His guess was that Judy Lowery was Daphne's sister. Or maybe her cousin. He hadn't noticed the physical resemblance until they'd stood side by side on Daphne's front porch.

And Judy's reaction to Daphne's absence had been that of someone with an emotional investment in Daphne's life. Like a family member.

And Daphne was renting from Judy. That in itself wasn't enlightening, but added to the other details, it seemed to lend credibility to the idea that they were related.

Well, he thought, selecting a barstool in a far corner, if he had his way—and he usually did—one day soon they would all be related.

"What'll it be, Mr. Estevez?" the bartender asked. He was an older man. Seasoned. He had advice on everything from fashion to child rearing.

"Bloody Mary, please, Howie."

"Coming up. You okay tonight? You look preoccupied." He smiled as he dipped the rim of a barrel glass in salt. "The elegant blonde?"

Vic tried to remember if he'd ever brought Daphne back to the lodge. He hadn't.

Howie read his confusion as he righted the glass and shot in some vodka. "Saw you with her at the bookstore. Beautiful woman. And she has a beautiful child. You're dead when a woman's children like you."

Oh, he was dead, all right. Vic acknowledged that with a nod and took a handful of nuts. "She told me goodbye just an hour ago."

Howie added tomato juice and spices, then an onion, a pepper, and a green bean on a skewer. He placed the drink on the bar, then braced his hands on it, obviously prepared to philosophize. "Women are always doing things that seem final. They give you ultimatums, they tell you it's over, they leave you."

"Really."

"I think it's because they like to test our devotion, but for one reason or another, they don't really trust us to come through. So they put us in these do-or-die situations. Then if we're still there when it's over, they consider us worth having. It's like a very sophisticated test, you know what I mean?"

"Yeah, I think so."

"So, even though she said goodbye, she's probably expecting you to stay right by her side."

Even though he knew he wasn't going anywhere, Vic knew *she'd* meant the goodbye. And that made it almost feel final.

Howie folded his arms on the bar and leaned toward him. "But, you know, if you want to glimpse the future, we've got an astrologers' convention coming in on Friday. Maybe one of them can tell you what's going to happen with you and the pretty blonde.''

Vic smiled a thank-you for the advice as Howie moved down the bar to wait on a pair of newcomers.

The only thing Vic could imagine that would make his situation more otherworldly and potentially explosive would be the addition of an astrologer.

''THESE PANTY HOSE ARE killing me,'' Judy grumbled. She stood in front of the long, lighted mirror in the lodge's ladies' room and tugged at the waist of a tropical-print dress.

Britt, standing beside her, pulled Judy's hands away and readjusted the raffia belt her tugging had disturbed.

''Judy, it's just for a few hours. I know you hate dresses, but we chose this one because it was the least confining and you can't *always* look like a grunge queen.''

''Particularly tonight,'' Daphne added, ''when the Tyler Ladies' Club honors you for your accomplishment in being published.''

Judy stood still while Britt readjusted the neckline of the dress, fluffed out her shoulder-length hair.

''Aren't you glad you listened to me and had your hair done?''

Judy frowned at her reflection. ''I look as though I've taken one volt too many.''

Britt swatted her shoulder. ''You do not!''

''Did anyone say they liked the book?'' Judy asked nervously. ''Nobody's said anything about it. Do you think they all hate it?''

''Everybody loves it.'' Britt grinned at her in the mirror. ''Didn't you hear them talking?''

''Brick Bauer bought ten copies to distribute to

friends. He said it was very accurate," Daphne added. "Mrs. Green from the bookstore told me."

Judy's face brightened. "She did?"

"And I loved it, too."

"Of course, you did. You're my…"

Daphne's eyes widened at her in the mirror.

"Friend," Judy concluded. She glanced quickly at Britt, who now stood behind her, working at the back of her hair, and didn't seem to have noticed anything.

Daphne punched Judy's arm punitively. "Relax. This is supposed to be a fun night for you."

"Right."

The ladies'-room door flew open with a jolt, and a full-figured woman Daphne guessed to be in her middle-to-late fifties walked in. She wore a diaphanous midnight-blue caftan dotted with star-and crescent-moon-shaped sequins, and walked with her arms extended so that she gave the appearance of the night sky on a swift rotation of the earth.

Her hair was a bright, artificial red, piled haphazardly on her head, and her still-beautiful complexion was rouged and powdered. A star-shaped mole rested just below her left eye.

She smiled warmly at Daphne and her companions. "Hello! Can you feel the excitement in the air?"

"Ah, yes," Britt replied. She pointed to Judy. "We're here to celebrate our friend's success."

"Oh?" The woman smiled again, then raised her right hand as though she were waving, but passed it in a shallow arc several inches from Judy. Then she beamed at her. "You will have *great* success. Far beyond what you know now."

Judy just stared at her.

She turned to Britt and made the same motion with

her hand, smiling as if to herself as she did it. "Happiness for you. Great happiness. But seven children is a big job."

Britt laughed lightly. "I only have five."

The woman patted her cheek and turned to Daphne. She made that swath in the air near her and frowned. Then she did it again and seemed to relax a little. Finally she looked into Daphne's eyes and smiled maternally.

"You're going to prevail," she said softly, "and find what you've always wanted."

"I will?" Daphne breathed.

"You will," the woman assured her, then disappeared into a stall.

Daphne, Britt and Judy filed out into the hall and stood in a startled little knot in the green-carpeted corridor.

"Who was that?" Daphne asked.

"She's not with the Tyler Ladies' Club," Britt said wryly.

"Maybe the Mars Ladies' Club?" Judy suggested.

Before anyone could comment on that, a woman in a severe gray suit, her dark hair in a bun, stopped to ask them anxiously, "Have you seen Mother Mirabai?"

"Who?" Britt asked.

The woman's gaze narrowed on them. "You're not with the astrology convention, are you?"

"No," Judy replied. "But sparkly blue dress and red hair?"

The woman's eyes brightened. "Yes!"

Judy pointed to the ladies' room.

"*Thank* you!"

Daphne, Britt and Judy looked at one another as the woman in the suit disappeared into the rest room.

"Spooky," Judy said.

Britt laughed softly. "Actually, I think a few of the astrologers staying here are on *our* program tonight."

"You're kidding."

"No. We thought it would be enlightening. And fun."

Daphne put an arm around each of her companions and ushered them back toward their banquet room. "And we're all in for good stuff according to Mother Mirabai, so we can relax."

Britt frowned at Daphne. "But she said you were going to prevail. Over what?"

She didn't want to think about it. The look in the woman's eyes had suggested things were going to get worse before she "prevailed." "Who knows?" she forced a smile and caught Judy's commiserating glance. "Maybe dinner's going to be awful."

Dinner was not awful. It was chicken parmigiana with pasta and vegetables, and absolutely delicious.

Judy spoke briefly about working for a publisher in Boston before moving to Tyler four years before. She'd found home here, she told her friends, after a lifetime of searching for all the things she felt her life had lacked.

Daphne watched and listened with pride and empathy and a desperate need to hold back tears.

Judy, eight years older than she, was the daughter of their mother's first husband, a senator, who'd taken his own life when Judy was eight. She'd been away at school when Daphne's own father was killed, and came home to offer her little sister the comfort their self-involved mother failed to give.

She'd come home for Daphne's birthdays and for

Christmas, but continuing disputes with their mother kept her from more regular visits.

Daphne remembered clearly the Christmastime after their mother had married Gordon. Judy had guessed something was wrong, but Daphne had been stunned, terrified, uncommunicative, under a feeble pretense of good cheer.

And then, for almost three years, it had all been too big and ugly to fight, too horrible to explain to anyone.

When the day finally came that Daphne couldn't stand another moment, she was fifteen. And she'd had no illusions about making her living any other way. The critical necessity was to make enough money to support herself so that she could *stay* away, and at her age, there were few other options.

A friend had told her that Judy had walked up and down Hollywood Boulevard for several days, looking for her. But Daphne had remained hidden, feeling too dark and dirty to reconnect with the sister she loved.

It had taken the desperation of needing to get Jenny to safety after the last close call with one of Celeste's private detectives that had made her call Judy. Daphne had been hiding in Manchester when she'd seen the follow-up show Oprah Winfrey did on Britt's yogurt company. The television cameras had gone to Tyler, and there among Britt's friends had been her own sister. Daphne had stared in disbelief. Then she'd called Tyler, Wisconsin, Information and found her listed. She'd called, but when Judy picked up, Daphne had been unable to speak. Loneliness for her sister had overwhelmed her, but not enough to allow her to ask for help. And then Celeste had closed in eight months ago and she'd had no choice.

Now Daphne found consolation in the fact that the

loss of Trey and the destruction of her life had resulted in the reestablishment of her relationship with her sister. Judy had welcomed her warmly and without question, and done everything in her power to secure her anonymity and her safety.

When Judy finished her speech, Tyler's head librarian, Elise Fairmont, who served as mistress of ceremonies, introduced Mother Mirabai. The astrologer spoke briefly about the stars' influence on an individual's life and how that was affected by the individual's own determination and sense of purpose.

Then she introduced several of her fellow astrologers, who volunteered to develop charts for anyone in the group and set up a table at the back of the room.

Rob Friedman followed them to photograph the process.

"Did you see tonight's *Citizen?*" Britt asked quietly as Daphne stood to stretch her legs.

"No," she replied. "Why?"

"Rob's review of Judy's book is in it."

Daphne stopped at the dry tone of Britt's voice. "Oh, no. He didn't like it?"

"He said it was *competently* written," Britt replied just above a whisper, "but that it was predictable—" she closed her eyes before adding "—and verbose."

Daphne drew her breath in with a grating sound. "Thank God she never reads the paper or he'd be fish food... What is she *doing?*"

The words about Rob's life expectancy were no sooner out of Daphne's mouth than she saw Annabelle Scanlon in a corner of the room handing the newspaper to Judy, who'd taken a place in the line of women to see Mother Mirabai. Annabelle always knew what was going on in town and loved being able to pass on the latest to the uninformed.

Rob, unaware of impending doom, turned his camera to the small groups of women who stood around the room in earnest conversation. Then he spotted Britt and Daphne and started in their direction.

"I'm off to powder my nose," Daphne said, slipping between Britt and a nearby table in an attempt to avoid the reporter and his camera.

"Coward!" Britt whispered after her. "You're going to miss the bloodshed."

The corridor felt cool after the perfumed confines of the banquet room, and Daphne leaned her weight against the wall for a moment and closed her eyes against her narrow escape. Between Rob Friedman and his ever-present camera, and her sister and her increasingly frequent slips where their relationship was concerned, it was becoming harder and harder to maintain the charade.

She drew a deep breath to regain her equanimity and caught a whiff of something herbal and familiar. Vic.

She opened her eyes to find him standing directly in front of her in a sports jacket over a tab-collared shirt. He looked darker than usual in the moody lighting, his cheekbones more pronounced, his smile more lethal.

"You all right?" he asked, his eyes going over her features with slow deliberation, just as she explored and savored his.

"Fine," she said, her heart rapping against her ribs like someone knocking on a door. "We're having a party for Judy in the banquet room and Rob's all over the place with his camera. You can understand why I don't want to end up on the front page of the *Citizen*."

"Of course."

Vic put his hands in his pants pockets to restrain him-self from touching her. It had only been four days since he'd kissed her in the kitchen of the House of Three Gables, then on her front porch, but it seemed like an eternity.

He'd deliberately kept his distance because, for the moment at least, he wanted her to believe he was com-plying with her wishes. But he'd thought about her con-tinuously and longed for her in a way that he never had for another woman. The feeling was more than greed. It was need.

"How's Jenny?" he asked. He liked the way Daphne's eyes watched his mouth, the way her own lips parted as though she imagined his lips on them.

"She's...fine." She smiled, her eyes moving up to his. "We lost one of Bear's shoes yesterday and had to retrace our steps all the way back to-TylerTots. It was in the street against the curb. We must have lost it get-ting into the car. She really loves...those shoes."

Her eyes slipped to his mouth again, and he felt the pull of that small movement. He lowered his head as she lifted hers, and he felt the warm, faintly coffee-flavored touch of her lips.

Then there was a burst of sound as the banquet-room door opened and Rob emerged.

At the sight of him, Daphne fled with a quick, apol-ogetic smile.

"I'm beginning to think," Friedman said as he watched Daphne disappear into the ladies' room, "that that woman deliberately avoids me."

"Well, I know you're just doing your job." Vic caught his shoulder and turned him toward the lounge, away from Daphne. "But a lot of people are very pri-vate and don't like having their pictures taken. They don't like other people to know all the details of their personal lives." He indicated the entrance to the lounge at their right. "Buy you a drink?"

Friedman blinked at him. "This is Tyler, Wisconsin, and I'm covering a ladies'-club meeting—simple local news. I'm hardly looking for scandal." He studied Vic speculatively as they stopped in the doorway to the lounge. "Or is there more here than that?"

Vic shrugged a shoulder. "Got me. Is there?"

Friedman measured him. Vic knew the look. He hadn't been made, but Friedman suspected something here wasn't as it should be. "I buy the retired-cop story. You look like one. But I can't see you choosing to live in Tyler. I think you're here for another reason."

"What would that be?"

"I don't know," Friedman admitted, "but it has something to do with her, hasn't it?"

"Who?"

"Daphne. And something to do with the way she disappears every time she sees me."

Vic's mind was fabricating an excuse for Daphne's behavior when the banquet-room door flew open again and Judy appeared in the hallway. There was something lethal in her stance, Vic noted, and in her eyes.

"Oh, good," Friedman said under his breath. "A confrontation with Tank Girl. Just what I need."

Vic thought he'd never seen Judy Lowery looking so seductive. She'd done something to her hair that made it look fuller, curlier, and she wore a dress that defined a small waist and revealed a trim thigh through a seductive side slit. She seemed supremely feminine, although there was nothing vulnerable about her.

She ignored him and addressed herself to his companion. "Mr. Friedman," she said in a voice that scraped along Vic's spine. The smile that accompanied her words was incongruous though quite pretty. ''I understand you're a literary critic besides being a backwater hack.''

Friedman took the verbal punch in the face with what Vic considered laudable calm. The reporter smiled back at her.

''I don't think *Murder by Moonlight* would be considered 'literary' even under the most liberal standards,'' he replied. ''But I consider myself a fair pulp critic.''

She regarded him with an upward tilt of her brows. Vic felt the air crackle. ''Do you? The *Chicago Sun-Voice* said it was an impressive first book.''

He shrugged a shoulder. ''Some people are easily impressed. Actually, to your credit, I think a good editor would have helped you a lot.''

Vic saw Judy's cheeks go an alarming shade of violet.

''About that drink…'' he reminded Friedman, hoping to get him out of harm's way, should the ''violet'' woman blow. But he seemed determined to hold his ground.

''The plot was good,'' Friedman conceded, ''though you took the predictable turn at the end, rather than the more interesting possibilities, and you tend to drive home a point with the same hammer you bring to conversation.''

Oh, God. Vic judged the distance from where he stood to the safety of the backside of the cigarette machine just inside the lounge.

''Subtlety,'' Friedman added, ''is something you might apply to your next book. Then the effectiveness of your plotting will shine through.''

Judy glared at him, fidgeting from foot to foot, obviously at a loss for a reaction.

Vic understood her dilemma. His criticism had been brutal, but couched a considerable compliment.

Then, apparently making a swift decision, she reached out to grab the camera that hung around his neck and yanked it off him. Then she focused on him and shot. She handed it back to him with a vicious jab to his midsection.

"There's a front-page picture for you," she said in a voice strangled by anger. "Paleolithic man discovered in Tyler."

"Judy!" Daphne, emerging from the rest room, saw Judy's angry thrust with the camera. "What...?"

Judy stalked off. With a puzzled look at him and Friedman, Daphne followed.

"The woman hates me," Friedman said, his tone seeming to reflect surprise.

"Yeah, well." Vic ran a hand over his face, wishing he'd had more time with Daphne. But Friedman and Judy's confrontation had cut that short. "I'm not sure how smart it is to be that mercilessly honest with a woman."

Friedman frowned up at him. "I'm a reporter. Honesty is my business."

"Women aren't business," he explained patiently. "Particularly if—"

He stopped short as a plump woman in yards of glittery blue fabric drifted past them, her precarious red hairdo tottering atop her head. One of the astrology group, Vic guessed.

She stopped suddenly as she drew abreast of them. She turned to him and, raising her hand like a child in class, waved it in an arc near his face.

She seemed to concentrate for a minute, then she looked into his eyes with an expression that combined scolding condemnation with motherly acceptance. He got the feeling she'd "read" every event in his life from the first step he'd taken as a toddler to what he'd just had for dinner.

"The only thing that'll save you," she said cryptically, "is that you'll turn out to be everything she thought you were."

She moved to Friedman and repeated the waving gesture.

Friedman gave Vic a vaguely worried look but remained still.

"Ah," she said after a moment. "That's where it was coming from."

"What?"

"The turbulence."

"The turbulence just went that way." He pointed in the direction Judy had taken.

The woman smiled at him. "Yes. That one. But she's connected to you."

"No," Rob said. Vic thought his tone sounded a little frantic.

She shook her head at him, the gesture regretful. "I'm afraid so. You're tied to her success. And everything that will come before."

"What…will come before?"

She shrugged. "I don't know. Turbulence. Adventure."

Rob eyed her narrowly. "I don't want turbulence and adventure."

The woman's eyes grew merry. "That's too bad." Then she turned back to Vic and shook her finger at him. "You be careful of the game you play, young man." And she toddled off, a sparkling mound of blue.

Vic turned to Friedman, a curious sensation running along his spine. "Who *is* that?"

"Mother Mirabai," Friedman replied grimly. "Astrologer and seer, if you can believe her publicist. Can I take you up on that drink now?"

CHAPTER NINE

"THE MAN'S A SWINE." Judy lay on her back under Daphne's kitchen sink, at work with a wrench on the elbow pipe. Water stood in the sink—the reason Daphne had called her sister to fulfill her role as landlord.

"Judy, really." Daphne peeled potatoes at the kitchen table while Jenny rode around and around on her tricycle. "It's been a whole week. Let it go." She knew it had been a week because she'd lived every long hour of every day, wondering where Vic was, what he was up to, if he'd found a house he liked better than the House of Three Gables. She hoped not. Even though she couldn't have him, she wanted to be able to think of him there.

"Rob Friedman has a right to his opinion," she continued. "And please be careful what you say. Jenny's starting to pick up words."

"I didn't call him a *pig,* did I?" Judy asked, her voice curiously disembodied and echoing in the small space under the sink. "I used the cultured word for pig."

"He said you were a good plotter."

"*After* he said I had a big mouth."

Daphne kicked gently at the waffle sole of the booted foot at the end of the leg protruding onto the tiled floor. "Well, sis, you do. Let's face it."

"When I get this off," Judy threatened with a grunt

as she struggled with the pipe, "I'm going to hit you with the wrench."

"Violence isn't good for Jenny, either," Daphne returned. "You sure you don't mind staying with her this afternoon? Britt doesn't usually call me in on a Saturday."

"I don't mind at all. We'll just hang out and watch old movies. But I thought Barbara worked Saturdays."

"She does. But Britt asked me to come to the plant, not the shop. She wasn't specific, she just asked me to come. Something about advertising."

"You don't know anything about advertising. Do you?" There was the ripping sound of metal scraping metal. "Almost got this."

"Just that it costs a fortune." Daphne pushed her chair away from the table and stood to look into the sink. It was still full of water. "Judy," she said quickly, "before you take that off, I have to…" She reached for a bowl and something to bale with, but not quickly enough.

"Got it!" Judy exclaimed victoriously, then followed that with a shriek as the standing water rushed down the drain—into the pipe that wasn't there.

While Daphne stood against the counter, a hand to her mouth, Judy emerged from under the sink—soaked to the waist, her face wet, her hair plastered to her head.

"I'm…sorry," Daphne said from behind her hand, afraid removing it would release the guffaw that waited there.

Judy rose to her feet with dignity. "It's all right," she said flatly. "I don't think we were ever baptized." Then she handed Daphne the four-inch-long plastic figure of the Disney character, Jasmine, that had obstructed the flow of water. "Next time you pull the highchair up to the sink so Jenny can watch you wash veggies, keep your eye on what she's throwing in your water."

"Yes, ma'am." Daphne's voice was choked and very faint.

Jenny, on her circuit of the table, saw the figure in Daphne's hand and reached out for it as though it were a brass ring. "Mine!" she cried.

Daphne handed it to Jenny and she rode on, ringing the bell on her handlebars.

Judy's fierce expression cracked into a smile and Daphne wrapped her in her arms, laughing uproariously.

"DAPH, YOU KNOW SANDY, our marketing director, of course. But have you met Kika Mancini?" Britt drew the attractive, fair-haired young woman toward the middle of her plush office, where Daphne stood.

"Yes, of course. She brings Melody to TylerTots." Daphne offered her hand. "How are you?"

The young woman was a casting director from Minneapolis who'd come to Tyler on a search for a toddler to use in an ad campaign for Fancy Furniture.

Daphne remembered the panic she'd felt when someone had recommended that Jenny apply as the Fancy Baby. Fortunately, the furniture company wanted a red-headed baby, and Annabelle Scanlon's granddaughter Melody had been chosen. Then, in true storybook fashion, Kika had fallen in love with Melody's widowed father and married him right before Labor Day. His two boys also seemed to adore her. That was no surprise to anyone. The young woman emanated energy and good cheer.

But Daphne already suspected this interview meant trouble.

"Yes, we know each other," Kika said. "Melody

loves her. Did you know she knows all twenty-some verses to 'Davy Crockett'?''

"Such talent," Britt exclaimed. "Let's sit at the table. The men should be here any minute."

Men? Daphne wondered, as Sandy Stirling, Yes! Yogurt's vivacious marketing expert, explained to Britt that Drew, her husband and Jake's cousin, would be late for the meeting because of some crisis with his eccentric grandfather, who lived at Worthington House. Clarence was always causing a ruckus at Tyler's old folk's home, it seemed.

With a laugh, Britt led the three women to the oval conference table at the far end of the comfortable office on the plant's third floor. Afternoon sun slanted in through the miniblinds and made a geometric pattern on the carpet.

They had just sat down when the door opened, admitting Jake, Britt's husband.

"Hi, darling," Britt called. "Did you find him?"

"Of course." Jake held the door and let Vic Estevez precede him into the room.

Britt's heart rose into her throat. No. She was finally beginning to adjust to his absence from her life and here he was. Now she would have to start over, fight off all the lust and longing she'd just begun to bring under control.

The men came toward the table, Vic dressed in gray wool slacks and a green-and-gray sweater. The sweater's gray turtleneck was a flattering contrast to his dark features.

Jake bent to kiss the top of Britt's head and took the chair beside her, gesturing for Vic to take the one between Daphne and Kika.

Britt introduced Vic to Sandy and Kika, then Vic

turned to smile politely at Daphne. "Hi, Daph," he said. His tone was easy and friendly, as though they were simply acquaintances—as though that was all they'd ever been.

She should have been pleased that he was behaving in precisely the way their goodbye warranted, but she wasn't.

"Okay, I'll get right to it," Britt said as Jake leaned back in his chair beside her. "The Yes! Yogurt team has developed a few new products, and with the National Flavor Test blue ribbon on our name, we thought it was time to do some serious advertising."

Daphne couldn't imagine how this related to her, but she had a feeling she wouldn't like it.

Vic simply listened quietly, his chair pushed away from the table, one ankle angled on the other knee.

Britt smiled at the casting agent. "So we consulted with Kika to see what she thought about faces to represent us, and she suggested a glamorous approach rather than the homespun look that's been our stamp so far." Now she looked from Jake to Daphne. "And we both have difficulty believing this, but we think two of the most glamorous-looking people anywhere are right here in Tyler—the two of you."

Daphne refused to panic. All she had to do was refuse. Certainly they'd considered that she might.

"What do you say?" Britt asked, her smile glowing with enthusiasm. "Will you be our models?"

As Daphne stammered over an answer, Britt's smile dimmed. "Vic?"

Daphne looked at him, trying not to let her desperation show, but sending him the clearest message she could, certain he understood. *No. Say no.*

He turned to look doubtfully at Kika. "You want a

Latino face on an ad campaign that isn't to promote salsa or garden pottery?''

"Absolutely," she replied. "It's a strong and handsome face without a suggestion of prettiness. It's the male look Britt wants. And let's face it." She shrugged and smiled without apology. "Latinos are box office right now."

He laughed lightly. "So I owe this proposal to Andy Garcia and Antonio Banderas?"

"No," Britt said, "you owe it to your own charisma. And the fact that Sandy and I both think you're gorgeous."

"Watch it," Jake warned mildly and without moving.

Britt reached back to pat his hand and acknowledge the teasing caution. Then she turned her eyes on Daphne. "Daph," she said reasonably, "you could make a lot of extra money on this. We'll pay you modeling scale. You'll have something to say about all—"

"No," Daphne said. She had to physically force the word from her lips. Britt had given her a job when she'd needed it desperately, then had offered her her friendship. And all Daphne had done in return was lie about everything she was.

It was all about to erupt on her; she felt it coming—beginning with the churning emotions inside her.

"Daphne, we plan a very tasteful campaign," Sandy assured her. "We intend—"

Daphne pushed away from the table. It wasn't Britt's fault, of course, but for the last few weeks every time she'd turned around there'd been a camera in her face. Daphne was feeling pursued. It occurred to her with a sense of gallows humor that that, of course, had been her situation, even before Britt suggested putting her in a national ad campaign.

"I'm sure you'll do something wonderful, but I'm afraid I can't be involved. I have a small child and two jobs, a house that requires my—"

"Daphne, we'll work around your schedule," Britt said. "I understand Jenny is your priority. But we'll—"

Daphne picked her purse up off the floor and stood, shouldering it. "I'm sorry, Britt. I don't want—"

Vic caught her wrist, his eyes looking directly into hers. He was trying to send her a message, just as she'd done to him moments ago. *Calm down,* his gaze said. *Relax. You're only making yourself look suspicious.* "Daph, why don't you just listen to the plan?" he suggested quietly. "Maybe we can—"

And that did it. She added a sense of betrayal to her feeling of pursuit.

How could he suggest that she consider having her face projected across the country when he *knew* she was hiding? What was wrong with him? He was a man, that was what was wrong with him!

She turned to Britt, too agitated to even try to force a smile. "I'm sorry, Britt. I can't do it. But this town is full of pretty faces. You'll find someone else." She glanced at Jake and saw the surprise and speculation in his eyes. God. Now she'd done it.

She said a polite goodbye to Kika and Sandy and hurried from the room.

There were tears streaming down her face as she fairly ran down the sunny sidewalk. She didn't understand why this should happen now. She hadn't cried since Trey's death. Not when she'd barely gotten Jenny away from Celeste's thugs in Malibu, not when she'd had to run three blocks in Allentown with Jenny in her arms, not when she'd hidden in the water-heater closet for twenty minutes in her apartment in Lexington while Celeste's men ransacked it.

But now, because she'd been approached about a silly ad campaign, she was on the brink of hysterics.

She ran around the corner, through the middle of a family group that stopped to watch her tearful progress, then saw her car just halfway down the block. Suddenly it represented safety.

She was just a few steps from it when a steely hand caught her arm and pulled her to a stop.

"Daphne, wait!"

Daphne was spun around and found herself looking into Vic's face. She saw impatience in his eyes, and that added fuel to her already burning anger.

She tried to yank away from him but he held firm. So she stood quietly, waiting for her moment. "Wait for what?" she demanded. "To listen to the plan, as you suggested in there? Haven't you heard a thing I've told you? Have I been pouring my soul out to myself? I'm *hiding!*"

Vic looked up and down the street, which was fortunately quiet at the moment, then at her. "Then it's probably not a good idea," he said softly, "to shout it at the top of your lungs in midday traffic."

She looked surreptitiously around her and saw no evidence that anyone in the passing cars or in the group of people looking in a store window down the street had heard her.

"Give me your keys," he said.

"Why?"

"So we can find a quiet place to discuss this calmly."

She tried to yank her arm out of his grasp, panic inching up her internal barometer. She didn't want to talk about it. She didn't even want to think about it. She wanted to go home to Jenny and Judy and hide.

His fingers gripped her elbow a little tighter. "I'm not going to let you go, so you may as well relax. We are going to talk about this, and you're too upset to drive."

"Because *you* were acting like you thought the ad campaign was a good idea, when you *knew*…"

He was shaking his head. "I was just trying to play out your cover. You have a lot to learn about undercover work. We could have agreed to think about it, planned to talk it over, and no one would have been suspicious when we finally told Britt we didn't think it would work out. She'd have presumed it was our antagonistic relationship at work."

Vic shook his head at Daphne reprimandingly. "But the way you reacted in there, they're probably trying to decide if you're dying of something terminal or just having a nervous breakdown. Now, will you please give me your keys and get in the car?"

Daphne dug them out of her purse and handed them to him, avoiding his eyes as he unlocked her door, helped her inside, then locked and closed it.

They were at Timber Lake in fifteen minutes, on the shore opposite the lodge. It was less manicured here, more unspoiled.

Daphne looked around at the golden afternoon, the trees growing more colorful as each day passed, the lake deep blue, its migrant Canada geese already diminishing as flocks headed south for the winter. Mallards remained among the last holdouts and swam with a serenity Daphne wished she could capture for herself.

Vic pulled to a stop near the lakeshore, then came around the car to help her out.

She still felt quarrelsome and edgy. "We're not going to skip stones or lie on our backs and find pictures in the clouds, are we? I'm really not in the mood for rustic pursuits, thank you."

Apparently unaffected by her ill temper, he caught her hand and led her to a trail through a tall stand of spindly white birches. "No, I thought we'd take a walk," he said, "and burn off some of this cussedness."

She hung back. "I don't want—"

"Sure you do," he said, tugging her along with him as he set off at a steady pace. "You've been in hiding too long. You need fresh air to clear your thoughts."

With little choice but to follow or be dragged, Daphne fell into step beside him.

The trail looped along the shore, trees and shrubs standing sentinel. All but the latest autumn asters and goldenrod were gone, but the cool air was rich with the fragrance of pine and the sweetness of a breeze off the lake.

As they walked, pine needles crunched underfoot, and the sunlight shot through the trees like laser beams.

They walked some distance in silence, then the hand that held hers moved to her shoulder. "You warm enough?" Vic asked gently.

The annoyance with which she replied was half pretense. She *was* beginning to relax. "This is a fine time to ask me, after you drag me half a mile down a cold forest trail."

He rubbed his hand gently up and down her arm and pointed ahead, toward a clearing in the trees. "Sunlight up there. We'll stop and soak it up."

Daphne's sweater was thick, and she was really quite comfortable. She'd complained simply to be difficult.

But if he stopped, he would probably want to talk, and that was the last thing she wanted to do at the moment.

"I'm fine," she said coolly. "Let's just keep going and get this walk over with."

"That's not the point of it."

"Yes, it is. You take a walk to get somewhere."

"No, you take a walk to enjoy nature and your companions."

"*My* companion," she said querulously, "is pushy."

"Your companion," he corrected, "is concerned for your welfare." They had left the shadowy corridor of trees, and he tugged her toward a clear patch of grass on the sunny bank of the lake.

"We decided that we don't have a future together," she reminded him, following along desultorily as he sank to the ground near a shady maple and pulled her down between his knees. "You have no responsibility for my welfare. And you're going to get your slacks all grass stained."

"*You* decided we have no future." He wrapped his arms around her so that her back leaned against his chest. "I'm convinced we do. It's just more efficient not to argue with you. Comfortable?"

She was. It was heavenly to have his arms wrapped around her. But every time she was forced to push him out of her life, the chore grew more difficult, the pain of separation harder to bear. And although his persistence was flattering and consoling, things couldn't be the way he imagined.

But the upset of the afternoon had left her drained of energy and, momentarily, at least, of resources. So she rested her weight against him and tried once more to explain. "Vic, I told you that Jenny has to be my—"

"The focus of your complete attention," he interrupted quietly. "I know. I understand. And you have to understand that you and Jenny have become the focus of *my* attention."

"No," she said firmly. "You know that can't be."

"I'm sorry. It is. I see all of us in that farmhouse with the gables."

Daphne could see it, too. That made it hurt that much more, to know it couldn't be.

"I explained my situation," she said with a sigh. "I might have to leave at a moment's notice."

He tightened his grip on her, and she felt his lips in her hair. "No. You're not going anywhere. We're taking a stand, here."

She didn't like the steel in his voice. She didn't like that aggressive string of words. She turned in his arms to look at him, bracing herself with an arm on his shoulder. "Vic, you don't know what you're talking about. Celeste has men, weapons, money at her disposal. She's filed a court order for Jenny, but her maneuvers to find us have been contrary to legal guidelines. She has thugs working for her. You are *not* getting involved in this."

"Too late," he said, brushing windblown strands of hair from her face. "I already am. We're going to get Celeste out of your hair, clear up the court thing, then we're getting married."

Her heart cramped in her breast. She hadn't wanted to tell him. She'd wanted to be able to think back on this time with Vic a year from now and remember that deliciously lustful look in his eyes—delicious because it was always wrapped in tender adoration. He thought she was good. He didn't know about the other life.

She didn't know how else to turn him away from this course he intended to take. She had to tell him.

Vic saw it coming in her eyes. That dark mystery

that always lay at the bottom of her gaze came to the surface, deepening the light blue color. He would have saved her this if he'd been able, but until he had the answers from Heath and he could choose a course of action, he had to protect his own cover. If she discovered who he was, she wouldn't sit still long enough for an explanation. And Vic wasn't letting her out of his life.

She sat up so that they no longer touched, although his legs still bracketed her.

"I have to tell you something," she said heavily, drawing her knees up and wrapping her arms around them.

Guilt clawed at him because she had to go through this. But he forced himself to remain still. There was no other way. "You only have to tell me what you want to tell me."

She braced herself on a hand and leaned back to look into his eyes. Her expression was questioning. "What do you mean?" she asked.

He tried to give her an out. "I mean, if you're heading toward…past indiscretions or something, I'm not asking for confessions, and I have every intention of keeping all my stupid moves to myself."

He'd seen that heroic look in her eyes before. He prepared himself to take the news, even though he knew what she was about to tell him. It wouldn't hurt him, but he knew it would hurt her.

She turned to face him, sitting back on her heels. Her hair blew, her face was pale and her eyes were so stricken he had difficulty looking into them. But she was making such a point of honesty that he made himself meet her gaze.

"I *have* to tell you this," she said.

"Okay." He raised a knee, rested his forearm on it and held her gaze. "Tell me."

"When I met Trey," she said, her voice soft and tight, "I was working in Vegas." She hesitated.

He nodded, still hoping to divert her. "You told me that."

"I didn't tell you," she went on intrepidly, "that I was working as a call girl. A prostitute."

Daphne made herself add the word that removed whatever mystery the term "call girl" might retain. And she felt both the release of a huge burden and the addition of a great weight. The sensations negated each other, and she realized grimly that she remained trapped.

The confession was therapeutic, but when made to the man she loved, it was also decimating. Her hands trembled and she locked them together.

She waited for Vic to betray shock, disgust, anger.

But his expression remained steady, calm. So she went on. "I started at fifteen," she said, "and was almost twenty-three when I married Trey."

He nodded. She saw acceptance and pain in his eyes. "Eight years," she said. "I did it for eight years."

He nodded again. "I can do the math."

Tears pooled in her eyes. "The stepfather I told you about…began molesting me almost immediately after he moved in with us. I saved my baby-sitting money, and left when I was fifteen. I found other girls living on the street who did it for a living, and…" She hunched a shoulder in a gesture that suggested acceptance, endurance. It broke his heart. "I'd already been trained for it." A sob escaped her. "What are you feeling?" she whispered.

Vic tried to analyze what he would be feeling if he

hadn't known that part of her past, if he'd fallen in love with her as he had and this had come as a complete surprise.

Then he realized he'd have reacted no differently. He felt anger and disgust, all right—but not for her.

He tried to pull her toward him. "Come here," he ordered softly.

She stared at him in obvious surprise, and a tear spilled over, but she pushed against him. Her hands balled into fists on his shoulders. "Don't you understand?"

"Yes, perfectly," he said. "You were victimized by a man you were supposed to be able to trust, and you did what you had to do to survive in an impossible situation."

He tried to reach for her again, but she drew away. "You're not...horrified?"

"Daph, I was a cop," he reminded her. "I've seen the outer limits of everything you can imagine. I know how hard life can push you. Some big strong men don't emerge with as much strength and savvy as you've put together."

Daphne wanted to believe his nonjudgmental response, his easy tolerance. But she'd been so sure for so long that she would never be able to explain to any man what had happened, and that if she did, he would never be able to understand.

Faced with the opposite reaction, she felt her world tilt and fall over. Things she knew to be true were suddenly erased. Possibilities she'd always deemed *im*possible—at least for her—now dangled just beyond her reach.

"Will you please come here?" he asked her, trying to pull her into his arms.

But the world was too confused suddenly. She wanted him more than anything, but he couldn't be thinking clearly.

She got to her feet.

He followed, and caught her arm when she wandered aimlessly away from him.

"Now," he said, looking into her stunned eyes. "You have to stop the pattern. Turn it around."

"I haven't..." she began.

He shook his head. "I don't mean that. I mean you don't believe in anybody but yourself. I'd be the last one to blame you, because I've been out there all alone, betrayed and abandoned by the people in whom I'd placed my trust. But there comes a moment when you realize that the job—or the world—is too big for you to fight all alone, and you have to take a risk and trust someone again."

Daphne looked into the love in his eyes and couldn't shake the notion that he simply hadn't understood. "Vic," she said, taking his forearms and shaking him. "I made love with men for money for eight years!"

He dropped his arms from her and spread his hands in a gesture of complete frustration. "I got that, Daphne! How do you want me to react? You want me to shout and scream at you? Well, I could, but then fairness would force me to tell you that in my undercover work, I've tricked men and women into friendships with me that resulted in the destruction of their futures and sometimes their lives, all in the name of getting drugs off the street. It's not that different from prostitution, and I loathed myself for a lot of it. I just had to believe that in the end, good things would result from what I'd done. I'm sure that's all you hoped for—security and a little peace."

Her face crumpled, and she wrapped her arms around his neck. He enfolded her against him and held her closely while she cried.

Daphne clung to him and felt the world stabilize. But it didn't change her situation with Celeste. She sniffed and drew back from Vic, her arms still looped around his neck. "When this is over," she said, "maybe we can talk about—"

"Not when it's over," he insisted. "Now."

She shook her head adamantly and leaned it against his cheek. "I'm too tired to think about anything right now. Will you let me take you back to your car, so I can go home to Jenny?"

He didn't want to. He wanted to take her home with him and make her feel the extent of his love for her. But in view of the discussion they'd just had, it was a proposal he was afraid would make him sound like too many other men she'd known. So he agreed.

They parted on the sidewalk around the corner from the Yes! Yogurt plant. As she came around the car to take the keys from him and slip into the driver's seat, he kissed her desperately but tenderly, all the dreams he had for the two of them and Jenny invested in the communication.

"I love you, Daphne," he said when he raised his head. "And I'm going to get you out of this. You have to trust me."

"I trust you," she said, running the pad of her thumb over his bottom lip. "But I don't want to involve you."

"I told you. You no longer have a choice. I'm involved. And I'm going to fix it."

She hugged him fiercely for one long moment, then got into her car, blew him a kiss and drove away.

CHAPTER TEN

THE LODGE MANAGER hailed Vic from behind the desk as he returned.

"A message, Mr. Estevez," she said with a smile as she handed him the slip. "And you have a guest." She pointed behind him to a plush sofa flanked by potted palms.

Vic turned, a spark of excitement flaring in him. Had Daphne changed her mind and beaten him back here? He felt the separation from her like an ache.

But a uniformed police officer rose from the sofa. The leather of his utility belt creaked as he met Vic in the middle of the room.

Vic recognized him instantly. Brick Bauer—Britt's cousin, who'd questioned him when he'd found him watching Daphne leave her aerobics class.

Vic offered his hand.

Brick shook it. "Buy you a cup of coffee?" he asked politely. His gaze was even, steady, but Vic knew the look—he'd used it often enough himself. Brick knew something about him he wasn't pleased with. Hell.

"Sure," he replied.

They walked side by side into the coffee shop and took a booth in a quiet corner. A cheerful, full-figured waitress was there immediately to pour coffee. Brick apparently knew her, made small talk with her, then told her she didn't have to fuss over them, that they just wanted to talk.

Vic watched him at work and thought he reminded him of an old small-town sheriff, the kind who knew everyone in his jurisdiction and guarded each individual possessively.

Vic did his best to look innocent. "What's on your mind, Captain?" he asked.

Brick leaned back in the booth. Leather creaked again. "You lied to me, Mr. Estevez. You're not here to relocate. You're a P.I."

So he'd checked him out; Vic had to give him credit. His acuity was going to be trouble, but Vic would have done the same thing in his position.

He smiled. "I'm a P.I.," he said, "looking to relocate."

Brick didn't smile back. "A former DEA agent who brought down the Rumorosa Cartel wants to settle in Tyler?"

Vic shrugged. "*You're* happy here."

"I was born here."

Vic tried another tack. "It's always been my dream to own a sporting-goods store in a small town where I can put the sludge behind me and start over."

Brick studied him, analyzed him. Only long experience prevented Vic from squirming.

"The only thing in your favor," Brick said after taking a sip of coffee, "is that you haven't lied about who you are. So I assume you're not hiding. That means you must be looking."

"I am. For a house and a storefront. Paul Bullard can verify that. He's been showing me around."

Brick gave him a look that condemned him for trying

to con him. "You've been spending a lot of time with Daphne Sullivan."

Vic nodded. "I have."

"Is she the subject of your investigation?"

Vic credited him with a good try. "We're called private detectives, Captain," he said politely but firmly, "because our proceedings are confidential until we have proof."

Brick leaned slightly toward him, his eyes lethal. "Anything that presents a danger to the people of Tyler is my business, Mr. Estevez. And I have the damnedest feeling you're trouble."

"I assure you I'm not," Vic said. That is, he didn't intend to be. "But if I do decide to settle here," he added with a smile, "it's a comfort to know Tyler's so well protected."

Brick studied him for a moment longer, apparently dissatisfied with their interview, then slid out of the booth.

"Watch yourself, Mr. Estevez," he cautioned, picking up the check.

"You too, Captain," Vic returned, taking the check from him. "Please. My treat."

Brick acknowledged the courtesy with a nod that coupled gratitude with threat, then walked away.

Vic heaved a sigh and pulled the message Sheila had given him out of his pants pocket. It was from David Heath.

He had solid data on Celeste Huntington, Vic discovered when he called his friend from the privacy of his room.

"Long history of wielding power ruthlessly," David reported. "My guess is that she has a few city and county officials in her pocket, judging by campaign contributions. And I checked into her butler and her chauffeur, as you suggested, and guess what?''

"Records?''

"As long as your arm. Assault, armed robbery, parole violations. Not what you'd expect to find in Palm Beach. What's this lady into, anyway?''

"Not sure. What about her family?''

"Husband was CEO of Huntington Industries when he died in '83. Her family, the Butlers, were big into oil, and were bought out by Huntingtons. One son— Butler Davis Huntington III, playboy, yacht racer, parents bought him out of trouble regularly when he was a kid, but he increased the Beach Boy Shops' assets when he took over in '88. Married Diane Majors in '92, killed in an automobile accident in '94.''

"His fault?''

"Unknown. Happened on a country road. Hit a phone pole. No witnesses.''

"Did you find anything on Diane Majors?''

"Well, that's interesting, too. She's Judy Lowery's half sister—same mother, different father. Lowery's father was state senator Jarvis Lowery, who was caught in the late sixties with another senator's wife. The men were on opposite sides of an environmental issue at the time, and the press deduced that he was after information. Or she was. It was a big deal. He finally offed himself in his study. Maid found him.''

Vic remembered Judy's explosive reaction to Rob Friedman at the lodge, and realized there'd probably been more involved in her reaction than his lukewarm review of her book.

"Lowery—the girl—went to BSU, worked for Minuteman Publishing for a couple of years, then moved to Tyler to write or something.''

Vic knew that. He was sure Judy and Daphne kept their relationship a secret so that Daphne couldn't be traced through Judy. "What about Diane?"

"Uh...tell me about this, Vic. Is your interest personal?"

"Just give it to me, Dave."

"Okay. Missing person at fifteen. A case opened by her sister in fall of '84 said she left Chicago for L.A. and was known to be working the street on Hollywood Boulevard, but nobody could find her. Funny. Her stepfather was Chicago police commissioner at the time and certainly should have had some connections to help in the search."

"No case opened by the parents?"

"No."

Maybe, Vic speculated, she hadn't been found *because* her stepfather was police commissioner. Finding her would have resulted in her ending up in the system and possibly revealing why she'd run away in the first place. And that would not have been good for the commissioner.

"She virtually disappeared. I found nothing after that, except that the kid in the picture Judy Lowery left police when she filed her missing-persons report looks a lot like the young woman in Huntington's wedding picture. They're one and the same?"

Vic sighed. "You don't call yourself a detective for nothing."

"Thank you. That's what I've always thought. Need anything else?"

"No. Thanks, Dave. I owe you big."

"Damn straight, you do. In real money."

"A check's on its way."

"If I get caviar in the mail, you're a dead man."

Vic paced the small area around his bed and thought with a private smile that he reminded himself of Jenny, going around and around the coffee table on her tricycle.

All right. This was it. No more skirting the issue to protect his relationship with Daphne. He had to tell her what had brought him to Tyler, why he'd continued to withhold the truth from her even after he'd become convinced she wasn't the jezebel Celeste claimed her to be. He had to insist that they take legal action against the woman immediately, and were then getting married.

Vic knew he was an optimist to even consider that she would still be listening after he'd told her who had hired him, but a future without Daphne was not an option. He had to think positively.

He glanced at his watch. Not quite 5:00 p.m. She would be feeding Jenny, and he didn't want to intrude upon that. He would spend an hour at the Y working off his frustrations and his guilt, then go to Daphne's and tell her who he was and what he intended to do.

He patted his pocket for car keys and wallet as he framed the thought—and stopped when his hand met only the rental-car keys. No wallet. He turned to check the dresser, the night table on which the phone stood. It wasn't there.

He thought back. He hadn't had a reason to take his wallet out of his pocket all afternoon, since he'd put the coffee with Brick Bauer on his room tab. Could he have dropped it, he wondered, when he'd been chasing Daphne? His complete attention had been focused on reaching her before she got to her car and sped away.

Her car. Had he dropped it there?

He'd just formed the question when a quick, light

knock sounded on his door. Preoccupied, he went to the door and pulled it open.

Daphne stood there looking long and leggy in jeans and his UC Santa Barbara sweatshirt. Her hair was loose and full, as though some sophisticated artist had curled and spun moonbeams.

She held her hands behind her back, and something subtle had resolved itself in her eyes and her smile. The mystery was completely gone from them, and now they were open—not just to the world, but to him specifically.

And he knew then without a particle of doubt that whatever else lay between this moment and their lifetime together, love was going to happen. She was his. He was hers.

Her smile was shy but honest. ''Missing something?'' she asked.

He reached around her waist and under the arms crossed behind her back to pull her into the room. He closed the door behind her.

The action brought her right up against him, so that his lips hovered a millimeter from hers. He felt her eyelashes brush his cheekbone. Startled surprise flashed in her eyes, but was replaced instantly by the same desire he felt at their body-to-body closeness.

''Yes,'' he whispered thickly. ''You.''

Then he closed his mouth over hers and felt the immediate ignition of her eager response. It was as though she'd come to some decision that had wiped away every caution, every fear where he was concerned.

Her tongue met his, toyed with it, drew on it. Her fingers delved into the thick hair at the crown of his head and tightened there, causing him a delicious pain he was sure would burn into his memory. Her free hand reached under his sweater, then pulled impatiently at the T-shirt she encountered until she could lay her palm against bare flesh. He swallowed her sigh of satisfaction.

This was no time for questions. After a long career of risks and near misses, he was usually the last one to challenge a benevolent fate, but he couldn't help himself. She was vulnerable now. And God, so was he.

"Daphne." He dragged his mouth from hers and tried to hold her away. But she was showering his face with kisses, moving to the underside of his chin, along his jaw to his ear. Everything inside him jangled. "Daph...we should talk about..."

He was interrupted by an insistent pair of lips and an artful tongue that wiped his brain clear of all thought.

Then she drew back for an instant, and he stared in spellbound wonder at the dark passion in her eyes, at the utter intensity of her delicate features as she focused on him and said with humbling sincerity and conviction, "I love you, Vic. I'd gotten home, and was about to get out of the car when I saw your wallet on the floor. And I was thrilled that I had a reason to come back to you. That's when I realized that it was foolish to pretend that I could simply hold off what I feel for you until everything else in my life is resolved." She kissed him again. "I adore you, Vic. Jenny adores you."

Her eyes softened and grew suddenly uncertain. "If you're sure the other life doesn't matter...then, I need you so much."

He didn't know how to reassure her except to make her forget the other life, and that there'd ever been anyone but him.

He lifted her into his arms and walked around the bed with her to deposit her against the pillows. With a deft yank he pulled the spread and blankets down until there was just a cool sheet under her.

Daphne wanted him to make love to her more than she wanted anything, except to keep Jenny. But she felt an emotional storm building inside her, a sudden rush of shame and longing that was all curiously entangled.

She'd been so sure about this when she'd left the house to come here. She loved him. He loved her. She was certain of both of those facts. So, why now? Why, after she'd come on like a woman who knew what she wanted, should she be plagued by a past he'd told her he could forgive?

She didn't understand it, tried to fight it off by pulling the sweatshirt over her head as he drew the blankets down.

But it continued to rise up in her—all the anguish accrued over years of surviving by lying on a bed just like this.

Then he reappeared beside her with that handsome, smiling face filled with tenderness and that indulgent look that always made her feel like a fraud, and the sob erupted from her in a small, choking sound. She clutched the sweatshirt to her mouth and curled into a tight ball.

She felt his arms come around her, shielding her as much as holding her, and she wrapped her hands around them where they crossed over each other. But she wouldn't look at him.

"I've done this so many times," she sobbed, the tears burning as they fell.

He kissed her bare shoulder. "You've never done it with me."

"You don't understand." She choked. "I was married to Trey, and I loved him, but it was all over so quickly that sometimes, except for Jenny, it's as though those two years never were. And all I remember…is the other life.''

He rubbed her back in smooth, comforting circular strokes. "I understand," he said quietly. "The other life was a solution for a desperate girl with no other options. The woman you've become is someone else entirely."

She rested her wet cheek against his hand. "Oh, Vic," she said brokenly. "I'm sure the parents who taught you to walk a woman to the door wanted something else for you. Some innocent young woman who's never—"

"What *you* have to understand," he interrupted gently, "is that I couldn't love you more if you *were* virginal. I love the poor little girl who was left without choices, and the woman who survived to be a strong and loving woman. I love all of you. You don't ever have to hide anything from me. And you'll never have to do anything you don't want to do."

Daphne felt the girl inside her that Gordon had ripped apart heal at those warm and loving words. And as the girl healed, the woman she'd become slowly returned to life.

She turned into Vic's arms and wrapped hers around him, crying out the residual misery of years of guilt and shame.

Then she leaned away from him, her makeup wept away, her face clean, her eyes clear.

"Do you want to make love to me?" she asked. "It's all right. I'm…safe."

"I would love to make love to you," he replied without hesitation, his knuckle gently rubbing at her puffy cheek. "But only if that's what you want. If you're still upset, we can just lie here and rest or talk or stare at the ceiling, and then I'll take you home.''

She smiled at him, and he saw genuine amusement in the gesture. ''Then my car would be in the wrong place again.''

He grinned. ''I could take you home in *your* car.''

''Then how would you get back?''

''Maybe you'd invite me to stay.''

She kissed him lightly. ''Maybe we should just make love and I'll drive myself home.''

''Well,'' he said with theatrical uncertainty, ''if you really think that's best…''

He leaned over her to kiss her until he felt her complete relaxation, the melding of her long, slender body into his. She clung to him as though she needed him every bit as much as he needed her.

Daphne felt the tender touch of his hand against her bare back and realized with a sense of delicious discovery that the fears that had gripped her just moments ago had been banished. It was as though a new day had dawned.

The other life was dead.

His hand moved slowly across her shoulders, down the sensitive crenellations of her spine, then up again to grasp the nape of her neck and hold her still so that he could look into her eyes.

She smiled at the banked passion in his dark gaze, basking now in that look of adoring indulgence.

''I love you,'' she whispered.

''God,'' he said feelingly, ''I love you, too.''

As he rained kisses across her throat and over her breastbone, she tugged up on his sweater and T-shirt, needing to touch him, to feel him against her.

He rose up on his knees to let her pull them off him.

She noticed the puckered scar on his right shoulder. She put a fingertip to it, frowning. "What happened there?" she asked.

"A bullet," he said, then grinned. "Isn't that a romantic line? I have to learn to say it more heroically, though."

"From the DEA days?"

"Yeah. Long time ago. Uh, could I have your undivided attention, please?"

Lowering his mouth to hers, he kissed her until her mind could comprehend nothing other than his lips. Then he moved them down her bare flesh to ring one breast in kisses, then take it gently into his mouth.

Sensation rayed through her as though that little mound were a power source. His mouth moved to the other breast and she gasped.

Her skin prickled with life as he kissed a line down her body. He stopped at the waistband of her jeans and knelt to unbutton and unzip them.

She braced herself on her elbows to help him tug them off. Her pink panties caught at her hip, and he yanked them off.

She sat up to unbutton and unzip his pants, and pulled at them as he lowered himself onto his back. She tossed them at the chair and turned to him to find his arms open to her.

She went into them humbly, relishing the simple action of strong, loving arms closing around her. She leaned her weight, her life, against his muscled warmth.

Vic felt her put herself, at least for that moment, into his care. Love swelled in him, filled him.

He moved his hands over her, tracing the small span of her waist, exploring the delicate mound of her hip, the long line of her thigh.

She raised her leg for him as he traced a path back up over her hip, then down again. She planted kisses across his pecs, over his rib cage and under it, across his stomach.

She heard his indrawn breath, felt his tension and stopped to rest her cheek there, momentarily arrested by the wonder of possession.

He took advantage of her hesitation and used it to pull her up beside him. Braced on an elbow, he cradled her in his arm and rested his hand on her flat stomach, his fingers splayed.

She bent her knee for him and curled an arm around his neck.

"Still okay?" he asked against her mouth.

"Wonderful," she whispered.

His finger dipped inside her and she leaned her face into the warm hollow of his throat. Sensations sparkled within her, new and brilliant, as his finger explored her, moved deeper inside her.

She ran a hand down his side, felt the mild indentation of his waist, the long, straight line of his hip and thigh, then retraced her path when she could reach no farther.

His finger moved lazily within her, stroking, dipping, retreating, filling her with a restless wanting that had never been a part of this experience. The physical experience of approaching climax was familiar, but her body had never recognized it as desirable, had never yearned for it, waited for it, focused every particle of concentration and desire on it.

But now she felt as though she were balanced on the edge of infinity, trusting fate—trusting Vic—to cast her free and somehow keep her safe.

She moved restlessly, wanting him as much as she wanted the pleasure he offered.

She whispered his name as she moved against his touch, her hand slipping down the middle of him and grasping his manhood in silken fingers.

Fire billowed inside him and he had little choice then but to pull her over him and steady her hips as he thrust upward into her.

He heard her sigh of relief, and moved with her as her body began to circle on his. He clasped her waist, and she leaned forward slightly to grasp his arms.

Her hair fell over him, skimmed along the flesh over his ribs, his pectoral muscles. It was a sensation that locked into his memory, into his being.

Then he felt her shudders, heard her little gasps and lost awareness of anything but himself as he erupted inside her, with passion strong and deep, the love it expressed rolling over and over him until he was sure he must look as changed as he felt.

Daphne felt shaken to the very depths of soul and marrow. The echoes of climax still resounded inside her, and she marveled that, after all she'd known and been through, making love could feel this magical, this fresh, this profoundly affecting.

Always, before, it had been done in fear, with revulsion, out of necessity, according to someone else's notion of what gave pleasure. Except with Trey, and that had been good, but he'd been spoiled and a little selfish, and it had never been quite as much about her as about him.

She crumpled atop Vic's chest and wept with the deep-down wonder of someone whose life has been renewed.

Vic pulled her up beside him, drew the blankets over

them and settled her in his arms. He wasn't sure what these tears were about, but he judged by the way she clung that they didn't relate negatively to him.

"I never cry," she told him while doing just that. "And I promise I'm going to stop in a minute."

He kissed her temple. "Good," he said. "Because we have a lot of plans to make. We can shower and go downstairs for dinner."

She looked up at him, her eyes drenched, her lashes spiked with tears. "That sounds wonderful. Judy's watching Jenny. I should call her."

Judy. Her sister. Everything he'd learned about Daphne from Dave Heath surfaced in his awareness, and with it, all he'd learned about Celeste. And that reminded him of what had completely left his mind from the moment he'd opened his door and found Daphne standing there.

She still thought he was just an ex-cop starting over in Tyler. She didn't know he'd come here to find her for the mother-in-law she'd been running from for a year.

And now he'd made love to her. She was going to hate him for that unless he explained very carefully. God.

She put a hand to his forehead. "You're frowning. What is it? Are you worried about my mother-in-law?"

He caught her hand and kissed it. "Yes," he said honestly. "We have to talk about that."

"I was thinking," she said, hiking herself up on an elbow, her eyes bright, her cheeks growing pink. He smiled at how fresh she looked, how fresh she made him feel—except for the guilt. "Maybe you're right about going back to Palm Beach and confronting her in court. I was thinking I could leave Jenny here with Judy so Celeste can't try to take her from me until the issue is settled.'' She smiled hopefully at him, obviously warming to the idea.

''Her argument was that I'd resumed the old life after Trey died. I could get some people from here to testify that that isn't true, and if I could show them a reputable man in my life—an ex-officer at that—it should all stand in my favor, don't you think?''

He thought Celeste Huntington sounded more like a hood than an honest woman willing to accept a court's decision, but that was where they had to start.

''We'll work on it,'' he said. ''I'll take a shower while you're calling Judy, then it's all yours.''

''Okay. But all I have to wear to dinner is your sweat-shirt and my jeans.''

He smiled and kissed her. ''I'll try to find a dressier shirt for you.''

She grinned and rubbed her nose along his cheek. ''Really. If we're going to share your clothes, you could use a few more sequins in your wardrobe.''

He nipped her earlobe. ''Make your call,'' he said. He went to the closet, pulled out a pair of slacks and disappeared into the bathroom.

''OF COURSE, I DON'T MIND staying with Jenny,'' Judy said over the phone. But the suspicious tone of her voice belied the reassuring words. ''I'm just not sure your having dinner with him is a good idea.''

Daphne smiled at the receiver, wondering what her sister would think if she knew how safe that was in light of what she'd already done.

''I like him a lot, Judy.'' She knew all her sister could understand at the moment was the understatement. ''He's wonderful to me.''

"How wonderful?" Judy demanded.

"Very wonderful. I'll be home in about two hours, okay?"

There was a dispirited sigh on the other end of the line. "Okay. Can I have the Light Lunch manicotti thing in the freezer?"

"Of course. And the pint of choco-cherry ice cream, if you want it."

"Yeah, I saw that." Her sister's voice took on a humorous lilt. "I'm going to tell Britt you have a competitor's ice cream in your freezer."

Daphne laughed. "Well, Britt and Jake don't produce any high-calorie, gut-buster stuff for those moments of great stress. So I had to look elsewhere. If *you* eat it, then you can't rat on me because you're equally guilty."

"Yes. Clever of you. All right, I'll see you in two hours, and if you're one minute late I'll be nuts, so call me!"

"I promise. What's Jenny doing?"

"We're playing drive-in. She just pedaled by on her tricycle and I gave her half a baloney sandwich."

Daphne laughed. "Thanks, Judy. I love you."

"I love you, too. Watch yourself with that man."

"Don't worry."

"That's what big sisters do. Goodbye."

Daphne hung up the telephone and looked out the window at the changing light of early evening. Vic's herbal scent lingered on the sheet wrapped around her, and she buried her nose in it, thinking that her life had changed magically today. She and Jenny had a future again.

CHAPTER ELEVEN

VIC AND DAPHNE ATE dinner by candlelight in the lodge's dining room.

Vic couldn't take his eyes off the picture she made in his white silk dress shirt and a loud red-and-blue tie one of his sisters had given him. He'd packed the tie, thinking that maybe here in rural Wisconsin, where no one knew him, he would have the courage to wear it. But he hadn't.

Daphne, though, had picked it right out of the lineup of four other, more sedate ties. She'd tucked the shirt into her jeans and covered the whole with a vest that was part of his gray pin-striped suit.

She looked delectable, her delicacy dramatized by the masculine wear, her hair falling free to her shoulders and gleaming in the soft shadows.

She gazed into his eyes with a delicious adoration that made him feel unashamedly pleased with himself and humbly grateful at the same time. He also felt great guilt, but he pushed it away, unwilling to mar the moment with anything beyond the bounds of its perfection.

She reached across the table with her fork to spear a bite of shrimp from the pasta on his plate. She'd ordered a simple salad.

"So, we're to share a wardrobe," he said, privately pleased that she was showing signs of a restored appetite. "And the same dinner plate?"

Candlelight sparkled in her eyes. "Do you mind?"

He shook his head. "I think we should extend it to a life."

She speared another bite as she repeated his words, obviously confused about his meaning. "You think we should extend it..." She hesitated, then put her fork down as the significance came home to her. "To life?" she asked in a whisper. "Share...a life?"

He pushed his plate aside and leaned toward her, reaching for her hand. "And a name, and Jenny, and the House of Three Gables."

Daphne couldn't quite take it in. In a muted gray-and-blue-tweed sports coat over a white dress shirt, Vic looked at her with grave resolution in his dark eyes.

She could still feel his touch on and inside her body, and the radiating glow that had resulted. She was sure she could have lit the darkness for a hundred miles.

And he was suggesting that she could have that forever?

"You mean...?"

"I mean marry me," he clarified. "Right away. We'll get blood tests on Monday, then a license."

She gazed at him, speechless. The obstacles were too large and too many.

"I know," he continued. "Your mother-in-law. We'll take her to court together. You'll have a better chance against her married to a DEA agent with a few commendations to his name."

Her eyes widened. "Really? What for?"

He dismissed their importance with a small gesture of the hand that held hers. "Doesn't really matter. But it could come in handy in court."

She placed her other hand over his. "Tell me."

He moved the candlestick aside, afraid for her slender arm in the loose folds of his shirtsleeve.

"I was involved in an eighteen-month undercover operation to bring down a drug cartel operating in Mexico and Texas."

Eighteen months. She'd been on the run almost that long. She understood the pressures of hiding in another identity, unable to be yourself. Only in her case, she preferred who she'd become. But she related to the pressure it placed on you every moment of every day. And loathsome as Celeste was, she was probably less dangerous than a drug cartel.

"Is that when you got the scar on your shoulder?"

He nodded. "A fellow agent turned just before the raid we'd been working toward all that time. As part of the group, we'd lived lives of luxury for a year and a half, and he couldn't deal with the idea of going back to life on an agent's pay. So he gave me up to them."

Her nails dug into his knuckles. "How did you get away?"

He grinned. "Cleverness and skill, of course."

She frowned at him.

"Okay, okay." He drew a breath, and she saw with sudden insight that he would have preferred not to explain. "A young lady who'd grown fond of me slipped me a weapon. I got away, disabled their helicopter and their truck, and hid in the woods until the raid."

"She didn't survive?"

"No." He still had to brace himself to think about it. "Her brother was the leader of the cartel, a man named Santos. He shot her for helping me."

Daphne felt sick.

"I wanted her to run with me," he said, "but she couldn't imagine a middle-class life-style, either." He shook his head over old wounds, then put the grimness away again. "Anyhow...I was scared spitless the whole time, but a judge might be impressed. And I bet if we try," he continued, thinking of the information Heath had given him, "we can get a case together against your mother-in-law."

"But marriage is—is—"

"Is what I want," he finished for her. "You're not afraid of it, are you?"

"No," she quickly assured him. "I just never thought it would happen to me again. You know..." She made an uncertain gesture he interpreted clearly.

"I know. But we both accept each other as we are. That's all it takes."

She laughed lightly, her lingering smile brilliant. "Yes," she said, "I'd love to marry you."

Now, he thought. *I have to tell her now.* Or he could wait until after they were married, when her options for reaction were diminished. That was tempting, but lower than he was willing to sink.

He put his napkin on the table and reached for his wallet. "Come on up with me for a few minutes," he said.

She glanced at her watch. "I promised Judy...."

"I heard you. But you can't agree to marry me, then run off. We have to talk about a few things."

She conceded easily. "Why don't you just come home with me?"

That would work. She might be less reluctant to scream at him with Jenny in the next room.

The waiter picked up the bill and his credit card.

They were walking across the lobby toward the door to the parking lot when the night clerk called his name from behind the desk. The man held up a note. "Message for you, Mr. Estevez."

Daphne, between Vic and the desk, said cheerfully, "I'll get it," and took the half-dozen steps to retrieve the note.

Lulled by their lovemaking and their cozy dinner, her agreement to marry him still making music in his ears, Vic had lost his edge of vigilance.

It was only as he saw her smiling at the clerk and reaching for the note that he awoke to the potential danger.

It was some corroboration of fact from David Heath, Vic told himself bracingly. Or some communication from Paul Bullard that just couldn't wait.

Then he saw Daphne's attention snagged by the small square of paper she held, and her look of openmouthed shock as she stared at it for the space of a heartbeat, then looked slowly up at him.

He went to take it from her. It was a simple sheet from a message pad. Under For: was his name, and under From: in clear block letters, was "Celeste Huntington."

"Phone me ASAP," was the simple message.

Calling himself all kinds of a fool for letting Daphne find out this way, Vic caught her arm and pulled her to the stairs.

Apparently still sedated by shock, she was halfway up the stairs before she began to fight him. Then her assault was vicious.

"You bastard!" she breathed. She was livid with rage, her cheeks scarlet as she kicked and slapped at him.

Fortunately, they were past the landing and the only people on the stairway. Taking the most expedient solution available to him, Vic put his shoulder to her waist, pinned her kicking legs to his chest and carried her to his room.

The instant he locked the door behind him and set her down, he took her bony-knuckled blow right in the gut.

"You stay the hell away from me!" she shouted, backing toward the bed.

Curiously, her gut punch didn't hurt him. It was her eyes that ground his nerve endings to pulp and made everything ache. Because under the fury and the pain and the hate, he saw love she couldn't quite shake despite what had to look to her like betrayal.

He caught her wrist again, neatly dodged another swinging blow, then grabbed her other arm.

"You're going to listen to me," he said quietly, insistently, "while I explain."

She went limp in his hold and sank to the floor, expecting him to lean down and try to pick her up, giving her a chance to strike while he was doubled over. But he second-guessed the maneuver and sat on the edge of the bed, still holding her wrists.

She tried to kick at him, but he managed to turn her away and wrap his arms around her by wrapping hers around herself.

"If you keep this up," he said softly in her ear, "you're going to get hurt. And you know I have more muscle and stamina than you do, so settle down and listen to me."

"Do you really think," she demanded, her voice high and tight as she continued to struggle, "that I would believe *anything* you told me now? You liar! You rotten, cheating son of a...!"

He tightened his grip on her. "All I can do is tell

you," he said. "Whether you believe me or not is up to you."

"Then let me save you the effort. I will *not* believe you." She launched a violent struggle against him that lasted for only a minute. Then she went limp in his arms once more, breathing heavily, her energy spent.

"I'm a private investigator," he said while he had the opportunity. "Celeste hired me because I'd done work for a friend of hers. She told me you were an opportunistic young woman who'd bilked her son out of a couple of hundred thou, blackmailed him into marriage, then absconded with her granddaughter after he was killed. She said you'd gone back to prostitution, and she wanted to get her granddaughter away from you and into a healthier environment."

"It seems I *have* gone back into prostitution," she retorted, with a loathing glance at him over her shoulder. "That'll be five hundred dollars for this afternoon, please."

Anger was a nice change from guilt, and he used it to propel her up from between his knees and onto the bed. She landed on her back with a bounce, and rose to her knees to glare at him, big-eyed and dangerous.

"You know that lovemaking changed both of us," he said, glaring back at her from the foot of the bed. "So don't try to pretend it was just a page out of the other life, so you can go on hiding."

"You *lied* to me," she declared.

"No, I didn't," he objected. "I just never told you the truth. Now I'm telling you. I knew almost the moment I saw you that Celeste had lied, that you weren't at all what she claimed."

"Well, then, why are you still here? Why didn't you

go back to Palm Beach and tell her you knew the truth?''

''What good would that have done?'' he asked impatiently. ''She'd still be after you.''

''What difference does that make to you?''

''You know damn well the difference it makes!'' he shouted at her. ''You know what we have here—you just agreed to marry me! I *love* you. I wanted to hold off until I could earn your trust and hear your side of the story, then decide how to proceed.''

''Well, you've failed miserably earning my trust,'' she said, trying to clamber off the bed and past him.

He hooked an arm around her waist and sat her down again. She fell back on her elbows as he leaned a knee on the bed and looked down at her. He was at the edge of his strained patience. He understood her anger, but she was making no effort to understand what had led him to this point.

''You gave it to me,'' he reminded her grimly. ''You told me everything. You bared all your vulnerabilities and let me in. I know that was hard and risky, but I'm asking you to carry that trust a little bit further. I know it looks like I used you, but you just came to life in my arms, Daphne. Do you really believe that was all in the line of my duty to Celeste?''

She shook her head, her eyes cold. ''You told me this afternoon that it was time to turn my life around. To open up and trust you…'' Her voice caught and emotion moved in her eyes. ''And all the time…you were using me and planning to steal my baby. I hate you for that.''

That hurt like the blow of a spiked fist, even though Vic could see in her eyes that she might want to hate him, but didn't.

"If I'd wanted to steal Jenny, I'd have had ample opportunity," he reminded her. "But I didn't."

She looked uncertain for an instant, but the shock and anger she felt were still too great. She couldn't make the leap from how it looked to how it was. And he had no one to blame but himself.

Still, somehow, he had to turn her around.

"I don't believe you," she said angrily. "And I don't trust you. Not for a minute."

Desperate, at the end of his rope, he didn't know what else to do to make her see his position than to take the gloves off and be as hard on her as she was being on him.

"All right," he said with quiet steadiness, looking into her eyes. "If you just made love with me without trusting me enough to believe what I'm telling you now, then what we did wasn't love. You're still in the business. And I'm just another—"

"Don't you say it!" she threatened darkly, tears standing in her eyes. "I'll kill you if you say it."

She planted a foot against his shoulder and tried to shove him out of her way as she leaped past him.

But he caught her ankle and brought her down on the carpet between the bed and the door. She fought him wildly, but he had the advantage of weight and experience, and she was pinned on her stomach in a matter of seconds.

"Do we have to talk this way?" he asked, his knee planted lightly but firmly in the middle of her back. "Or can we sit down like two reasonable human beings?"

"I'm finished talking," she said, her voice tight from having her face pressed against the carpet. "And you should be, too, because I'm not listening."

Resigned to having to do it her way, he maintained

the pressure on her back, holding her hands behind her waist, knowing the instant he loosened his grasp she would be gone.

"Well, if you care about Jenny, you'd better listen," he replied.

He felt the sharpening of tension within her. "What do you mean?" she demanded stiffly.

"You were just going to run out of here, go back to the house, get Jenny and take off for parts unknown. Am I right?"

She didn't reply. But she *was* listening.

"That would take Celeste right to your daughter," he said.

He saw Daphne's eyelashes flutter, saw the profile of a frown. He let her up and sat her on the floor against the end of the bed. He knelt before her on one knee, the other bent to support his arm.

She eyed him suspiciously, rubbing her wrists. Her left cheek was pink where it had been pressed to the carpet.

"Celeste apparently had *me* followed," Vic said. "I didn't tell her where I was going because I prefer to work without client interference. But I'm better at my job than this. I was taking too long, and she knew it and got suspicious."

Daphne considered that, then closed her eyes as the obvious conclusion struck her. "So if she knows where you are, she knows where *I* am."

"Yes. My guess is that she knows you're in Tyler, but not where, specifically. Or she wouldn't have called me, she'd have simply picked you up."

She opened her eyes and glowered at him. "Now I really hate you."

He was beyond knowing what to do about her. All

he could do now was rely on all his old instincts to keep her and Jenny safe.

"Knock yourself out," he said, pushing himself to his feet. "Just don't try to leave the room without me."

He went to the window and peered down on the parking lot, looking for something, anything that would tell him they were being watched. Darkness had fallen.

"Is she here?" Daphne asked.

He didn't see any sign of danger, but that didn't mean it wasn't there.

"I doubt that she is personally. But she might have sent the butler or the chauffeur you told me about." He left the window and went to the phone.

Daphne tried desperately not to panic, but all she could think about was how far away she was from Jenny. How vulnerable her sister was, alone at the farmhouse. She watched Vic's calm, economic movements as he stabbed out a phone number, pocketed his wallet, cradled the phone on his shoulder as he pulled on his watch.

Betrayal burned inside her where love had been. Impotent rage made her want to leap up and beat him until he felt as battered as she did. Then she wanted to run to her daughter and find somewhere else to hide. Again.

But she had to think of Jenny.

"I'd like to speak to Captain Bauer, please," he said into the telephone receiver. He listened for a moment. "Then, would you get a message to him? Tell him Vic Estevez called, and that he was right about him. Yes. Right about him. And ask him to meet me at Daphne Sullivan's house. Yes. Thank you."

He broke the connection, then carried the phone to the bed and handed the receiver to Daphne. "Call Judy," he said. "Tell her to make sure all the doors and windows are locked, and to not let anybody in but us.''

Daphne watched him throw his clothes into a bag while she answered Judy's anxious questions and listened to her I-told-you-so's.

He pulled on a short leather jacket and tossed the bag over his shoulder.

"Where are we going?" she asked.

"To get Jenny," he replied.

"You just said that if I drove home, I would—"

He cut her off with a look. "But I know how to make sure I'm not being followed."

"That's right," she said coldly, going to the door where he waited. "You're the professional deceiver."

He put a hand on the doorknob and sighed patiently. "Could we just stow all this until we're safely out of here?"

"When I'm safely out of here," she said, shouldering her purse, "you're out of my life."

He shook his head at her. "That's not how it's going to go. But this isn't the time to fight about it. Come on."

She went. Uppermost in her mind was getting safely to Jenny.

He settled his bill at the lodge with a credit card and a broad, natural smile for the night clerk, a young man with whom he'd obviously made friends.

"You're going *now?*" the clerk asked. "But we were going to go trout fishing before the season ends. I thought you were moving here."

Vic nodded, his smile easy. "I am. But I have a few things to settle first. I'll be back."

Vic turned to leave. Daphne snatched the receipt he'd ignored from the counter, then thrust it at him as they walked across the carpeted lobby. "Here," she said. "You'll want to turn this in to Celeste with your expenses."

He cast her a mildly threatening look. "If you don't ease up," he said quietly, smiling at a fellow guest lounging on the sofa, "I'll take Jenny to safety and let Celeste have you."

"Judy would never let you have Jenny."

"I can handle Judy."

Daphne made a scornful sound. "I'd like to see you try."

Vic stopped her just outside the lodge door, his face suddenly hard and angular. He caught her elbow and held her at his side when she would have started down the steps. His eyes scanned the parking lot.

"All right." He stepped forward, holding her beside him. "Where's your car?"

She pointed across the lot to a dark corner.

He made a disparaging sound. "Didn't anyone ever teach you that a woman alone should park under a light?"

"I wasn't expecting," she said coolly, "to still be here when it *got* dark."

He slanted her a disbelieving look, then continued to prowl the lot with his eyes as he picked up their pace. "Right. That's why you were all over me."

"I was all over you—" her voice was breathless as she hurried to keep up with him "—because I thought you were what you said you were."

"I am."

"You..." She began a hot accusation, but saw three forms take shape out of the shadows at the far side of the lot. "Vic!" she whispered harshly.

"I see them." He pulled Daphne to a stop, dropped his bag and pushed her behind him.

Her heart thumped and she found it hard to swallow.

"Head back to the lodge," he said.

She turned to gauge the distance and found that it was considerable. Loud music escaped into the parking lot from a live band in the lounge.

She saw two men walking slowly, purposefully toward them from the shrubs near the porch.

"Can't," she said. Now she had a grip on the back of his jacket. "Two men there. What? What're we going to do?"

He turned them toward the road as the men began to spread out in an effort to surround them.

"Are you generally good with your fists?" he asked in a tone she considered far too casual for the circumstances. "Or do you just like hitting me?"

She pushed up the sleeves of the silk dress shirt she was wearing and took a firm-footed stance behind him. She could scarcely breathe. She was sure it was simply lack of oxygen that prevented her from screaming in fear.

"Celeste's goons will be every bit as satisfying to hit as you," she replied in a high, strained voice.

"Steady," he said.

A Jeep Cherokee sped suddenly into the parking lot, bright headlights on, temporarily blinding them. Daphne threw an arm up against the glare. The Jeep turned in the direction of the three men, who quickly scattered behind parked cars. She gaped in disbelief. Rob Friedman?

But the two men coming from the direction of the lodge took advantage of the confusion and ran at her and Vic. She screamed Vic's name as she flung herself at the smaller of the two and rocked him off balance. They fell together onto the back of a Karmann Ghia, then slid off it onto the pavement.

Now that they were body-to-body, Daphne found terror dissolved by a sudden, violent outrage. She slapped and clawed, but her efforts to scream were quelled by a beefy hand.

Vic's opponent was strong but witless. He delivered a swift one-two combination that felled a fleshy young man badly in need of a regular schedule on a Nordic-Track.

Vic glanced at Friedman, saw him coping well with a burly man his own size, and turned again in the direction of Daphne's cries. He found her being dragged backward by the hair by a middle-aged thug dressed completely in black.

When he saw Vic, the man drew a gun and put it to Daphne's head.

Vic held his hands out to the side to show he was without a weapon, but continued to approach as the thug backed away toward a van.

"Stop!" the man ordered, cocking the pistol. "Or I'll shoot her."

Daphne felt the cold bore of the gun against her temple. She was terrified, but a weird sort of calm glazed over her fear as Vic kept pace with them, advancing while the man dragged her backward. She'd recognized him as Celeste's "chauffeur."

Vic looked so calm, and although his eyes never met hers, remaining relentlessly on her captor, she felt that curious sense of safety she always experienced in his presence. It seemed strange, considering the hatred she now felt for him, but she didn't question it. It was a comfort in that moment of terror, and she held on to it as her scalp stung from the meaty fist pulling her hair.

"Mrs. Huntington won't like that," Vic said, looking past the terror in Daphne's face to the cold determination in the man's eyes. *Celeste must pay her staff extremely well.* "Then you'll never find the baby."

"We've got the baby," he said.

Daphne stopped struggling immediately. "I'll come with you. Vic, stop," she said, stretching a hand toward him to hold him away. "I want to go with him."

Vic wasn't sure how he knew the man was lying. Maybe because he'd looked into the faces of so many liars in his career.

"They don't have her," he said. "You're not going with him."

The man straightened his arm and aimed the gun right between Vic's eyes. "We've got her. Now back off, or I swear to God I'll kill you."

It was a move Vic had been hoping for. As the man backed away, bringing Daphne with him, he tried to make it look like just another step as he pitched his weight forward, then swept up his leg in a kick that caught the hand that held the gun and flung the weapon upward.

The man screamed in pain, the gun flew, Vic grabbed Daphne with one hand and dropped the man to his knees with the other. One more punch and he went down like a fallen tree.

Vic pulled Daphne back to the Cherokee, where Rob was besting a man taller but slower than he was. Vic leaned her against the car door and caught her chin in his hand to inspect her face. It was still set in terrified lines, but unharmed.

She caught his wrist and tried to pull his hand away.

"How do you *know* they don't have Jenny?" she demanded. "How do you know?"

"Because if they had her," he said calmly, "they wouldn't have come for you."

She didn't look convinced.

"Trust me," he said. "They don't have her."

The first two words came out automatically, and he knew instantly that they were the wrong ones. She glared at him.

"It'll be all right," he amended.

Her eyes denied that, although her voice quieted. "No, it won't. Not until I have Jenny in my arms."

"We'll get her. I promise." Rob Friedman dealt the finishing blow to his opponent and staggered back to the Cherokee. Vic caught him as he sagged wearily against the side of the vehicle. Rob's lip and his forehead were split, and he had a swelling bruise under his right eye.

He frowned at Vic's face. "You don't have a—a mark on you," he said, panting heavily.

Vic shrugged and grinned. "I kind of do this for a living. The object is to not let the other guy hit you. What are you doing here?"

Rob touched a finger gingerly to his lip. "It's called investigative reporting. I happened to be covering a fiftieth-anniversary party here tonight and saw what was going on as I pulled in. I thought you needed a hand."

Vic slapped his shoulder. "Thank you."

"You're welcome. What the hell *was* going on?"

Vic pulled the nearest man to his feet. He coughed and groaned and shook his head.

"You don't have rope, do you?" Vic asked Rob.

Rob opened the Jeep and pulled out a coil of thin, rough cord.

"That's twine," Vic objected.

Rob unwound a length and cut it with a pocketknife. "I bundle newspapers with it to take to the post office for mailing. It's more durable than you think. And it's rough. It'll hurt like hell to struggle in it."

Vic bound the man's hands behind his back, then patted him down and retrieved a gun and a wallet. The gun he pocketed, and he handed the wallet to Friedman. "You want to tell us who hired you?" he asked as he worked. "And what the plan is?"

Rob opened the wallet and held a pocket flashlight to it. "His name's Chester Biddle. Florida license."

"Well, Mr. Biddle?" Vic prompted.

"Sure," Biddle replied, his voice raspy. "It was Sylvester Stallone. He filmed the fight and left."

Vic tightened the twine. The man winced.

"You don't mind doing time for a vindictive woman?" Vic asked.

"Never said I was working for a woman," Biddle said.

Vic sat him down on the pavement and tied his ankles. "She's safely tucked away in Palm Beach and you're going to jail. Is that fair?"

"Anything's fair," the man replied with complete unconcern, "if the money's good enough. And anyway…" He looked into Vic's eyes and smirked. "She sent an army," he said, "when we told her we found you. They might even be here now. She's bigger than the cops, you know. She's got you."

Vic saw terror darken Daphne's eyes. Tension tightened in him.

He hooked an arm in one of Biddle's. "Take his other arm," he told Rob, and together they dragged the man under the light near the parking lot's side entrance.

They tied up the other men and placed them out of each other's reach along the grass.

"I've got a cell phone in the Jeep," Rob said. "I'll call the police."

"Good. I'll…" Vic began, then stopped at the tinny sound of a motor. He swore softly and got to his feet. Across the parking lot he saw two red taillights heading for the exit.

Rob sprang up beside him. "What?"

"Daphne, no!" Vic shouted, already running toward the faded red car speeding out of the parking lot. It turned onto the lakeshore road and raced away.

Vic let fly several multilingual profanities, then pushed Rob toward the Cherokee when the reporter caught up with him. "Come on," he said. "We've got to follow her."

"These goons probably have friends out there," Rob said as he leaped into the Jeep.

"Precisely," Vic said grimly. "Head for the highway and turn east."

"But she's out of sight." Rob turned with a squeal of tires and headed for the exit.

"Doesn't matter." Vic held on as they hit a bump at high speed. "I know where she's going."

"Where?"

"Home to get her baby."

"At the risk of sounding repetitious," Rob said, peeling out of the parking lot without even a perfunctory stop, "what the hell is going on?"

CHAPTER TWELVE

DAPHNE THOUGHT THE NIGHT had never looked so dark, nor the dark so hostile. She'd long ago passed the road back to town and was coming up to the turnoff to Britt and Jake's place. Her headlights picked out three reflectors on the post that marked their road, then met darkness again as she sped on toward home.

She knew it wasn't safe to drive so fast in the dark, but she'd traveled this road so often she knew every curve and pothole in it. And her mind refused to obey any instinct but the need to get to Jenny.

Remembering the violence of the attack on her and Vic in the parking lot of the lodge, she prayed that he'd been right when he'd said he didn't think Celeste's thugs had her daughter. The very thought of her child in the hands of violent men made nausea rise in Daphne's throat. The thought of Jenny living out her life under Celeste's care made her want to scream with anguish.

As she sped through the night, she could hear the labored sound of her own breathing mingling with the rumble of tires on dirt and gravel, and the near hysteria of the sobs swelling in her chest.

She had to get a grip on herself. If Vic was right and Jenny was still safe at home, Daphne would terrify her if she arrived like this.

If he was wrong and Jenny had been taken, she would have to think logically about what to do.

That very notion accelerated her panic, and she burst into tears. Celeste had a court order. If Jenny was already on her way to Florida, getting her back would be a long and tedious ordeal, and Daphne wasn't sure she could survive without her for the length of time it would take.

She hit a pothole at high speed and fought to keep the car under control. And that jarred her into composing herself, into realizing that whatever happened, she would have to cope with it.

Tires squealing, she turned into the driveway of her home and saw with a jolt of terror that all the lights were out. The form of the house, with its peaked roof and long porch, barely stood out in the shadowy darkness. It looked ominous, somehow. Threatening.

Her heart pounding, stifling her breath, Daphne dashed out of the car, fell up the steps and pounded on the door.

"Judy!" She screamed. "Judy, answer me!"

The door opened suddenly, and someone reached out of the dark and yanked her into the house.

The living room was suddenly bathed in light, and Daphne found herself looking at the lethal gleam of a butcher knife.

Then she focused beyond it on the determined set of her sister's face.

Judy dropped the knife to her side when she recognized Daphne, then slammed and locked the door behind her.

"You scared me to death!" she scolded. "You call and tell me to lock all the windows and doors, that you think Celeste is here to get Jenny, then you—"

Daphne ran past her into the bedroom where Jenny slept and found her in her crib. The soft glow of the nightlight revealed that her face was buried in her pillow, her round backside was sticking up.

The scene was so normal, so familiar, that for an instant Daphne couldn't believe her eyes. Then she pulled Jenny out of her crib, blankets and all, and crushed her against her, sobbing.

Jenny fidgeted fussily, then nuzzled against her and went back to sleep.

Judy pulled Daphne back into the living room, sat her down on the sofa and placed a steaming cup before her on the coffee table.

"I'm sorry I frightened you," Daphne said wearily to Judy. "But Vic and I were attacked in the parking lot of the lodge, and one of the men told me they had Jenny. Vic insisted they didn't, but I thought they might..." She shook her head and leaned back against the cushions, holding Jenny even tighter.

"Where *is* Vic?" Judy asked. "I can't believe he's let you run around alone at night if Celeste..." She stopped at Daphne's guilty glance.

"He didn't let me leave. I just took off while he and Rob were busy tying up the men who attacked us."

Judy blinked. "Rob Friedman was there?"

Daphne explained how he'd arrived at the opportune moment. "He blinded them with his headlights, then jumped right in to help us." She smiled thinly. "He's a lot meaner than he seems."

Judy made a scornful sound. "His mouth certainly is. Did Vic follow you?"

Daphne shook her head. "I didn't even glance in the rearview mirror once. I just pointed the car toward home and never looked back." Then she closed her eyes and winced. "And he may just decide to leave me to my own devices anyway."

"Why? What do you mean?"

She poured out the story of her confession to him that afternoon, of going back to return his wallet and staying to make love with him. Of going to dinner, then being stopped by the desk clerk with the message, and her resultant discovery that Vic was a private detective hired by Celeste.

Judy's face flamed with rage and indignation.

"He insisted," Daphne explained, "that he knew right away that Celeste had lied to him, and that he stayed around to learn my side of the story."

"Then why didn't he tell you who he really was?"

"Because he knew I'd bolt with Jenny and the issue would go on, unresolved."

Judy studied her assessingly. "And that mattered to him," she said finally, "because, in the meantime, he fell in love with you."

Daphne expelled a sigh. "That's what he said."

"But you don't believe him?"

Daphne rubbed at an empty spot in her breast. Her maternal self felt whole again with Jenny in her arms. But the part of her that was simply woman ached with a love she couldn't shake but now was afraid to trust.

"I guess I believe why he did it," she said, her voice strained. Judy put the coffee cup in her hands. Daphne sipped and swallowed and felt the warmth soothe the tightness in her throat. "I just…resent that he lied."

She held Jenny to her as she put the cup down. Then she rubbed at her eyes. They felt gritty and sore. "Of course, I guess I lied to him, too. I let him believe I was what he thought I was. Just a young widow with a baby…"

Then something occurred to her that she'd never considered when she discovered that Celeste had hired him.

Celeste must have told Vic about her past when she put him on her trail.

But Daphne had never seen a suggestion of condemnation in him. Not a trace of superiority or judgment. In fact, she remembered his affectionate teasing, his chivalrous care of her and Jenny and, more than anything, that look of indulgence, as though she were some rare and precious treasure he'd just discovered.

And all that time, he'd *known*.

She felt a violent rattling of everything inside her. It wasn't as though he'd fallen in love with her and then learned the truth and been forced to cope nobly with it. It was that he'd known, and had *still* fallen in love with her. She remembered his fierce defense of her in the parking lot and had no doubt that what he felt was love.

The knowledge was staggering.

"What?" Judy asked, touching her shoulder.

Daphne put a hand to her pounding head. "I said awful things to him when I found out he was a detective."

"I'm sure he knew the chance he was taking by not telling you," Judy replied gently. "He must have gauged the risks and decided his plan was worth it."

Daphne looked into Judy's eyes, her own filled with regret. "I wish I'd been more like you—confident and brave, but smart enough to think before acting."

Judy rolled her eyes at the praise. "You're looking at me through a veil of sisterly affection. I think to most people I'm pushy and reckless, and always looking to protect myself. That's what comes of having a father who had too many regrets to live with. I swore that would never happen to me." She narrowed her gaze on

Daphne and put a gentle hand to her hair. "I wish I'd understood what you were going through with Gordon," she said softly. "I wish I'd been more available so that you'd have been able to confide in me. I'd have had you out of there—"

Daphne caught her hand and held it. "I made my choices. They had nothing to do with you. You were wonderful. I just wish I were half as fine."

Judy swatted her arm, her eyes grave. "You're everything I prayed you were becoming when I didn't know where you were."

Daphne opened her mouth to protest, but Judy stopped her. "No. All those things happened to you, but they aren't you."

A sudden explosion of noise came from the direction of the front door. Daphne leaped to her feet and Judy reached for the knife. The sound came again and the front door flew open, revealing the large burly man who'd kicked it in and an equally unsavory companion.

Judy pushed Daphne in the direction of the kitchen and the back door. "Run!" she screamed, and placed herself squarely in the middle of the room, the knife held purposefully in her hand.

Daphne hesitated for an instant, torn between getting her child to safety and not wanting to abandon her sister.

Then Judy shoved her again. "Go! Get her out of here!"

Holding Jenny to her, Daphne ran through the kitchen, choking on her heartbeat as she fidgeted with the back-door lock. She heard shouts and shrieks behind her as she tore open the door, ran onto the dark porch and down the steps. The moon was hidden by a cloud and left the field behind the house in utter blackness.

The sweet fragrance of damp grass mingled with the pleasant bite of woodsmoke as she tore across the yard toward the lane that led into a woods. Her mind accepted the awareness as incongruous in this nightmare of renewed flight.

Frantically she prayed for Judy as she pounded across the grass. Jenny was now awake in her arms and screaming with fright.

Daphne realized she'd been a fool to leave Vic and head off on her own. He'd told her Celeste's men didn't have Jenny, that the chauffeur had simply used that ploy to gain her cooperation.

But she hadn't known whom to believe at that point, and she'd decided to trust herself. Big mistake. She'd done precisely what Vic had warned her against: She'd led them to Jenny.

And Vic wasn't here to save her this time.

Exhausted, her arms aching, she heard footsteps gain on her, felt a whoosh of air behind her. Arms locked around her knees and brought her down.

Jenny flew out of her arms, and Daphne landed with a thud that knocked the breath from her lungs. She felt a man's body pin hers to the grass, grab her hands and hold them roughly behind her back.

She tried to scream Jenny's name, but she had no breath with which to do so. Agony filled her at the sound of Jenny's desperate cries for her somewhere in the darkness.

Then the weight was suddenly lifted off her and her hands were free. Her attacker scrambled away in the direction of Jenny's cries.

Daphne pushed herself to her feet, and in a sudden burst of moonlight saw him just ahead of her. She leaped onto his back, wrapping both arms around his neck.

He staggered backward with a cry of surprise, and she braced herself for sudden impact with the ground.

Instead, she was grabbed from behind and peeled off the man. Then her attacker was wheeled around and took a grinding blow to the jaw.

He groaned and flew backward, but regained his footing.

Vic and her assailant squared off again as a high-pitched, indignant wail directly ahead of her told Daphne where Jenny was. She found her in seconds and pulled her into her arms.

There was the sound of flesh striking flesh in the darkness, and Daphne tried to locate the movement as the moon disappeared again.

Then she saw the white of Vic's shirt flashing in the shadows of the maple tree. A darker shadow moved toward him, then fell back against the tree trunk with a sickening thud and slid to the grass.

"Daphne!" Vic shouted, his voice breathless.

"Here!" She went to him, Jenny still screaming and clinging to her.

"Are you all right?" he demanded, wrapping her in his arms. He put a hand to Jenny's back. "Is she all right?"

"I don't know. I think so," she replied. "I can't see her."

"Come on." He started to pull her toward the house. She hung back. "But there were two men—"

"Not anymore. Brick arrived the same time Rob and I did. Jenny, come here, baby."

Whimpering, Jenny opened her arms to him and let herself be settled against his shoulder.

Vic caught Daphne's hand and pulled her with him as he headed back to the house. There was anger and tension in his grip, and she felt her own relief suddenly diluted by it.

She frowned as the back-porch light went on and a man in a tuxedo suddenly came through the back door at a run. He stopped halfway down the steps when he saw them approaching. He was dark-haired and handsome, and it took her a moment to recognize him in the stand-up collar and black bow tie. It was Brick Bauer.

"They okay?" he called.

"Think so," Vic called back. "Let's get them in the light."

Brick offered Daphne his hand to help her up the steps, then kept an arm around her as they went into the kitchen.

"You leave another one out there?" he asked Vic.

Vic nodded. "Under the tree."

Judy, her left arm bloody, wrapped Jenny in her right one. "Thank God!" she exclaimed. "Is she all right?"

Vic stood Jenny on the kitchen counter, and Daphne looked her over. Her little face, though contorted in angry tears, was without blemish, and the way she wheeled her tiny arms and legs to get back to Vic suggested that her limbs were sound.

Daphne laughed softly in relief. "I think she's fine."

Judy hugged her sister to her.

"Oh, Judy!" Daphne cried, pushing her away so that she could look at her bloody arm. "I didn't *want* to leave you. Oh, God. How bad is it?"

"It's not bad at all," Rob Friedman said, taking hold of Judy's sound arm and maneuvering her onto a kitchen chair. "And might even stop bleeding if she'd sit down and quit moving around."

Daphne noted that he held a linen handkerchief folded into a square, and a roll of gauze. He'd apparently been trying to bandage Judy's wound. Daphne put a hand to Judy's shoulder to hold her in the chair while Rob applied the makeshift dressing.

Beyond them, in the living room, she saw two men, bound hand and foot, lying facedown on the carpet. One of them, too, had a bloodied arm.

"We have to get you to a doctor," Daphne said urgently.

"I'll do that," Rob offered, "as soon as you and Vic are on your way."

Judy looked up at him, her pale face startled. "On their way where?"

Rob bounced a glance off Vic, who was pacing back and forth with a clingy Jenny. Brick was making a phone call.

"I'm taking Daphne and Jenny away with me," Vic said. "To an old family place."

"When?"

"Right now. Tonight. Celeste has more men on the way, and there just aren't enough of us to deal with them." He gave Daphne a reprimanding look. "And how many times do we want to do this to Jenny?"

Judy shook her head. "But Celeste won't stop."

"I'm going to stop her." Rob knotted the ends of the bandage and gently lowered her arm.

Judy looked at him impatiently. "How? With a bad review?"

Rob unraveled a length of gauze strip and held it an inch from her mouth, as though measuring.

Judy swiped at it with her good hand.

"Daphne mentioned something to me the other day that I've been thinking about," Vic said as Brick joined them at the table. "The day of Trey's accident, his own car had run out of gas, and he'd used hers. Daphne had a lunch date that she canceled so he could take her car. The accident was on a rural road and there were no witnesses."

"Are you suggesting," Brick asked, "that the car might have been tampered with?"

"It crossed my mind. And the strong-arm tactics employed tonight suggest serious determination on Celeste's part. She always wanted Daphne out of the picture, and she seems to be getting pretty aggressive about it."

Brick tried to dig his hands into his pockets and realized that in the tuxedo he was wearing, he had none. He folded his arms, frustrated.

"In most states," he said, "when there's a fatality and no witnesses, the state police send an accident reconstructionist to check out the scene and the vehicle and determine what happened. If the vehicle had been messed with, there'd have been an investigation, possibly even charges filed."

Vic shrugged a shoulder. "*If* the state had been called in. It'd be interesting to see if that happened in this case." He grinned across the table. "Rob's going to look into it for us while I get Daphne and Jenny somewhere safe. If there was a problem there, we might be able to put Celeste Huntington away, and Daphne can stop running."

Brick shook his head. "I don't like it. I'd rather there was a legal way to confront this woman now."

"I've thought about it." Vic rubbed Jenny's back. "But I can't come up with one. Celeste has a court order out for Daphne, and, if we can believe one of the men who attacked us back at the lodge, she's sending more men than your force could deal with. So the best thing to do is get her out of here until Rob can build a case.'' Vic looked into Brick's eyes. ''Will letting us slide by the court order be a problem for you?''

Brick shook his head again. ''No one's brought my office into it. I suppose by the time they do, you'll be gone.''

Judy looked worriedly at Vic. ''You mean, the three of you could be in hiding for God knows how long, and your return will depend upon—'' she cocked her head in Rob's direction ''—his ability to collect evidence against Celeste? The accident happened in southern California. How's he going to do that and run a newspaper?''

Rob smiled blandly at her. ''Nice of you to be concerned. I have contacts everywhere from my days on the *Sun-Voice*. And I have a staffer at the paper to help me out should I have to be away.''

''Right. The Eber kid. A cartoonist.'' Judy rolled her eyes. ''God. I'll never see my sister and my niece again.''

''You, Miss Lowery,'' Rob said, pointing an index finger at her, ''are going to eat those words in the near future.''

He smiled encouragingly at Daphne. ''I can do this. You just take off and rest easy. It might require a little time, but if there's anything at all to go on here, I'll find it, and I'll wrap your mother-in-law up for you so tightly she'll never get away.''

Daphne slipped her arms around him. ''Thank you, Rob. And will you do me a favor?''

''Anything.''

She drew back to look into his eyes. ''Keep an eye on Judy for me.''

"Anything but that," he said quickly.

Daphne swatted his chest. "I don't know if Celeste knows we're related or not, but—"

"You're related?" Brick interrupted.

"Same mother, different fathers," Daphne explained quickly. "We'd been...apart for a long time, until I went on the run with Jenny and called Judy for help. Anyway, I'm afraid if Celeste can't find me, she'll come down on Judy."

Judy fixed her sister with an indignant stare. "Who defended your escape?" she demanded. "I'm perfectly capable of—"

"Of getting yourself sliced up," Rob finished for her. "You shouldn't wield a knife if you're going to let an attacker take it away from you. And I believe Brick and I defended *you,* while Vic got Daphne away from the other guy."

Judy looked up at him aggressively. "Who asked you?"

He smiled blandly at her sister. "I'll be pleased to keep an eye on her for you. It's bound to be character building."

Rotating lights flashed through the kitchen window, and Brick left the room to greet the officers who'd arrived to take away Celeste's men. "They also picked up the four you left at the lodge," he came back to report.

"A fifth one got away," Rob said. "You might stake out their van in the parking lot. Maybe he'll try to return for it."

Brick went back to advise the officers.

Vic met Daphne's eyes. He remained tense, holding up a barrier between them. She understood, of course. She'd said terrible things to him, had hidden behind his muscle in the parking lot, then ignored his directions and headed off without him, bringing about the threat to her sister and her daughter.

She wanted to apologize, to make amends, to tell him he'd proved himself worthy of her trust several times over. But time was short and the room a little crowded.

Vic came around the table to place the now sleeping toddler in her arms. "Bundle her up, and pack one soft bag with warm clothes for both of you. Judy, can you help her?"

Daphne's sister gave him a look that combined displeasure with acceptance. "I was without her for ten years, you know. If you let anything happen to her—"

He shook his head before she'd finished speaking. "You have to trust me. I'm good at this. And I'd die before I let anyone touch either of them."

She studied him a moment, then sighed. "All right. I'm going to hold you to that."

"Fair enough."

After they'd disappeared into the bedroom, Rob turned to Vic. "You going to tell me where you're going? Someone has to know."

"Minnesota," Vic replied quietly. "Just north of the Cloquet Valley State Forest. Goose Lake."

"Northern Minnesota?" Rob whispered incredulously as he followed Vic to the service porch beyond the kitchen, where Vic retrieved an empty cardboard box. "No one goes there in the winter."

He placed it on the kitchen counter and began to pile boxes and cans of food into it. "Makes it a good place to hide. My uncle bought a place there years ago. He used to take me there. We were the only ones in the family who could sit quietly long enough to enjoy fishing. My cousins vacationed there in the summer."

Rob checked drawers until he found a can opener, and tossed it, too, into the box. Vic acknowledged the addition with a grin. "I'd have hated myself if I'd forgotten that."

"I've done it often enough. You have a weapon?"

"Took a Smith and Wesson .357 off the guy that chased Daphne out." Vic fitted a precious supply of Cheerios into a corner of the box. "What I don't have," he added with a significant glance at Rob, "is a reliable vehicle."

Rob returned his look without obvious reaction, then winced. "You want me to keep an eye on Judy the Terrible *and* lend you my Cherokee?"

"I know it's a lot to ask—especially since you got roughed up saving our hides at the lodge."

Rob shrugged that off. "I've taken a few punches in my career as a reporter. It's just hard to believe that kind of tactic is being used to claim a baby."

"Daphne's mother-in-law is a power freak. I just hope you'll be able to prove it."

"I will. Count on it." Rob slapped the counter as though a deal had been made. "I'll move the baby-seat thing into the back of the Jeep while you finish up here."

Vic stopped to clap his shoulder. "Thanks, Rob."

"Sure."

Vic grabbed the roll of paper towels and several sets of utensils and added them to the box. There was a general store just a mile from the cabin, but he was trying to cover the eventuality of trouble along the way. He didn't think it would happen once they were clear of Tyler, but he knew better than to take anything for granted.

"There's a thermos in that cupboard to your left."

Daphne's quiet voice came from just behind his shoulder. "We can put the rest of the coffee in it."

He reached for the cupboard door without turning to look at her.

She materialized suddenly in front of him, wearing a high-necked green sweater and green tights. Her hair was tied back in a ponytail secured with a sliver clip. The green gave her eyes a pale aquamarine quality. They rested uneasily on him.

"Let me rinse it out first," she said, taking the thermos from him.

He handed it over, then, noticing cups in the cupboard, hooked two pottery ones and a third small plastic cup with two handles, which he presumed was Jenny's. By this time the box was full to overflowing.

Daphne poured the contents of the coffeepot into the insulated cylinder, then secured the lid and placed it beside the box.

He started to lift the box to carry it out to the Jeep, but she put a hand on his arm.

"Thank you," she said in a breathless rush, "for following me. I'm sorry I didn't believe you about Jenny, but I was terrified you were wrong."

"Doesn't matter now," he said, and tried again to pick up the box.

She stopped him once more. "It does," she insisted. "I know it does. I just want you to understand why I ran off on you."

"I understand why," he said, though she thought his expression looked anything but understanding. "If you don't let me put this in the car, we'll starve along the way."

She retained her hold of his arm. "I have to say one more thing."

He shifted his weight and abandoned his grip on the box. "Say it. Preferably before Celeste's army arrives."

"I'm sorry for all the mean things I said." She spoke hurriedly, although her eyes were grave and she still held his arm. "But it was a shock to see Celeste's name on that message for you. Certainly you can see how it looked to me."

He relented slightly. "I understand your reaction," he said reasonably. "That was all my fault. I should have told you sooner. But after, when I tried to explain, you didn't even want to listen—when you'd just made love with me as though you'd rediscovered life in my arms."

She gritted her teeth stubbornly. "Well, you'd made love to me," she reminded him, "while keeping that important bit of information from me. It's a two-way street, fella. If you expect my trust, you have to trust me."

"I was trying," he said with exaggerated patience, "to do what was best for you."

"And I," she countered, "was thinking of my daughter's safety. But I said I was sorry, and that I appreciate your coming after me."

He picked up the box. "You appreciate my coming after you," he said quietly over the top of it, "because I saved Jenny for you, not because it brought me to you. I understand Jenny's your priority—that's as it should be. But you trust me in so far as I can keep your daughter safe, and that's it. What was between us is gone. I can feel it."

"How nice for you that you can understand complicated feelings so clearly," she retorted, an edge of irony in her tone. "Does clairvoyance come with a P.I.'s license? Maybe all you're *feeling* is a guilty conscience."

That snapped what was left of the control he'd maintained when he'd watched her speed out of the lodge's parking lot, when he'd run through the front door of her house and had a screaming Judy tell him she was being chased out the back, when he'd followed the sounds of cries and footsteps into the black night, then watched a sudden burst of moonlight reveal Daphne leaping onto the back of a man twice her size. His heartbeat still hadn't settled down.

He put the box down again, all that restrained anger smoking in his eyes. But he was tired of her insults and accusations.

"Guilty conscience?" he asked with quiet vehemence, jabbing her shoulder with his index finger. "I'm not the one who endangered my daughter and my sister by ignoring caution and common sense and running off on my own—leading the enemy right to them."

Daphne glared into his eyes, tears standing in hers. "No. You're just the one who brought the enemy here in the first place!" She stormed away.

Vic picked up the box and walked out to the Jeep with it. Rob had transferred Jenny's car seat to the back, and he now took the box from Vic and wedged it into a corner.

"How often will you be in touch?" Rob asked.

"Every couple of days," Vic replied. "I'll call you from the general store."

"How can I get in touch with you?"

"You can't. It's better that way. I found Daphne originally through telephone-company records. Whoever found me for Celeste has to be at least that smart. If there's something you have to tell us, wait until I call." Vic grinned, then closed the Jeep door as the police car drove away with the three men who'd attacked the house safely cuffed in the back. "Or you can come and visit."

Brick approached them. "I checked with my officers, and I called County, and they report very little traffic on the road. If an army's coming, it isn't here yet. I'll follow you to the county line to make sure you get safely on your way."

Vic shook his hand. "Thanks for all your help, Brick."

"My pleasure. And Britt'd kill me if I let anything happen to Daphne."

Daphne emerged from the house carrying a duffel-type bag, the diaper bag and her purse. She wore a red, hooded parka over her sweater and tights.

Judy followed with Jenny in her good arm, Bear dangling from her fist by an ear. Judy's face was puffy and red, and Daphne had obviously been crying. Jenny, apparently sensing the tension, was crying, too.

Vic took the duffel from Daphne and put it in the back. Rob went to take Jenny from Judy. Judy hugged the child, then backed away, her lips moving unsteadily.

Daphne wrapped her sister in her arms and held on for a long moment.

Rob handed the toddler to Vic. "Don't let Daphne worry about Judy," he said. "And I promise you I'll get the goods on Celeste Huntington."

"That'll keep Daphne going." Vic put Jenny into her car seat and was surprised when her tears suddenly stopped.

"Bye-bye?" she asked hopefully.

"Right," he replied. "Bye-bye. A couple of days' worth. How about a handful of Cheerios?" He dug into the box and sprinkled a dozen little O's onto the tray attached to Jenny's car seat.

She shoveled them into her mouth one by one with great efficiency.

Vic backed out of the Jeep to find Daphne hugging Rob.

"You promise you'll watch out for her?" she asked again.

"I promise," he said. "No matter how hard it is, no matter how much she aggravates me, or how difficult—"

Judy socked him with her good hand. "You have no idea how hard I'm going to make it for you," she threatened.

Daphne waved a dismissive hand. "She's all talk, Rob. Underneath, she's a pussycat. And you'll take her to the doctor as soon as we're gone?"

"The minute you're out of sight."

"Well." She looked from her sister to the reporter, aware that there was nothing left to say. She smiled feebly at Judy, then climbed into the Jeep.

Vic locked her in.

He shook hands with Rob, then gave Judy a quick hug. "I know it's easier said than done," he told her, "but don't worry. As soon as Rob does his job, I'll bring them back to you."

She looked into his eyes, wanting to believe him. "I'll be waiting," she said.

Vic climbed into the Jeep.

Brick pushed his door closed for him. "I'll be right behind you," he said. "Good luck, guys."

Daphne blew him a kiss.

Vic waved and turned the key in the ignition. The motor sparked to life, and he backed out of the driveway.

Judy made a move toward the Jeep, but Rob held her

back, keeping her there with an arm around her waist. He said something to her, and she forced a smile and waved.

Daphne waved back, a dry sob erupting from her.

Vic turned onto the road. He put a hand to her knee as he pulled up at the stop before the highway.

"You'll celebrate Christmas with Judy," he said. "I promise you."

"Unless your disposition improves," she said tearfully, "you're not invited."

"I'll be at the House of Three Gables."

"You bought it?"

He nodded.

She burst into noisy sobs. Jenny, alarmed, joined her. With a groan, Vic turned north onto the highway.

CHAPTER THIRTEEN

"NANA, MOMMY?" Jenny asked from her car seat.

It was early morning and they'd driven all night except for a brief stop for gas. Jenny had slept most of the time, and Daphne had dozed off now and again, although never for very long.

She recalled the night as long and dark and fraught with tension from the possibility that they were being pursued, and from the hostility that still simmered between her and Vic.

A road sign told them they were approaching the Minnesota border.

Daphne unfastened her seat belt and leaned over the seat back to search through the box of food Vic had packed. She found the canned fruit cups she always kept on hand for Jenny.

"No bananas," she said, digging for a spoon. "But how about fruit?" She held up the can Jenny always recognized, trying to make it look appealing. "Yum!"

"Nana," Jenny repeated, looking belligerent. Then she pushed emphatically at her car seat.

She'd been cooperative longer than they'd had any right to expect, but her expression suggested that that time was over.

"Sweetie, Vic didn't pack any bananas," Daphne said in a cajoling tone, the shift of blame deliberate and very satisfying. "You'll have to be happy with fruit."

"Na-a-a-ana!" Jenny shrieked, banging on the restraining bar of her seat. "No fruit! Nana! Nana!"

"We're coming into a small town," Vic said with a scolding glance at Daphne for the banana remark. "She's probably really ready to get out of that seat."

"Vic's going to stop," Daphne told Jenny, running a comforting hand over her warm cheek. "Then we'll find you a banana."

Jenny roared over the delay and pushed her mother's hand away. Daphne settled back into her seat, wincing at Jenny's screams.

"There was a big bunch of bananas on the counter," she said defensively as Vic took the marked turn off the highway.

He cast her a grim glance. "Then why didn't you put it in the box?"

"You were packing the food."

"Sorry. I was distracted by a little matter of keeping you alive at the time."

Daphne folded her arms and remained silent. She didn't know what to say to that. And she didn't know why she was blaming him for everything. She was the one who'd lived the life that had wound its circuitous way to this point, anyhow.

The little town's main street looked just as it must have at the turn of the century. It reminded Jenny of Tyler, only it was considerably smaller. She saw the spire of a church, the smokestack of a probably abandoned power plant, a tree-shaded thoroughfare lined on both sides with shops. It was about 9:00 a.m., and the sun had a new, frosty gleam as it picked out shop windows and the cross on top of the church.

Vic braked to a crawl behind a slow-moving Chevy

coupe, which had a banner on the bumper that read Caution: Student Driver.

Daphne smiled and forgetting again that they were angry with each other, shouted to Vic over Jenny's screams, "I once wiped out power on the entire south side of Hollywood while learning to drive."

"I did in a whole bank of azaleas," he shouted back. "And two mailboxes on a rural road. Even my father's dashboard Saint Christopher fell over." He grinned at the memory, watching the slow car ahead. "My mother took it as a sign that I shouldn't drive, because the saints had abandoned me."

Daphne laughed. "How did you convince her otherwise?"

He shrugged a shoulder. "My father did it. He always had a way with her. My older brother claims the skill isn't inherited, though. His wife is less amenable to his suggestions."

The tension in the car, which had been relieved for a few moments, suddenly stretched a little tighter. "Maybe you'll be different," she said.

He gave her a significant glance. "Obviously not." Then he added, "Keep your eyes open for a restaurant."

A neon sign of a smiling pink pig wielding a pancake on the tines of a fork promised fifty-two varieties and a never-empty coffee cup. Daphne pointed. "How about there?"

Vic pulled up front of it as the student driver continued at a snail's pace down the main street. Jenny was now crimson with rage and catching her breath between screams.

Daphne was exhausted after the long night, and her head ached abominably. She pushed her door open, taking a moment to breathe in the pungent fragrance of fall before reaching into the back for her daughter.

But Vic already had Jenny out and set her on her feet on the sidewalk. She took off instantly, and her tears turned to laughter at the exhilarating freedom.

He strode after her, staying between her and the street, laughing with her when a Labrador retriever being walked on a leash responded to her gentle pat with a slurp at her face.

Daphne watched as Jenny slowed down and caught Vic's hand, then pulled him toward a toy-store window. She pointed excitedly, and he squatted down beside her to look.

Theirs was a match made in heaven, Daphne realized. And less than twenty-four hours ago, she'd thought she and Vic had the same kind of relationship. Then everything had fallen apart on her.

He lifted Jenny onto his shoulders and started back toward the restaurant. Giggling from her high perch, Jenny slapped at awnings and reached for pigeons that swooped just out of reach.

Had everything fallen apart? Daphne wondered as they made their way back to her. Or had life just been so difficult that she was too accustomed to thinking in those terms? Vic was angry at her, but he was still with her. If he didn't care, would he have accompanied her into exile?

She felt hopeful for a moment, then realized that he probably would. He was a good man. He would see the project through to its completion.

She smiled against a sinking sense of loss as Vic lowered Jenny to his hip and opened the restaurant door for her.

"Not feeling well?" he asked, his eyes doing a cursory examination of her features as she walked past him into the restaurant. It smelled of bacon and coffee.

"Just a headache," she said, avoiding any further conversation by heading toward an empty booth.

Jenny ate a pancake and a side dish of bananas and cream. Daphne worked on bacon, one egg and toast, while Vic put away a ham-and-cheese omelet with all the accompaniments.

"How remote is this place we're going to?" Daphne asked, enjoying a second cup of coffee.

"It's about a mile beyond a little store and gas station, which are a couple of miles from a town. But we have to walk in that last mile."

She looked concerned. "With all our stuff?"

He shrugged. "It shouldn't be that hard." He glanced at his watch. "If we hang around long enough for the stores to open, we can pick up a backpack for Jenny."

Daphne raised an eyebrow, glancing at the child on the booster seat beside her, awkwardly eating banana slices with a spoon. "You're going to make *her* carry things?"

Vic dropped his fork, put a hand to his eyes and ran it down his face in an exasperated gesture. "I meant," he said finally, "a backpack to put her in."

For a moment Daphne forgot the strain between them and laughed at her own misinterpretation. She saw him fight an answering laugh, then finally succumb to a fractional smile. He shook his head at her, then returned to his breakfast.

"So, do you think we got away?" she asked when he pushed his plate aside. "You don't think we were followed?"

He sipped at his coffee. "No. I think the goons in the parking lot and the thugs at the house were it. At least then. And I doubt even Celeste has enough men to send in all four directions, looking for us. So they'll have to figure out where we've gone before trying to follow."

Daphne sighed. "I'm worried about Judy."

Vic shook his head. "They won't hurt her. Celeste can't risk that, especially with Brick aware of the situation, and Rob watching out for her."

Daphne put her now empty cup in its saucer and leaned toward him on folded arms. "You really think Rob Friedman will be able to build a case against Celeste?"

Vic picked up the check and grabbed his jacket. "He won a Pulitzer for digging up the truth on a politician in Chicago when he was on the *Sun-Voice*. I'm betting he can do it again."

She sat up, stunned. "I didn't know that. He never said—"

"All he wants now is to live in Tyler and put out the *Citizen*." He grinned. "And maybe needle Judy a little."

"When did he tell *you* all this?"

"We had a few drinks at the lodge the night of the dinner you ladies held for Judy."

She digested that information, then asked reluctantly, "How long do you think it'll take him to build this case?"

"I imagine it'll take a while. Celeste is sure to have covered her tracks very well."

Daphne wondered about conditions in the cabin they were heading toward. The word *cabin* implied small— one room, possibly. How were they going to cope for an extended period of time, confined in a small space with so much tension crackling between them?

She had no idea. But she decided that they had half a day's travel before she had to deal with that problem. She would put it aside until then.

"Jenny and I have to go to the ladies' room," she said, wetting her napkin in her water glass and wiping Jenny's mouth and hands. "We'll meet you in the car."

He handed her the car keys. "In case you get there before I do," he said.

Jenny had to wash her own hands, had to use soap, then had to have hand lotion. Then she had to weigh herself and use the hot-air blower. The fact that she already had lotion on her hands didn't seem to matter.

Daphne finally caught her hand and led the way out to the car.

VIC SPOTTED A SMALL MARKET across the street from the restaurant and several doors down. Since there was still no sign of his charges, he hurried over in search of bananas for Jenny and aspirin for Daphne.

It was a small, cluttered store, with hardwood floors and narrow aisles crowded with old and new products. Gardening tools leaned in one corner, and in another were baseball bats, hockey sticks, and fishing poles.

Vic paid for his purchases, and when a glance through the window showed that Daphne and Jenny still hadn't emerged from the restaurant, he skirted a pyramid of grapefruit and stopped at a small rack of magazines and newspapers.

He was perusing the newest *Field and Stream* when he heard the sound of a motor. He couldn't have said what alerted him to the sudden danger, except that the sound was too loud for the quiet little street.

But suddenly he found himself looking directly into

the grill of a Chevy that was heading straight for the store.

For an instant his mind couldn't comprehend why this was happening. Then Vic realized this was the student-driver car, and that the bumper sticker that had advised Caution should have read Danger!

The car was coming straight at him. The parking meter in front of the shop splintered off its moorings as he watched, and he heard the sound of the plate-glass window exploding on impact as he dived for the shelter of the checkout counter.

DAPHNE WAS UNLOCKING the Jeep door when the student-driver they'd seen earlier suddenly roared out of the parking lot of the bank down the street. The driver apparently changed her mind about a left turn when a persistent pigeon in the middle of the intersection ignored the approaching vehicle and continued to peck at the contents of a torn fast-food bag. In either confusion or panic, the Chevy headed straight for a window bearing the sign, Harry's Market.

Daphne gasped as the car crashed through the window and buried its hood halfway into the store before bouncing to a stop.

There were shrieks from inside the market.

She pushed open the door to the restaurant and shouted for the cashier to dial 911. Then, heart pounding, she scooped Jenny into her arms and headed for the market. She was vaguely aware of people pouring out of other establishments along the street and staring, openmouthed.

The teenage girl behind the wheel of the car was crying hysterically, although she seemed unharmed. Fortunately, the windshield hadn't broken.

Beside her, a thin, bespectacled male instructor sat as though stunned. "That wasn't your best effort, Marjorie," he said, his eyes suddenly focusing on the student. "Not at all."

Daphne went around the wood-and-glass debris to enter the store. Several people, apparently shoppers, were pulling splintered wood and a pileup of grapefruit off two pairs of masculine legs. The upper bodies were obscured from her view, but on one she saw a white apron hanging to the knees, and on the other—

Her heart stopped. She saw black jeans and long feet clad in Rockports. Oh, God. It was Vic.

She elbowed a man and two women aside, handed Jenny to one of them and removed the last plank of wood from Vic herself. His eyes were closed, there was a bruise on his cheekbone, and he lay absolutely still.

He was dead. Of course, he was. Men like Vic Estevez didn't happen to the likes of Diane Majors Huntington, otherwise known as Daphne Sullivan. It had just been a bright promise dangled in front of her, a brutal reminder that she would never have a father for Jenny, love for herself, life in the House of Three Gables.

She sank to her knees beside him, remembering with a swell of nausea the speed with which the car had been traveling when it crashed through the window.

On the scuffed hardwood floor beside him lay a bunch of bananas and a bottle of aspirin. Pain ripped through her with agonizing thoroughness, like a serrated knife.

She wasn't thinking of the danger she and Jenny would face, alone again against Celeste. Daphne was trying to imagine what their lives would be like without Vic's warmth and attentive kindness, without his laughter. The picture refused to form in any detail, it was just there—impenetrable blackness. Eternal blackness.

"Vic." The strangled sound came from deep in her throat, deep in her heart, where part of her was broken, bleeding.

The man in the apron groaned loudly and pushed himself up on an elbow.

"Harry? You okay, Harry?" a voice asked. Daphne's mind absorbed the fact that someone was helping Harry to his feet, that Harry was responding to questions.

She heard a siren. She heard Jenny crying. She heard her own heart rending.

She placed a hand on Vic's chest. "Oh, darling," she said. Tears flowed down her cheeks and onto him. "Please stay with me. What will Jenny and I do without you? We need you. We love you. God, I love you so much. Vic, I…"

And then she surfaced from her grief long enough to register the strong thumping under her palm. It was his heartbeat! She caught the slightest movement between his eyebrows—a not-quite-conscious registering of pain.

"Vic!" she screamed. She leaned over him, grasping his shoulders. "Vic, speak to me! Are you okay? It's Daphne! Say something, darling! Say something!"

He groaned, his right leg moved and he raised his hand to his head.

The two ladies behind Daphne squealed with delight.

Jenny cried for him over and over.

Daphne grasped his arm and helped support him as he sat up. "What…happened?" he asked, wincing as he rubbed his neck.

In answer, she wrapped her arms around him and burst into tears.

Then an emergency medical technician peeled her away from him and laid him back down again to examine him.

"Your husband's going to be fine, sweetheart," the woman holding Jenny said. "You'd better sit down yourself before you fall down."

But Daphne was too exhilarated at the sight of Vic moving, at the sound of his voice answering the technician's questions.

She thanked the woman and took Jenny from her.

"Vic, Mommy!" Jenny said worriedly, pointing to him.

"I think he's going to be fine, sweetie." She hugged Jenny to her and squeezed, hot tears still flowing freely.

Jenny patted her shoulder in sympathy.

After a few moments, the medical technician helped Vic sit up again. He looked fine, Daphne thought, if a little pale. *Please be fine,* she prayed. *Please, Vic.*

"I think you're okay," the technician said, closing his bag. "But it'd be a good idea to let the hospital look you over. You stay right— Whoa!"

At that moment, Harry, who'd been leaning in the doorway, inspecting the damage to his shop window, suddenly collapsed. The technician ran to him while his companion put the occupants of the car into one of two ambulances.

Vic got gingerly to his feet.

Daphne tried to push him down again. "He said for you to st—"

Picking up his fallen purchases, Vic took her arm and began to lead her toward the back of the store, while everyone gathered around Harry.

"I'm fine," he insisted. "And we're getting out of

here before we become a police or a hospital record that Celeste can trace.''

Daphne pulled against him. "Vic, I don't think—"

But he dragged her along, down a narrow corridor to the back door of the store and out into the chilly morning. They made their way down the alley and back to the Jeep, unnoticed by the crowd gathered around the car protruding from the market's window.

Vic opened the driver's-side door for Daphne while she put Jenny into her car seat. But Daphne refused to cooperate.

"I'm not getting in unless you agree to let me take you to the hospital," she said stubbornly.

"We do not want a record that Celeste can trace," he said again. "Now, will you drive so that I can rest my head for a few minutes, or shall I do it myself?"

She glared at him for one more moment, then climbed in behind the wheel. He got into the passenger side, buckled his belt, leaned back against the headrest with a groan and closed his eyes. "Don't laugh," he said, "but I don't think the car hit me. I think I was beaned by an avalanche of grapefruit."

"Serves you right," she said, "for that sour disposition."

As Daphne turned the key in the ignition, she noticed the ambulance pulling away from the curb.

She glanced at Vic, and saw that his eyes remained closed. With a resolute set to her jaw, she followed the ambulance to the hospital.

Vic did not become suspicious until she slowed to a stop. Then he opened his eyes, saw the one-foot letters that spelled out EMERGENCY on the outside wall of the small community hospital, and sat up abruptly.

"Damn it, Daphne, I told you…" he began.

But she was already out of the Jeep, hailing a nurse who was pushing an empty wheelchair across the parking lot. Daphne opened the passenger-side door and said mildly, "Please don't swear in front of Jenny. She picks up everything. Oh, thank you, nurse. My husband was in the same accident as those two in the ambulance."

Vic sputtered a protest, but the nurse was already pulling him out of the car with a no-nonsense efficiency he apparently didn't know how to fight without making a scene.

His glance at Daphne told her she would pay for this later. She simply stared back at him as he'd done to her so often.

THEY WALKED OUT of the hospital two hours later, Jenny between them, holding their hands. Vic had been X-rayed, tested, prodded and poked, and his mood was grim.

"What in the hell did you think you were doing?" he demanded.

Daphne gave him a smiling glance. The doctor had declared him healthy, if a little unsteady for the next few hours. She felt wonderful. "Don't say 'hell' in front of Jenny."

He expelled an impatient breath. "This opens a trail wide enough to find us."

She sent him a scolding glance. "You're exaggerating. I doubt very much that Celeste will be checking hospitals to find out which direction we went. Lighten up. Life is good. I'll drive until you feel better."

He stopped her before she could insert the key in the passenger-side door. His eyes were still smoky with temper, but under that was a vague confusion. He didn't seem to like that. She loved it.

"Look," he said, shaking his index finger at her. "Let's get something straight right now. I didn't make much of a point of it at your place last night because I understood the concern for Jenny that made you run off like that. But you have to grasp that I'm in charge of this little adventure. I'm the one with field experience. And if you're going to get cute every time—"

She smiled winningly. "Do you really think I'm cute?" she asked as she held out a wisp of hair at her temple. "I'm really not a blonde, you know. My hair is brown and kind of ordinary. I went blond to hide from Celeste, but now I kind of like it. What do you think?"

His eyes went to her hair. He seemed to be distracted by it for a moment, then he shook his head and said sternly, "Daphne, I'm trying to be serious here."

"Oh, I know," she said, lifting Jenny onto her hip, "but let's try being happy instead. We've shaken Celeste, at least for the time being. The doctor says you're healthy, we have this beautiful child and we have each other." Her smile widened farther, and this time with the heartfelt sincerity of a woman in love. "That's more than I've ever had at one time in the whole of my life. Please be happy with me."

Vic tried to hold on to the gravity of their position, to the possible far-reaching consequences of a moment of carelessness, but her eyes were brimming with love, her entire demeanor alight with hope. He felt himself drowning in her happiness.

He tried to get a grip on just where he stood here. "*We* have this beautiful child," she'd said. *We have each other?*

He prepared to ask her for details, but Jenny reached out of her mother's arms toward him. "Vic!" she said gleefully, as though she'd just discovered him, and wrapped her little arms around his neck. "Bye-bye?" she asked.

Vic held her to him, feeling love, possession, a connection that couldn't have been stronger had she been his biologically. Daphne's sudden glow began to seep inside him, warming every dark corner.

"I love you, Jenny," he said into her little ear.

She gave him a noisy kiss on the cheek and beamed at him, pearly rows of baby teeth flashing. "Nana?"

He laughed and handed her to Daphne, who put her in the car seat and handed her a banana, peeling it halfway down. Then Daphne ducked out of the back seat and closed the door.

"Ready?" she asked, trying to reach around him to open his door.

He didn't move, but remained in her path, six-foot-plus of solid male apparently determined to have his say. Deciding that she was probably looking at a lifetime of this, Daphne waited patiently.

"I'd like to clarify a few things," he said. His eyes were free of anger, although there was a dark resolve in its place that might be just as difficult to deal with. But she was intoxicated with the possibilities of life.

"I know," she said, happiness making her reckless and giddy. "You'd like your word to be law, like your father's is, and you're the captain of this adventure and I will be expected to—"

He stopped her with a swift but thorough kiss. Now they were getting someplace.

"I was talking," he reminded her.

She had to think to draw breath. "Sorry. Go on."

He pinned her between himself and the car with a

hand to the roof on either side of her head. "I want to know what's on your mind," he said. "All of it. Now."

"Love is on my mind," she replied simply, looking straight into his eyes. "That's all. But it's huge, enormous. I can feel it in the pit of my stomach, in my fingertips and behind my eyes. It's warm and alive and it's all for you."

He studied her, obviously trying to comprehend how her vitriol of the night before had metamorphosed into this. She could see him reassessing the situation, reevaluating his position.

"How can you love someone you don't trust?" he asked finally.

She made a wide-open gesture with her hands. "I do trust you. With Jenny, with my love for you and all the other emotions that are entangled with it."

She drew a deep breath, because explaining love seemed to require so much energy. She had done it only once with Trey, and then he'd wanted everything put behind them.

"When I learned Celeste had hired you," she continued, "I went a little nuts, but you've come to my rescue twice since then. I'm convinced that you love Jenny and me, and that keeping all that from me was the result of having to cope with a difficult situation."

She drew another breath. One more moment, she thought, and she would hyperventilate.

"And if I was at all confused about how I felt about you," she added, "that straightened out when I saw you lying on the floor of that little market and I thought we'd lost you."

Vic saw her eyes reflect the horror she'd felt. Every need to make his position clear disintegrated in the strong need to comfort her. He gathered her into his arms and felt her dissolve in his embrace.

"When I saw you move," she said, "it was more important to make sure you weren't hurt and risk leaving a trail Celeste could follow, than to risk losing you." She drew back, and her eyes pleaded with him. "Tell me," she whispered, "that when this is all over, you'll still want to marry me."

"Oh, Daphne." He held her close and kissed the rim of her ear. "I love you. I'm sorry I barked at you, but you scared the hell out of me." He pulled back slightly to grin at her. "I know. I shouldn't say "hell" in front of Jenny, but 'scared the heck out of me' just doesn't express it. "And I think I was angry at myself that I let you learn the truth that way. I wouldn't have hurt you like that deliberately for anything."

She kissed him lightly on the lips. "Can we just go around that and think of this time up here as the beginning of our life together?"

He returned her kiss, but lingered over it, savored it. Then he raised his head and saw to his satisfaction that her eyes were bright with love and dark with desire.

"We'll marry ourselves when we get to the cabin," he said. "Then we'll have a serious wedding when we're home in Tyler. All right?"

She raised an eyebrow. "Marry ourselves?"

"Sure. That's all you do in a wedding ceremony, except that a priest or minister acts as a witness. But we make the promises."

She smiled with a tenderness that ground his spine into powder. "I love it."

He kissed her again. "I love *you*."

CHAPTER FOURTEEN

THEY DROVE THROUGH Duluth late in the afternoon and continued north.

They passed through a little town bustling with end-of-the-business-day activity, then drove along a heavily wooded road until they reached a small general store. Above it, a hand-hewn sign read Goose Lake. Pop. 63. The sun was low on the horizon.

Daphne stayed on the planked porch with Jenny, who squealed delightedly over a "tuxedo" cat sleeping on an old wooden rocker. Vic went inside to make arrangements to park the Cherokee in the rickety lineup of garages used by residents of the lakefront properties.

"Are there this many people up here?" Daphne asked as Vic pulled the car into a stall and began unloading their belongings.

"In the summer most of the garages are full. But I doubt there's anyone here but us right now."

She wrapped her arms around his neck, distracting him from his duties. "Good. I want to be alone with you. Really alone."

Jenny wedged herself between them and banged her hand against Vic's knee. When he pushed Daphne back to look down, the toddler raised her arms to him.

He scooped her up. "I don't think we'll ever be really alone," he said wryly. "This kid has a way of making her presence felt."

Daphne kissed the tip of Jenny's nose. "You won't mind that, will you?" she asked Vic.

He kissed her, then Jenny. "Of course not. But maybe we can give her a sister to keep her occupied."

Daphne smiled her approval of the idea. "That's inspired. We'll have to get right to work on it."

"Agreed," he said. "However, we have to get to the cabin first. And since we weren't able to stay in town long enough to buy a backpack for Jenny, we'll have to carry her at least part of the way. The trail's pretty level, but it's a good mile."

"We can leave one of the bags," Daphne suggested, "and come back for it in the morning."

He grinned at her. "*My* bag, I suppose."

She made a flat-handed gesture of innocence. "My bag has Jenny's toys in it. If Jenny's unhappy, we all pay for it."

"Good point." He put his bag back in the Jeep and locked it up. Then he locked the garage and pocketed the key.

Daphne shouldered her purse and the diaper bag, and lifted Jenny into her arms.

Vic slung his duffel across his back, then picked up the food box. They started up the trail lined with pines and ferns.

They shifted and exchanged burdens several times along the way, but Daphne was gasping for breath and tugging a slow-moving Jenny behind her when they finally reached the cabin.

"You'd think my aerobics classes would have made me stronger than this," she said after he'd gone ahead to drop his burdens on the porch, then come back for them. He lifted Jenny onto his hip and pulled Daphne to his side to lend her support the rest of the way.

He kissed her cheek. "You carried a twenty-five-pound child a lot of the way," he said. "And you still don't eat enough to maintain good health. But that's all going to change. You need good old Mexican rice and beans to plump you up."

The cabin was locked, but one of the front windows opened without effort. He deposited Jenny inside, climbed in after her, then helped Daphne over the sill.

"Not good for security purposes," he said, "but convenient for the moment."

The interior of the cabin was musty smelling and filled with shadows.

"You and Jenny stay here," he said, "and I'll get a light."

He disappeared across the room and into a closet, then the farthest corner of the room bloomed with soft light as he placed a Coleman lantern on a low table. He went around the room pulling sheets off the furniture.

"Oh!" Daphne exclaimed, pleasantly surprised. The room had a brick fireplace with a sit-down hearth, exposed beams, a comfortable collection of mismatched furniture and colorful braided rugs.

Vic tossed the sheets into a closet, and showed her a bedroom and a bath with a chemical toilet off to one side, a kitchen on the other. He opened cupboards to reveal a considerable supply of canned goods.

"It's a wonderful place," Daphne said, running a hand over an old-fashioned water pump.

"That's picturesque," he said, "and we may need it, depending on how long we stay, but we're always well equipped with bottled water." He opened a lower cupboard to reveal several dozen jugs.

"Goodness." Daphne put a hand to her heart. "I'm

glad I wasn't on the expedition that had to carry *those* in.''

''Every visitor to the cabin has to leave provisions for the group that follows. That's the rule. I think my cousin Hector brought those in. He comes in with a motorcycle pulling a trailer.''

He patted a small two-burner stove on the countertop. ''Stove works on butane, and we have a spare canister in the shed in the back.''

Daphne looked through the kitchen window to a small, rickety structure several yards away.

''There's still a sled in there, too, for when we get snow.''

Daphne smoothed Jenny's cheek. ''Jenny will love that.'' Then she moved her hand to Vic's cheek. ''And I'm going to love being here with you. We're here because this is where we want to be. That's how I'm going to think about it.''

He gave that thought his blessing with a kiss.

''So, do you want me to start dinner?'' she asked.

''Not yet,'' he replied, catching her hand and pulling her toward the door. ''First, we're getting married.''

''Oh, well. I'm for that,'' she said, following him as he ran lightly down the steps and across the clearing in front of the cabin toward the pinewoods. ''But where are we going to do this? It's starting to get dark.''

''We're going to the lake,'' he said. ''Just beyond the trees.''

They wound their way through a dense thicket of trees for about fifty yards, then emerged on a pine-needle-carpeted shoreline that rimmed a lake about a quarter of a mile long. It was at least as wide across.

Jenny shrieked with delight when geese flapped suddenly into the air, honking noisily as they rose against the dusky sky.

A long, slender pier stretched into the water, and a little boat was tied to it, bobbing gently.

Vic put an arm around Daphne and led her out onto the dock, going to the very edge. Then he helped her sit down, handed her Jenny and sat beside her. Jenny stood between them, a hand on each of their shoulders, while her mother held her steady.

Daphne thought she'd never seen a place more beautiful, more serene. Pines stood all around the lake, their pointed tops creating a ragged rim of shadow against the dark, dusky blue of the sky. Stars were already visible, and a sliver of a crescent moon lay among them as though in some exotic design.

And she'd never smelled air like this, even in Tyler. The bite of pine mingled with the purity of unpolluted air and all the sensory mysteries of night. She drew a deep breath and felt it fill her to the brim with newness.

"In the summer," Vic said, pointing across the lake, "you can see lights all around us. And during the day, somebody's always out there fishing. But it looks as though right now it's just us."

A cold wind whipped in off the water. Vic turned to pull on Jenny's hood and zip up her coat.

Daphne watched him, saw Jenny wrap her arms around his neck, and thought she felt happy enough to expire. Except that she had so much to live for.

Vic pulled Jenny onto his knee and turned toward Daphne, catching both of her hands. She turned toward him and held fast. Jenny, always eager to be included, put her little hands atop theirs.

Darkness closed in on them, but Daphne could see the love clearly in Vic's eyes.

"I promise," he said, "to do everything in my power to make you and Jenny happy, to keep you safe, to share all the hurts I can't protect you from, and to love you every minute of every day and night until my very last breath."

For a moment, Daphne's throat was too tight to allow speech. Then she swallowed and tightened her grip on him. "I promise to try to be as dear to you as you are to me, to spoil you and comfort you and do all in my power to fill your life with laughter and good cheer. I promise to never hold anything back—to love you and to trust you with openhearted honesty until my last moment on earth."

Then they leaned over Jenny to seal their promises with a kiss.

Daphne swore she felt a blessing cover them like the sweep of a cloak.

"I love you so much," she whispered into the encroaching night. "I imagine that one day we're going to be ecstatically happy in the House of Three Gables and that your family will come and visit and we'll string paper lanterns and play music and sing and dance. But I can't imagine being happier than I am right now."

He brought her hand to his lips and kissed it. Jenny's came with it and she giggled.

"Neither can I." He wrapped his arms around both of them. "But I wish I had a hay wagon to take you on a ride. We'll do that first thing when we get back to Tyler."

She snuggled into him. "That'd be nice. Maybe we can ride to our wedding reception in it."

"Good idea. What are we going to do about your

name? Shall I still call you Daphne, or do you want to go back to Diane?''

She gave him a blissful smile, her eyes incandescent with her love for him. ''You may call me Mrs. Estevez.''

continues with

PUPPY LOVE

by Ginger Chambers

Tyler's vet, Roger Phelps, has had a crush on Gracie Lawson for fourteen years. Now she's back in town and he still wants her madly. But Gracie couldn't possibly carry on romantically with the boy who used to pack her groceries. Even if the man he turned out to be is gorgeous, gentle, funny and passionate....
What would people say?

Here's a preview!

PUPPY LOVE

THERE WAS SOMETHING about the way he stood...

His quizzical gaze remained steadily on her. Why was he looking at her like that? Then his smile broadened and he winked...and Gracie realized after a shocked moment that he was flirting with her. With her!

She turned away swiftly. How ridiculous!

Yet when she ventured another look, being careful not to draw attention, he was gone. He might have been a figment of her imagination.

The large, wood-paneled dining room at Timberlake Lodge was filled with people. Gracie moved through their midst, smiling at familiar faces. Occasionally someone stopped her to talk about the afternoon's competition, or ask if she would join their table, but she was supposed to be at the table reserved for officials and judges of the show.

She'd just found her seat and was looking around to see who she knew when she noticed who was in the chair across from hers. She blinked. It was him. The same young man who had winked at her earlier. But who *was* he?

He spoke like a local, but she didn't remember having seen him before. Of course, any number of new people had moved into the Tyler area while she'd been devoting herself to the kennel. No one introduced them, as if she ought to know who he was.

From the conversation she gathered he was Dr. Phelps. The only Phelpses she knew were members of the George Phelps family—or what used to be a family. At one time, Dr. George Phelps had been chief of staff at Tyler General Hospital. He'd had a son named Roger. She furrowed her brow. What had she heard about Roger? He'd dropped out of medical school. Gracie smiled to herself, thinking Sheila would be proud of her for putting together so much Tyler gossip.

She leaned forward for a better look at the handsome young Dr. Phelps. He caught her gaze and winked. Again. In front of everyone!

Such an outward display made her uncomfortable. Gracie chanced a quick glance at the other people around the table and saw that no one had noticed. Relieved, she buried her nose in the menu. Why was he doing this? She refused to look at him, and as soon as the meal ended she jumped up, ready to make a quick getaway.

The president of the poodle club stopped her. "I was wondering, Gracie. Would you mind taking charge of Dr. Phelps for a bit? I don't think he appreciates all the attention Mrs. Wilcox is showering on him—all that coquettish laughter. Doesn't she realize how ridiculous that looks in a woman her age?"

Gracie hedged. "I'm very busy, Diane."

"It's only for an hour, then Mrs. Wilcox will be safely back in the judging ring. I'd do it myself, but I promised the AKC that I'd—"

Gracie felt concerned. "But he's a grown man. Can't he take care of himself?"

"One would think." The voice came from over her shoulder.

Gracie spun around. Him! He had heard! She looked

up—a long way up. Now what was she going to do? How could she possibly get out of this?

"You don't remember me, do you?" he asked.

"Should I?" She feigned interest in something at the end of the hall, aware that they were being overheard.

"I used to bag your groceries at Olsen's the summer before you moved away. I had a huge crush on you."

Gracie's head spun around. He was going back fourteen years! To a time when so much had been happening in her life... "I'm sorry," she said levelly, "I don't remember you."

His brown eyes took on an even more amused look. "Nor would I expect you to. Tragically for me, my feelings weren't returned no matter how carefully I packed your eggs."

Gracie smiled for the first time. "How old were you?" she asked.

"A man of fourteen," he replied. "I'd already started to shave."

"I would have guessed ten," she murmured.

"You don't believe in pulling punches, do you?"

"It's one of the prerogatives of growing older."

"How old are you?"

She was taken aback. "Do you enjoy annoying people?" she asked. "And isn't that rather juvenile behavior?"

He wasn't intimidated. "People usually comment how mature I am for my age."

"Which means you're perfectly capable of taking care of yourself."

"I've been doing that for most of my twenty-eight years."

He was twenty-eight. A little older than she'd originally thought. "Well, Dr. Phelps," she said with deceptive sweetness, "I suggest you continue to do exactly that. You don't need my help." She spun on her heel and prepared to stalk away, but she wasn't prepared for him to reach out and stop her. Nor was she prepared for her reaction to feeling the warmth of his hand on her body....

Spirit Junkie

SPIRIT JUNKIE

A Radical Road to
Self-Love and Miracles

Gabrielle Bernstein

THREE RIVERS PRESS
NEW YORK

Library of Congress Cataloging-in-Publication Data
Bernstein, Gabrielle.
Spirit junkie : a radical road to self-love and miracles /
Gabrielle Bernstein.
p. cm.
1. Self-acceptance. 2. Self-esteem. 3. Self-realization.
4. Course in Miracles. I. Title.
BF575.S37B47 2011
158.1—dc22   2011009236

ISBN 978-0-307-88742-9
eISBN 978-0-307-88741-2

Printed in the United States of America

Text design by Ellen Cipriano
Text photographs courtesy of Sam Bassett
Cover photography by Christopher Lane
Graffiti art courtesy of 5Pointz Aerosol Center, Inc.

10

First Paperback Edition

*For my mother. Thank you for being
my spiritual running buddy.*

Contents

PART 1 The Detour into Fear

Contents

Foreword

Gabrielle Bernstein is both a teacher and a storyteller, looking to the truth she's found in her own everyday experiences to mine the gold that is her gift to others. She realized years ago—as I once did myself—that if there were a force that could turn her messy life around, then she'd be compelled to share her story.

Spirit Junkie teaches clearly and entertainingly how to apply spiritual principles to practical concerns, by demonstrating how Gabrielle has done so herself. From love to career to other issues involved in simply being alive in these times, you can see her trip, fall, and come right back up. Then you see her get to the point where she doesn't even fall anymore. And, ultimately, you realize that you've learned so much from her that you think you can get there, too. A miracle for her has become a miracle for you.

Gabrielle has reminded me of our first encounter. Years ago, having stood in line to speak to me after one of my lectures, she asked how I would apply the principles of *A Course in Miracles* to people her age. To that I responded, "Read and study the *Course*. Then ask God how you should share it with your generation." I figured that that was her job.

I was right. And she has done it well.

This book is the story of Gabrielle's personal journey, but it is a story that instructs us all. Her sincerity, her willingness, and her true humility before the teachings of *A Course in Miracles* give her the requisite power of a genuine teacher. May her teaching grow, flourish, and deepen with the years. She has clearly been assigned a most beautiful task, helping legions of people move beyond their psychological and emotional darkness to a spiritual light that she herself has seen. With *Spirit Junkie*, she continues her work. Thereby, may she and all her readers be blessed.

—*Marianne Williamson*

Spirit Junkie

Introduction

The journey that we undertake together is the exchange of dark for light, of ignorance for understanding. Nothing you understand is fearful. It is only in darkness and in ignorance that you perceive the frightening, and shrink away from it to further darkness. And yet it is only the hidden that can terrify, not for what it is, but for its hiddenness.

—A COURSE IN MIRACLES

●—◆—●

For more than twenty years I kept a journal. In it I wrote about heartbreak, anxiety, and eating disorders. I wrote about trying to quit drugs while high on drugs. Pages and pages are filled with self-loathing, self-doubt, and a running calorie count. I wrote the same romantic mini-drama with dozens of different names attached. My journal entries were my only outlets from the turmoil and deep-rooted pain I lived with every hour of every day. Through writing I'd release my fears onto the page and get honest about my sadness as I scribbled over my tears.

Today my journal entries are much different. They reflect an empowered woman who is happy and bleeds authenticity. Instead of dwelling on my diet or obsessing over romance, I use my journal to honor myself. The words on the page are tinged with pride and compassion. I've overcome my addictions to love, drugs, food, work, fear—you name it, and I've recovered. I worked hard, and man, was it worth it. Today each of my journal entries shows a deep desire to continue growing from the inside out.

My primary guide on my journey to self-love has been

the metaphysical text *A Course in Miracles*. The *Course* is a self-study curriculum emphasizing practical applications for relinquishing fear in all areas of life. The *Course's* unique thought system uses forgiveness as the road to inner peace and as a guide to happiness. I was first introduced to the principles of the *Course* through the spiritual teacher Marianne Williamson, known throughout the world for her best-selling books and her international speaking circuit. Marianne is the leading teacher of *A Course in Miracles* and is a straight-up spiritual rock star.

The *Course's* lessons have taught me to view my life and how I experienced it in a totally new way. I've learned that much of what I feared in my life was not frightening at all, or in many instances even real. I've learned that fear is simply an illusion based on past experiences that we project into the present and onto the future. For instance, I came to realize that my experience of being dumped by my high school boyfriend had morphed into an illusion that I held on to for more than a decade. This simple adolescent breakup managed to morph into a belief system of unworthiness and debilitating fear of being alone.

The lessons of the *Course* allowed me to see how I replayed this fear from the past in all my relationships from high school onward. In every new relationship I began, I'd drag the baggage of that breakup in with me. Even as I was basking in the happiness of being with someone I liked, in the back of my mind lurked a constant fear that my happiness could be snatched away at any moment, and I'd be faced with the same heartbreak and trauma I'd experienced in that high school relationship. Ultimately that fear would cause me to sabotage my new relationship. When the relationship was over I'd try to anesthetize my pain with food, work, and—worst of all—drugs. I'd do whatever it took to avoid feeling my fears from the past. I was unable to savor simple pleasures and happy moments because I was constantly on guard against fear. This cycle was endless. I'm thankful that the *Course* taught me that the fear I had been lugging around for so many years wasn't even real, that it was just an illusion I had created and was projecting onto my current experiences. Once I experienced this realization, I was able to work through the fear. The more I committed to this new belief system, the less I replayed my past in the present. In time I began to release those fears and witness miraculous changes. This realization was revelatory in that I'd awakened to the fact that if I stuck to the *Course*'s plan I could truly relinquish my fearful patterns.

Admittedly, when I first began reading the *Course*, the language and many of the concepts were extremely foreign to me. Each time the text would refer to "God" or "the Holy Spirit," I'd totally freak out. But, ultimately, I came to realize that getting bogged down in semantics was a silly distraction. What mattered most was the guidance the *Course* had to offer me at a time when I needed it most. The words were just a vehicle to all the valuable lessons that were available within its pages. I learned that what really mattered was how relevant the *Course's* teachings were to my life, and my absolute willingness to be guided to change.

It was with that burning desire for change that I set out to purchase the *Course* to begin with. Upon entering my local bookstore, I noticed the sturdy-looking dark blue book with the title *A Course in Miracles* scrawled in gold lettering across the cover. Instead of being daunted by it, I found the thickness of the volume inviting and reassuring. So much so that I smiled as if I had received a wink from the Universe as I grabbed the book off the shelf. Then the most auspicious thing happened. The book literally dragged me to the counter. No joke. I physically felt the book dragging me to the register. It felt strange and yet oddly comforting. Intuitively, I knew I was in for something good. I bought the book immediately and walked out of the store. As I stood on a busy New York City streetcorner, I flipped the book open to its introduction and read, *"This is a course in miracles. It is a required course. Only the time you take is voluntary. The course does not aim at teaching the meaning of love, for that is beyond what can be taught. It does aim, however, at removing the blocks to the awareness of love's presence, which is your natural inheritance."* This passage sent chills down my spine. I'd found what I was looking for, a guide to removing all the crap that had been blocking me from inner peace and love. In that moment I made a commitment to myself to become a student and a teacher of the *Course*—a sacred contract that would change my life.

One year later, I went to hear Marianne lecture. Afterwards I had the opportunity to speak with her about my introduction to the *Course* and my desire to spread its message to my generation. I asked her for suggestions as to how I might proceed with this goal. She replied, "Read the *Text*, do the *Workbook*, and study the *Manual for Teachers*. Then get on your knees and ask God how you should share this work with your generation." I did just that.

Through reading the *Text* I was guided to understand the mission of the *Course*. Simply and succinctly, the *Course* states that *"its goal for you is happiness and peace."* The *Text* also gave me a deep understanding of the basis for my fear and guilt, and how they could be overcome. Finally, the *Text* taught me the meaning of "the miracle." The miracle is simply defined as the shift in perception from fear to love. Then I embarked on the *Workbook for Students*, which consists of 365 lessons, an exercise for each day of the year. This one-year training program began my process of transforming my own fears to love. The *Workbook* guided me to know a relationship with what I call my *~ing*, an inner guide, or, as the *Course* calls it, an Internal Teacher. This relationship with my *~ing* became my primary tool for restoring my mind. (I'll explain *~ing* further in chapter 1.)

Then, when I was ready, I began to practice the *Manual for Teachers*. This section of the *Course* prepared me to share its lessons in a way that was authentic to me. As a result of my dedication to the *Course*, I was blasted open to reconnect with my true inner spirit, which is love.

My intention and my hope is that this book will act as a conduit through which I can share the beautiful, life-changing lessons that I learned as a student of the *Course*. Through the telling of my own life's stories, I will relate how the lessons of the *Course* led me to release my fears of the world and become a full-on Spirit Junkie. These days I'm addicted to finding my happiness and love inside myself. Thus the title. With this book I want to show you how to tap into your own spirit in your search for happiness. This is not a book on *how to get happiness*; rather, it's a guide to releasing the blocks to the happiness that already lives inside you. I will guide you on a journey of new perceptions and show you a whole new way to view your life. Your hangups will melt away, resentments will release, and a childlike faith in joy will be reignited.

Throughout the book I'll share personal anecdotes of how I overcame the stronghold of my ego (my fearful mind) with the help of *A Course in Miracles*. Through my *Course* work I've learned that my darkest struggles in relationships were by far my greatest teachers. To drive home this message, throughout the book I'll often refer to my parents, friends, and former lovers. (For the record, I have tons of love for these people today and am deeply thankful for the lessons I've learned from our relationships.) Through my interpretation of the *Course's* principles you'll learn that all the safety, security, and love you're seeking is not "out there," but inside yourself. Trust me: I spent more than two decades looking for happiness in all the wrong places. I thought happiness was in a credential or a boyfriend or a new pair of shoes. I thought that if I accumulated or achieved enough, my misery, insecurity, and anxiety would somehow disappear and be replaced by joy, confidence, and lightheartedness. It never worked. Turning inward can seem like an insurmountable challenge, but by committing to the *Course* you'll learn that inward is the only place to go. When you truly know this, you can release the *need* to be saved, stop controlling, and let life flow.

I will be your teacher on this journey. Before we begin down the path, I'd like to tell you a little about myself. As a speaker, author, mentor, and coach I've made it my life's work to help others release the blocks that stand between them and their inner joy. My work has been received well throughout the world because, let's face it, who doesn't want to be happy? But let's put titles and credentials aside. The most valuable gift I have to offer you is life cred. I've lived every word in this book and transformed myself through the stories you're about to read. I once was a strung-out drug addict seeking self-worth from the outside world. Today I turn inward and receive all the happiness I'd been seeking.

The journey we're about to embark on together in this book is broken up into three parts. The first leg of the journey is Section One, "The Detour into Fear," which will explain how our minds go wrong and why we become so accustomed to fearful ways of being. Then, Section Two, "The Answer," will provide a road map to serenity. This section will give you the necessary tools for reconditioning your mind back to peace and joy. Then, in Section Three, "The Miracle," you'll be guided to maintain your happiness and share it with the world.

To help further illuminate your journey, I've created guided meditations that you can download on my site, www .gabbyb.tv/meditate. There is a meditation for each chapter. These meditations will help you reconnect with your true essence, which is love, and your birthright, which is access to miracles.

The *Course* teaches that each time we shift our perception from fear to love we create a miracle. The more miracles you add up, the more extraordinary your life will be. The outside world and all your relationships will be enhanced as a result of your inner shift. Serenity will kick in, fear will subside, and once and for all you'll know that all the love you need is inside you.

Sounds like I've got the keys to heaven, doesn't it? That's right, I do! And I can testify to these tools because I work them like a full-time job. Just breathe, be willing, and show up for the suggestions along the way. Remember you are not alone. Even if fear has you in a headlock, I'm here to remind you that happiness always wins.

PART 1

The Detour into Fear

1

A Tiny Mad Idea

All shallow roots must be uprooted, because

they are not deep enough to sustain you.

—A COURSE IN MIRACLES

For most my life I felt like a fraud. I worked super hard to be perceived as cool. I did everything I could to keep up, fit in, and be accepted. I dressed a certain way, studied specific subjects, tried different hobbies. In high school I wore Doc Martens, wrapped a flannel shirt around my waist, and tried to be cute by wearing my field hockey skirt to school on game day. I did whatever I could to fit in, but none of it worked. I never felt as though I was part of the group.

I now realize that behind all my striving was a search for meaning and purpose. I was searching for a sense of self-worth in relationships ranging from friends to family to romances. My outside persona was a loquacious, white, middle-class Jewish girl growing up in the 'burbs with her divorced hippie parents. But I had no clue who I was on the inside.

To make matters worse, I felt like my thoughts were totally different from those of the average adolescent. It seemed as though my contemporaries were content to focus on sports, the latest hit movie, and dating. My mind was obsessed with other things. I constantly wondered why I was this person in this body with this family at this time. I'd think, *Is this it? We're born, we get an education, we make some money, we get hitched, we have some kids, and then we die? Is that all there is to life?* I was an adolescent girl caught in an existential crisis. My inner turmoil had me questioning everything I was trained to believe in.

The world around me taught the thinking of inequality, separateness, and competition, and better-than and less-than. I was led to value money, a romantic partner, and success as driving factors for true happiness. The world taught me to believe in archetypes like mean girls, hot guys, rich dads, poor kids, cool crowds, and losers who sat alone at lunch. I was supposed to believe this world was real, but deep down I didn't fully buy it. In my mind a battle raged between what I was taught to believe and a deep-rooted intuition that there was something more. My inner voice was screaming, *Wake up, girl, there's a better way!*

Throughout my formative years I experienced fleeting encounters with what I was seeking: a peaceful world beyond what I was taught to see. This began at age sixteen. By that time my inner turmoil had gotten so bad that I was in a constant state of anxiety. I feared just about everything. I was scared of being alone, getting too fat, not being cool enough. Some days I didn't even have a reason—I was just scared. This anxiety made me feel like a freak. My brother and friends seemed to be totally chilled-out, whereas I was in a constant state of panic. My hippie mom chose to remedy this anxiety with what she knew best: meditation. I was desperate to ease my incessant thoughts and get out of the scary world I'd created inside my mind, so I took her up on her offer to learn meditation. Once I agreed to give it a shot, my mom lit some incense and sat my ass down on a meditation pillow. She taught me to sit cross-legged with my palms facing upward so that I could receive the so-called "energy" around me. This was far outside my comfort zone, but I was distressed and willing to try anything.

Early on in my mediation practice, I confirmed that my intuition was right. There *was* a better way. I found that whenever I'd sit long enough, my mind would soften and my anxiety would disappear. Then one afternoon I was led to know much more. In the middle of my meditation I felt a rush of peace come over me. My limbs began to tingle and I felt surrounded by a sense of love. I felt at home for the first time. This experience reassured me that my intuition was spot-on. There was more to happiness than shopping malls, TV, and being popular. There was a source of energy that was greater than me, which I could access if I sat long enough in meditation. Even though I was still totally confused about my existence, this gave me something to hold on to. It gave me hope that there was indeed a better way to perceive the world.

Unfortunately, I couldn't share this experience with my high school contemporaries. I couldn't very well show up at school and say, "Hey, guys, I meditated last night and my body was taken over by a loving energy. It was totally cool." There was no way in hell they'd believe me. As far as they were concerned, *what you see is what you get*. It seemed to me that they believed in a world of separateness, fear, competition, and prom. Had I shared my existential philosophies with my friends, I'd have been exiled. I was weird enough already.

So instead I chose fear. I turned my back on the feeling of love and serenity brewing inside me and took what I thought was the path of least resistance. I detoured into fear and forgot about my encounter with love. I made the decision to go along with the crowd and believe life was tough. As I got older and grew into this mindset, I focused on the form I'd projected onto my life. I saw myself as so-and-so's girlfriend, as a theater student, as a young entrepreneur, as a party girl mentioned in the gossip rags and someone worth Googling. I portrayed myself as better than others, but on the inside I felt less than everyone. From the outside it looked as though I had successfully created a "cool" existence for myself. But I couldn't ignore the voice in the back of my mind nagging me to remember that *there was a better way*.

However, I hid from that voice. I denied its truth. I chose to let fear take the wheel and navigate my life without a road map. This choice led me to some super scary dead ends, which included a slew of addictions—drug addiction being one of them—and unhealthy, drama-filled relationships. Luckily, I got lost enough times to surrender to that inner voice, listen, and pick up the map. That map was *A Course in Miracles*, and it became my guide back home.

Today I have the map in my back pocket and I'm psyched to share it with you. I know you must be longing for a guide. Maybe you're going through a breakup, coping with a job loss, or mourning a death. Maybe you're recovering from a form of addiction, you hate your body, or, like me, you're having some kind of existential crisis. Whatever it is I know it's not easy, and that in some way or another fear's running the show. Let's face it: you wound up in the self-help section of the bookstore, right? But that's cool. Your willingness to enhance your life is what guided you to me. Where you are is totally normal. This is where most of our minds end up sooner or later. That's because, early on in life, most of us separate from love and choose fear instead. We might have fleeting moments of inspiration and truth. We feel love through a song lyric or an image or after a warm embrace. We sense love, but we don't *believe* in it. We save our faith for fear. But ultimately, there is a quiet voice in each of us that longs for something better. That voice inside *you* is what led you to this book. Some way, somehow, your inner voice of love spoke louder than fear and said, *Maybe there's a better way*. And you listened.

Nice one! I'm proud of you. You did the best you could to get to this point. So let's get the ball rolling! I'm here to guide you to a whole new way to perceive the world. As I mentioned before, *A Course in Miracles* will be our map. Like most maps, the *Course* can be hard to understand at first glance. Therefore, it's crucial that you keep an open mind. I know this New Age stuff might be a little funky for you, but hang tight. All I ask is that you stay open to the suggestions. At times you may completely disagree with what I'm teaching. In fact, I'm sure you will. Most of what you'll learn in this book is the opposite of what you've been conditioned to believe. But that's cool. New ideas are what you need. Clearly your old ways haven't been working. I'm here to teach you that life doesn't have to be tough, that you don't need to feel alone, and that miracles are your birthright. So be willing to see things differently and you'll be led to all the happiness and serenity that you desire. I know this is a pretty ballsy statement, but I'll straight-up testify to it. As it says in the *Course*, "*There is a way of living in the world that is not here, although it seems to be. You do not change appearance, though you smile more frequently. Your forehead is serene; your eyes are quiet.*" Sounds totally awesome, right? Well, it is.

In this chapter I'll start us off on our journey by introducing the key principles of the *Course*, which identify *fear* as an illusion and *a shift in perception* as a miracle. For the most part, I'll be sticking to the *Course*'s language, but from time to time I'll Gabbify some stuff. I'll begin by reminding you of the state of mind we were born with, which I'll refer to as "love." Here, I'll take you back in time to the peace you once knew as an innocent child. Then I'll identify the key reasons you're no longer grooving in that way. I'll guide you to understand what the *Course* teaches is a major reason that we sink into unhappiness, which, simply put, is a separation from our inner state of joy. Then, I'll wrap up the chapter with an exercise designed to help you identify the negative thought patterns you've created in your mind. Taking inventory of those patterns is the first move toward shifting them. Our journey will begin with "love." What better way to start!

Born in Love

The love I'll speak of throughout the book is not to be confused with romantic love. The *Course* defines love as *"the right-minded emotion of peace and joy."* This kind of love is not something we offer to some people and deny others—this is one love that embodies everything and everyone. When we're in a state of love we see everyone as equal and we feel at ease all the time. This state is fearless and faithful.

Love is where we all begin. When we are born, all we know is love. Our ~*ing* is on! (If you haven't read my last book, *Add More ~ing to Your Life*, allow me to translate: ~*ing* is your inner guide, which is the voice of intuition, inspiration, and love. Throughout the book I'll refer to love, spirit, and ~ing interchangeably.) Our thoughts are aligned with love and our minds are peaceful. Our loving mind believes that all people are equal and that we are part of something larger than ourselves. We believe that we are supported and connected to everything everywhere. We believe that only love is real. We believe in miracles.

When I was first exposed to this lesson from the *Course*, it was hard for me to remember a time from my past when love fully ran the show. Even as a young child I felt anxious and skittish, and as if something were off-kilter. When I had that fleeting encounter with love during my early meditation days, I knew for sure that the presence of love was missing as a constant in my life. In that fleeting moment during my meditation, I felt it and it was real. Although I was unable to capture it and pin it down at the time, I was able to hang on to its memory for some sense of serenity.

A Tiny Mad Idea

So we are born into love, and then pretty soon thereafter fear is introduced. We begin to pick up the fear around us and are led to deny love. One tiny mad idea can hijack our loving mindset, and as the *Course* says, "*we forgot to laugh.*" This tiny mad idea could have arrived as early as infancy. Maybe Mom was anxious or Dad yelled a lot. As innocent babies we pick up fear from the outside world. All it takes is one tiny mad idea to make us detour into fear. A thought like "I'm not smart enough," or "Daddy doesn't like me, because he left," or "I'm not pretty enough" can separate us from love. The moment we take this tiny mad idea seriously, we get caught in a nightmare and forget to wake up.

With one fearful thought we lose love and are thereby separated from our *~ing*. This is what the *Course* calls "dissociation," which it basically defines as *"a decision to forget."* We chose to forget that we were equally as loveable and worthy as everyone and everything everywhere. Instead we chose to believe in fear and to perceive ourselves as separate in all ways. In some cases we believe we are better than others and special, whereas in other instances we believe we aren't good enough and are lesser-than. This thinking is destructive and unproductive: it leads us nowhere fast.

The tiny mad idea that totally seized my *~ing* arrived when I was eight years old and landed a national TV commercial. This was monumental, not because I was proud of my acting or excited about being on TV, but because it was the first time I remember my father ever noticing me. It's not that my father was a mean man or a bad parent; it's just that I don't remember having much of a connection with him when I was young. Then, once I got a taste of what his attention felt like, it became like a drug that I couldn't get enough of. From that point forward, I was on the chase for more. I became a love junkie.

Though I didn't realize it, that experience began to reprogram my mind. It taught me that outward success equals "Daddy loves me," and that I wasn't good enough without his attention. So I continued to do whatever it took to be noticed. That was when I *detoured into fear*. This one tiny mad idea became my root issue, and a whacked-out emotional blueprint was set down to be built upon for the next twenty years of my life. I lost my faith in love and fell for the fear instead.

The Ego

Upon learning of the tiny mad idea, we have two choices. As the *Course* says, *"You cannot be faithful to two masters who ask conflicting things of you."* Therefore we have to choose between the tiny mad idea and the love we came from. Most of the time we choose fear. This choice splits off our mind into another way of thinking, which the *Course* calls the "ego." (This is not to be confused with the ego of psychology.) In an instant we are separated from love and allow the ego to take over. The ego becomes like a bully in our minds. The ego's goal is to shut down the love parade and trap us on a dark and lonely street by making us believe we're separate from the loving mindset we were born with. The ego cannot survive in the light of our loving mind, so it will do whatever it takes to keep the light off. When referencing the ego, the *Course* states, *"Listen to what the ego says, and see what it directs you to see, and it is sure that you will see yourself as tiny, vulnerable and afraid. You will experience depression, a sense of worthlessness, and feelings of impermanence and unreality."* This lesson from the *Course* explained my deep-rooted anxiety and belief that I wasn't good enough. My loving mind had been captured by my ego.

The ego's sole purpose is to convince us that love isn't real so that we believe in the fearful thinking of the world. The ego is always revving up its game to take us down in a major way.

The *Course* says that *"the ego is totally confused and totally confusing."* To keep us in the dark, the ego separates us from love. We're persuaded to deny love by believing in issues around body image, relationships, career, low self-esteem, and so on. As an adolescent I chose to be faithful to the ego. I was totally obsessed with what other people thought of me, who I was friends with, and what I looked like. My moment-to-moment thoughts were consumed with fear about these issues. From childhood up until my late twenties I cannot remember a time when my mind was free of fear. To make matters worse, I was obsessed with the coolness of the girls in the popular crowd and with how uncool I seemed to be by comparison. I chose to see those girls as separate from and better than me. The ego convinces us that we are better or worse than everyone around us. The ego's illusion convinces us to believe thoughts like "I'm not good enough to get into that school," or "I'm incomplete without a man," or "I'm way more popular than that girl." Deep down we know these thoughts are false, but we believe in them nonetheless.

To further keep us in the dark, the ego's illusion leads us to attack others and ourselves. In my case, because I felt so misunderstood and disconnected from my contemporaries, my ego convinced me that *they* were the problem: "They don't get me. They're just a bunch of assholes." My ego made everyone else wrong, which made me the victim. The ego loves to make victims of us.

Projection Makes Perception

The ego's main job is to make sure we don't change our mind about fear. The fearful projection that the ego inflicts on us becomes what we perceive to be our reality. As it says in the *Course*, *"The world you see is an outside picture of an inward condition."* When we choose the ego's projection of sin, guilt, anger, attack, and fear, that's all we'll perceive. It's a nightmare. The *Course* states, *"Perception is a choice and not a fact."* My projection of the ego became my perception in many areas of my life—especially when it came to my romantic relationships. Because I chose the ego thought that I'm not good enough without my father's attention, I later projected that thinking onto all my relationships with men. Projecting this tiny mad idea onto all my romantic partners led me to perceive myself as less-than and not good enough. This led me to do whatever I could to hold on to a romantic partner because without him I believed I was incomplete.

We all have our own individual projections and perceptions. For instance, two different people get upset after watching a TV show together. Even though they watched the same show, they're upset for different reasons. One person is upset over the romantic struggles of the characters, whereas the other person is worked up over the violence. Each person was projecting their own ego onto the television show, and therefore perceived what they chose to project. *Choice* is the operative word. That's right: we *choose* to believe in this crazy shit. We choose to project ideas like "I'm too fat," "I'm unworthy," and "I'm just not smart." We made a decision to forget about love and we fell for the mad idea instead. As a result, we live in a world that is based on these limiting projections. We project these thoughts and therefore perceive them to be real. Worst of all, we believe deeply in our perceptions because we're the ones who put them there.

Starting early in life, we project a belief system based on grades, cliques, bullies, and societal crap about body image. We have no choice but to ignore our ~*ing* because the voice of love cannot coexist with fear. Fear spreads like a virus, contaminating our minds. All it takes is one tiny mad idea to separate our mind from love and create a pattern of thinking in which fear always wins.

The ego also re-creates your past fears in the present. This was totally the case for me. My fear of not being good enough without male attention became my Achilles' heel and affected nearly every area of my life. I did whatever it took to attain male approval. I spent years trying to prove myself to my father in order to feel good enough. I'd come home with stories of my daily accomplishments and speak loudly to make sure I was heard. I desperately needed to be acknowledged by him to feel safe. My father loved me and approved of me of regardless of my outside accomplishments, but on the inside I believed the opposite.

The ego is crafty. There are a number of tricks the ego turns to in order to keep us in the dark, such as causing us to believe that others are more special than we are, causing us to attack others, or getting us into the nasty habits of denying our greatness and believing we are inadequate. Each trick convinces us to believe in fear and forget about love. Eventually we get so hooked into the ego's illusion that we cannot remember the loving mind we came from. It's as if we've been roofied by the ego.

This sounds seriously effed-up, right? Of course it does, but in one or more ways we've all fallen for the ego's mad idea. One fearful thought takes over our minds and creates our very own illusions. We were all innocent children who once believed in love. But there comes a point at which we forget love ever existed. We choose fear instead. We fear just about everything. We fear our careers, our family, our friends—we even fear the possibility that love could be real. Most of all we fear our own greatness.

The truthful voice of our ~*ing* can only comprehend love. But because our minds detoured into fear, love became an afterthought. Our ~*ing* became a mere murmur in the midst of the ego's inner riot. I can safely say that the majority of people I know have more faith in fear than in love. My life-coaching clients often say things like "I know there is a better way, but I just can't find it." Deep down we remember that all the love we need is inside us, but the ego's darkness has smothered that luminous truth.

You need to take a look at the wreckage from your past to understand fully how to transform the ego's patterns. Accepting the fact that you chose fear and turned your back on love is the first step. Don't beat yourself up about this. You couldn't have known any better and you've been doing the best you can to cope with the ego's projections for your entire life. But now it's time to fully understand what went down in order to create change.

Please know that even if you've forgotten about love, it never actually left you. Your mind just separated from it. This separation ignited the spark that became the fire that burns through your loving mind. Unfortunately, you chose to detour into Fear Land when you took sides with the ego and turned your back on love. I'm here to remind you that the separation was merely a choice, and that you can choose differently now.

The Ego Isn't Real

Over time, fear becomes our companion. The ego goes wild, taking over the loving part of our minds and convincing us of what the *Course* calls "the real world." The ego's real world is the illusory nightmare that we've bought into. My "real world" was based on a belief system of being alone, separate, and incomplete without a romantic partner. I also believed that I wasn't smart and had nothing to offer the world. My ego projected my world as small and rigidly limited.

The world that the ego creates for all of us is based on belief in sin, attack, fear, competition, lack, sickness, and so on. The ego convinces us that we're all a bunch of separate bodies out to make more money, find a better spouse, or look better than the next person. None of this is real. It's all an illusion that our ego creates in our minds and repeats enough so that we believe in it. The repetition of the ego's illusion becomes a bad dream that we reinforce with every fear-based idea. We've saved our faith for fear. But deep inside each of us lives a soft voice reminding us that love is real.

The First Step out of the Ego's World of Illusion

The only problems we have are the thoughts we project. What's happened is that we think these funky thoughts enough times that we believe them to be true. Then the thoughts create anxiety, fear, anger, attack, and guilt. By recognizing that the thought isn't real we can release the perception. We must understand that the thought is something we created a long time ago and that we've just projected it onto our present and future.

Recognizing that the ego's projections are illusions is the first step to restoring your mind back to love. This was major for me. When I first began practicing the *Course*, I was relieved to witness my projections. By looking closely at my fears, I was able to stop perceiving them as real. For instance, when I wrote my first book, *Add More ~ing to Your Life*, I was rocked by the ego at first. All my childhood beliefs of not being smart enough rose to the surface. My ego said things like "Who are you to write a book? You're just a stupid girl with the writing skills of an eighth grader." By that point I was already practicing the *Course* and was therefore able to witness that these fearful thoughts were based on an illusion of being stupid that I'd picked up in sixth grade. I witnessed the fearful thought without judgment and was therefore able to weaken its power and write an awesome book!

I want these messages to sink in, and I hope to guide you to see how the ego has played a role in your own nightmare. At this point in the process, let's shine light on your own tiny mad ideas.

Negative Thought Pattern Exercise

With eyes closed, think of the negative thought patterns that cross your mind. Name each one as it occurs to you, and then call it out. Deny its reality by following the fearful thought with the loving response, "*Love did not create it, and so it is not real.*"

> *Examples:*
> Ego thought: *I am unworthy of happiness.*
> Loving response: *Love did not create the belief that I'm unworthy, and so it is not real.*
> Ego thought: *I can't make money.*
> Loving response: *Love did not create lack, and so it is not real.*

This exercise might not make sense to you at first. Throughout the text, the *Course* acknowledges that you may not fully understand the concepts it introduces at first, but teaches you to continue forward nonetheless. The *Course* states, *"The exercises are very simple. They do not require a great deal of time, and it does not matter where you do them. They need no preparation."* Therefore, all you need is an open mind and the willingness to be guided.

With your newfound willingness we'll move on to chapter 2, where we'll look more closely at the ego's illusion. Hang tight and know that each simple shift in perception creates miraculous change.

Quick Review

- We are all born into a state of love, in which we see everyone as equal.

- One tiny mad idea can hijack our loving mindset. We choose fear instead of love.

- This choice splits off our mind into another way of thinking called the "ego." The ego's goal is to shut down the love parade and keep us in the dark by making us believe we're separate from the loving mindset we were born with.

- The repetition of the ego's illusion becomes a bad dream that we reinforce with every fear-based idea. But deep inside each of us lives a soft voice reminding us that love is real.

- Recognizing that the ego's projections are false illusions is the first step to restoring our mind back to love.

2

Anxiety
and Ashrams

What is joyful to you is painful to the ego.

—A COURSE IN MIRACLES

•◆•

lashback to my teenage years. The tiny mad idea that had grabbed hold of me when I was eight took over and my anxiety got progressively worse. In an effort to help, my mother brought me to visit the ashram in South Fallsburg, New York, where her guru taught. At that point I was willing to do whatever it took to find some peace of mind. As we pulled into the ashram grounds, I saw people smiling with peaceful expressions on their faces. I felt a rush of love come over me, much like the experience I had while meditating. People smiled as we drove by them. Their eyes sparkled with a sense of lightheartedness and freedom. Then my body began to tingle and my hands went numb. I didn't speak up about what I was experiencing; I just allowed it to wash over me. In these new surroundings, I felt a sense of safety engulf me. Everything looked brighter here. It was like I was awake in a dream.

But the sensation was fleeting; as soon as we parked and began walking toward the main buildings, my anxiety returned. A voice in the back of my mind said, *That feeling was too good to be true. Nice try, sister!* As soon as I

heard the taunt of the familiar voice, my anxiety intensified. It was even worse than usual. I was experiencing an
overwhelming sadness, tightness in my chest, and panic for
fear that the sensation wouldn't go away. After only half
an hour spent walking through the ashram witnessing the
people, sitting in the meditation room, and getting accli-
mated, I couldn't bear my anxiety. I made my mother take
me home.

When we got into the car, my mother explained that I
was like a sponge soaking up the energy around me. That
was the reason my feeling of anxiety seemed even worse
than usual: I was not only reacting to the fear, but absorb-
ing the intense energy within the ashram itself. She went
on to say that this openness was a gift, but because I didn't
know how to control it, it left me unsettled and flustered.
Spiritual places like ashrams often attract people who
are not well and are in search of healing, she explained.
Because I was already in a fearful head-space, I was likely
to have picked up the anxiety of the others around me. My
ego met their egos, which compounded my own fear. So
not only was I totally freaked out about my own issues, but
I had picked up other people's fears, too. The entire experience infuriated me, and I began attacking my mother's
belief system. I was over her New Age approach to serenity,
I told her. It was time for me to take matters into my own
hands.

Numbing Out

In order to avoid my anxiety and fear, I reasoned that I had to anesthetize myself. So I rolled a joint and drank a beer. This remedy worked until one blowout night when it became clear that alcohol and drugs took me to some scary places.

My mother had gone out of town and left me home alone with my brother. You can probably guess where I'm going here. Yup, I threw a small gathering of thirty of my closest friends. As usual, we drank beer and smoked weed—nothing out of the ordinary. Then the paranoia set in. This didn't seem to be the typical pot-smoking paranoia. It was a whole other monster. I was crawling out of my skin. I felt overcome by fear and an underlying sense of guilt. I felt like I'd done something terribly wrong. This guilt/paranoia/anxiety cocktail was too much. I ended up kicking everyone out.

I called my mom the next day and told her what had happened. I felt safer outing my problems than hiding them. Her immediate response was "I expected this call." She went on to tell me that on the day of my party she'd gone to see an astrological reader. When she asked about me, the reader made a strong suggestion that I never use drugs or alcohol. The reader said that I was a very sensitive being and that I had a lot of psychic energy. She suggested that drugs and alcohol would take me to a place I didn't need to go, and that I'd struggle with this for some time.

I was surprised that drugs and alcohol had that effect on me. But my experience at the ashram and the astrologer's prophecies didn't make anything less crazy in my mind. In fact, I felt worse. I now perceived myself as a freak, soaking up the energy of others and unable to handle my liquor. This perception reinforced my feeling of being an outsider.

The Crafty Ego

In retrospect I can clearly see the craftiness of my ego back then. While at the ashram, my ego had sensed love coming over me when I first arrived. My ego couldn't survive in the light of this love, so it had to deny it to keep me in the dark. The ego can only survive when we're in pain. As the *Course* teaches, *"No one desires pain. But he can think that pain is pleasure. No one would avoid his happiness. But he can think that joy is painful, threatening and dangerous."* What I didn't realize at the time was that my ego had convinced me that "joy is painful," thereby weakening my faith in love. My ego had several nasty tricks at its disposal to keep me stuck in the illusion that my pain had purpose.

Remember, the ego is like a bully that takes over our minds. As soon as the ego sensed my mother's attempts to reconnect me with love, it bullied me into siding with fear to resist her efforts. My ego barged in to say, "Come on, Gab, that feeling of love is too good to be true. Don't believe your mom's hippie shit. That ain't real."

The Ego's Bag of Tricks

The ego totes around its bag of tricks in the same way we carry a favorite clutch. This bag holds space for what the *Course* refers to as the ego's "friends," namely sin, guilt, fear, denial, and attack. Whenever we start thinking loving thoughts, our ego reaches into its bag. The ego grabs on tightly to one of its "friends" to drag us back into fear. The ego reaches into the bag when it needs to defend against love.

Each trick is cunning and baffling. The *Course* says, *"The ego vacillates between suspiciousness and viciousness."* In order to overcome the ego's stronghold, we must understand its ways, so in this chapter we'll take a thorough look at the ego's crafty tricks. I'll guide you to witness the ego's commitment to keeping us in the dark. This will help you differentiate your ego from the loving voice of your *~ing* and give you more power to change your fearful patterns. The *Course* teaches that we must acknowledge our misery so that we can begin to change it.

The goal of this chapter is to guide you to understand

how the ego works. Toward that end, I've outlined the ego's tricks for you one by one. Use this breakdown as a guide, as these tricks will continue to come up throughout your journey inward.

The Nasty Tricks That Keep the Ego Alive

The moment at the ashram when love settled in, my ego freaked out. Remember that the ego cannot survive in the light of loving thoughts. If I'd chosen love, the ego couldn't endure. As it says in the *Course*, "*Whenever light enters darkness, the darkness is abolished.*" Therefore, the ego had to rev up its game and hook me back into fear. In order to keep me in the dark the ego reached into its bag of tricks. The ego's tricks convinced me to fear love.

Fear

One of the ego's first-line tools is fear. Fear was the primary feeling I experienced in my life before I began my *Course* work. At the time I couldn't actually express why I was afraid, but I felt fearful all the time. That fear is what led me to try to numb out with drugs and alcohol. The *Course* says, "*Being afraid seems to be involuntary; something beyond your own control.*" Fear is often a sign that you've turned your back on love and chosen to have faith in the ego.

Today I realize I was fearful back then for a few reasons. The first reason was entirely buried in my subconscious. I was afraid that I'd lost something—that I'd lost love. The voice of love had been beckoning me through moments of positive self-talk and the deep desire to perceive the world from a happier perspective, but time and time again I was tempted back to fear. By choosing the ego, I'd denied love altogether. This ignited an unconscious horrifying thought that I'd killed love forever. And the fleeting encounters with love that I found through meditation and at the ashram actually created more fear. Because my ego mind had become more powerful than love, I was afraid I'd lost love altogether. This fear led me into a deep depression. And what I feared most was that I would never get out of it.

The second reason for my fear was based on my own conscious decisions. I'd chosen to believe in fear. I'd chosen to believe in the ego's separate thinking that I was a girl living in a world of attack, war, separateness, anger, and discomfort. I was afraid of this world because it was the opposite of the love I remembered and because it was straight-up scary! I turned my back on love altogether and chose to believe this projected world was real. In other words, I chose to live in fear.

Fear of the Past

This world I'd projected was based on fearful past experiences that my ego clung on to—experiences of not feeling good enough, smart enough, pretty enough, thin enough. Things as simple as being told I was stupid or having acne were ways for the ego to run roughshod over my mind. My ego pulled these past experiences into the present moment and made them real over and over again.

I'd relive my past experiences daily. For instance, in middle school I was bullied. This experience of being attacked by others created a dark corner in my mind where I believed I wasn't good enough. I established a belief system in which the mean girls were better than I was. I carried this experience with me into high school. As a result of the belief system I had established, I was afraid of many of my female contemporaries and never found a true group of friends. I relived the experience of having been bullied in middle school daily when I walked through the halls in high school, felt alone in the lunch room, and sat in the front of the bus on school trips. This middle-school bullying gave my ego fuel to fire up a belief system based on separation, unworthiness, and lack. By bringing the past into the present, the ego stayed alive.

Fear of the Future

Once the ego has convinced you that the fear of the past is real in the present, it then hooks you into the future. I was so afraid of the present moment that I began to project more fear onto the future. I was totally freaked out about going to college because as it was I was barely able to make friends in high school. This fear-based thinking, which dated back to being bullied in middle school, was brought into the present and projected onto a future college experience that didn't even exist yet. Projecting fear onto the future is another way for the ego to control your mind. Future-tripping is totally whacked out because the ego convinces you to project forward to attempt to control future outcomes. None of this is real. No one can control the future because it doesn't exist. However, it's a sneaky ego trick that will hook you into fear time and time again.

Self-Attack

In addition to my past- and future-tripping, I also got great at letting my ego attack me. In order to keep me in the dark my ego led me to attack myself and feel pain on a moment-by-moment basis. Self-inflicted pain is perhaps the sharpest kind of pain there is, and it makes me cringe just to think about it. I spent years attacking myself in my mind and in my actions: overeating, making poor and impulsive choices, judging myself or telling myself I sucked and that I was unlovable. Using drugs and alcohol only fired up the ego even more.

The ego uses self-attack to ensure that we feel pain. The *Course* teaches that if there is pain there is no love. Our egos have a tremendous need to hurt us in order to prove that we suffer and keep us believing in pain. As long as we're suffering, we see ourselves as separate from love, and the ego remains real.

Attacking Others

To make matters worse, the ego starts attacking others. Whenever we feel threatened or hurt by someone, rather than forgive them and remember that they're love, too, the ego will "protect" us from hurt by attacking. This "protection" is actually another ego trick for keeping the illusion alive. As long as we're attacking someone, we're reinforcing fear, anger, resentment, and lack of forgiveness. This is a funky trick because the ego has convinced us that this attack is "protection." Actually, the attack only makes us feel worse because we're deepening the illusion and strengthening the ego's separation.

Attack Thoughts

Attack goes on in our actions and, even worse, in our minds. I began to believe in attack thoughts of separation such as "She's only cool because her family is rich," or "My mom's a crazy hippie who doesn't understand my tortured reality," or "I don't need a clique because I'm better than them." By attacking others I felt as though I were protecting myself. Meanwhile, the only things I was protecting were my ego's illusions. Each time I'd gossip, feel jealous, or think nasty thoughts, I was attacking others and deepening my faith in fear.

The Problem

The problem was not something on the outside; the problem was in my mind. The *Course* says, *"It is your thoughts alone that cause you pain."* The problem isn't what's in the ego's bag of tricks, but that I chose to reach for the bag in the first place. Why did I reach for it? Because I forgot there was another way. The ego had worked so hard to convince me to believe in fear that I'd forgotten that love was an option. I had no idea why I was so uncomfortable and upset, so I grabbed the bag of tricks to find a solution. I'd reach for the ego's tricks to deny love by attacking others in an attempt to protect myself and keep the ego alive.

Wow, I can only imagine how heady this must sound to you. Hang tight. Rather than overthink these new concepts, just let the upcoming tools guide you. It is important that you don't judge the ego. *A Course in Miracles* spends a lot of time instructing us to look at the ego and not underestimate its viciousness. In fact, what you learn about the ego can be quite terrifying. As you begin watching your own thoughts, you see the ego everywhere. Don't freak out. Remember that the ego has had all of us in a headlock— you're not alone. Just witness the ego's tricks without judgment. The *Course* teaches us not to be afraid of the ego. It says that the ego *wants* us to be afraid of its thoughts; being afraid of the ego makes us believe in it. The *Course* teaches that the only power the ego has is the power we give it. The source of the ego's strength is in our mind.

This is reinforced in lesson five in the *Course* workbook, which teaches, *"I'm never upset for the reason I think."* Our problems are not the issues of the world that we choose to believe in, or the people we attack. Our problem is that we choose to deny love. In fact, we only have one problem: that our mind chooses fear over love.

In this first section of the book, I'm your guide to taking a good look at how the ego took over your mind. It is imperative that you understand what went down. The first step is recognizing that things are not working. If you find yourself saying "I'm not happy," then you're in the right place. The work of looking closely at the ego's tricks will help you see how the thoughts you've chosen to believe work to create what you perceive as your reality.

By fighting, suffocating, or trying to obliterate the ego we just make it more real. All you need to do at this point is witness. Take it one step at a time. By witnessing the shadiness of the ego you'll take one more step toward setting yourself free.

In this chapter your only job is to focus on how the ego's tricks have wreaked havoc. By witnessing the ego in action you'll begin to see how your mind has separated from love. Taking an inventory of this separation will help you understand how much of your fear isn't real—that your fears are delusional thoughts created by your ego. This step will guide you to begin to slowly disassociate from the fears you've come to believe in. By seeing that your fears stem from the ego's tricks you'll have a whole new perspective.

Examining Your Ego

Before we begin the exercise below, I want to be clear that I'm not suggesting you attack the ego. Once again, the problem isn't the ego; the problem is your *belief* in the ego. But don't judge yourself for choosing fear. You couldn't have known any better.

Now it's time to take a good look at how the ego has worked to keep you stuck in that illusion. This will be our first step in the undoing of the ego. You'll begin by asking yourself a series of questions to become more aware of the ego's presence in your life. This is followed by a freewriting exercise that throughout the book I'll refer to as an ~ing-write (inner guidance writing). You'll ~ing-write each of your responses in a journal. Take your time doing this writing exercise. Allow your subconscious to come forward and try to be aware when it attempts a retreat.

The next step will be to take a daily inventory of your ego, acknowledging its trickster ways. Your ego will be weakened each time you acknowledge its tricks because when you look at darkness without judgment, you shine light on it. This is detrimental to the ego because it cannot survive in the light. Our work together isn't about blasting light onto the ego overnight, but rather one day at a time *shining* light on the darkness of the ego to reconnect with love. Therefore, be patient and committed to becoming aware of how the ego has played a role in your illusion.

Take a Close Look

The work in this exercise will guide you to become honest about how the ego has been playing tricks in your mind. Before you begin to take an inventory of the ego, let's start with a meditation. Looking directly at the ego can be scary because the ego is afraid of being found out. Therefore, in this meditation I will prepare you to witness your ego's patterns clearly and without fear. Immediately following the meditation, answer the questions below. Trust that your

Witnessing Meditation

(For the audio version, visit www.gabbyb.tv/meditate.)

Sit up straight in your chair, with your feet planted firmly on the ground.

Gently breathe in through your nose and out through your mouth.

Breathe in: I welcome guidance.

Breathe out: I am willing to see the truth.

Breathe in: I am fearless.

Breathe out: I release attack.

Breathe in: I let go of the past.

Breathe out: I release the future.

Breathe in: I welcome the present moment.

Breathe out: I allow my inner guide to lead me to what is real.

meditation will take the edge off and lead you to truthful responses.

Gently open your eyes to the room and answer the following questions:

1. *What am I afraid of?*
~ing-write your response . . .

2. *How do I attack myself?*
~ing-write your response . . .

3. *How do I attack others?*
~ing-write your response . . .

4. *How do I bring my past fears into the present and future?*
~ing-write your response . . .

Spot-Check Your Ego

For a week or more, spot-check your ego throughout the day. Take a small notebook with you and, on the hour, every hour, take a fearless inventory of your ego.

Every hour, write in your journal the answers to these questions:

Did I deny love, and how?
Did I attack, and whom?
Was I fearful? What was I fearful of?

Remember not to judge yourself for having these projections. Once again, you've been doing the best you can with a lot of fear thrown in your lap. Just continue to witness your ego in action and have faith in my plan. Know that I've got your back. In the coming chapters you'll receive beautiful tools for releasing the pain and suffering of the ego. Right now, though, it's all about becoming aware and acknowledging the pain. This may in itself bring you some peace of mind. When I began to perceive my fear as created by the ego rather than by my true self, I immediately started to feel better.

Reflecting

The process of reflecting on the ego's crafty work is very powerful. Understanding the ego's tricks will help you move forward. At times you may get confused. That is to be expected. Remember, we're reconditioning years of thinking. You've probably become so accustomed to the ways of the ego that you believe they are real. In fact, I'm pretty confident that's the case. Your ego likely has convinced you that your problems are your reality. Therefore, you may hear your ego's voice inside say, *This is craziness. What does she mean, my fear isn't real? Isn't the drama at my job real? Aren't those mean girls real? Isn't the fact that I hate my mother real?*

Of course this will be your response, because the world of these fearful thoughts is what you believe in. But I'm here to guide you gently to detach from these worldly fears and begin to see in a different way. My work is to help you see that these fear-based "realities" around you are simply choices you made. They are blocks to love.

Remember that our work together is not based on finding love on the outside. Instead, our work is to release the blocks to the awareness of love's presence on the inside. So be fearless about this inventory. Look closely and stay honest. Get clear about the blocks so you can begin to remove them. On this journey, one day at a time you will remove these blocks as I guide you to remember love. The *Course* says, *"Children perceive frightening ghosts and monsters and dragons, and they are terrified. Yet if they ask someone they trust for the meaning of what they perceive, and are willing to let their own interpretations go in favor of reality, their fear goes with them. When a child is helped to translate his 'ghosts' into a curtain, his 'monster' into a shadow, and his 'dragon' into a dream he is no longer afraid, and laughs happily at his own fear."*

Each time we acknowledge that there must be a better way, our loving mind can begin to intervene. When we recognize the ego's role in our unhappiness, we invite love in to intervene. We must not look at our ego with judgment. Instead, we must begin to see our fear as a curtain rather than a ghost.

Be proud of yourself for taking this fearless inventory. Each time you witness the ego in action, you can perceive it as separate from you. Seeing your ego as a separate entity reminds you that you are not your fear. When you recognize that *you are not your ego*, you become more connected to your loving spirit. Lifting the curtain of fear takes guts, and I'm here to guide you through each step. In chapter 3 we'll boldly examine one of the ego's craftiest tricks: the "special relationship." Stay committed to this process, knowing that with each exercise we are one step closer to removing the blocks to your loving connection with the spirit within you.

3

Somethin' Special

The special love relationship is the ego's chief

weapon for keeping you from Heaven.

—A COURSE IN MIRACLES

◆

My First Idol

In high school I fell hard for the ego's mad idea. I was consumed by fear. As a result, I often felt unsafe when I was alone. I was on an endless search for solace in someone or something outside of myself. My mother often said to me, "Why can't you spend time alone? Can't you read a book and be by yourself?" Little did she know that I was afraid to be alone. When I was by myself, I had nothing to distract me from my anxiety and fearful thoughts. I'd hide out in someone else's reality so that I didn't have to deal with my own. To be super clear, it's not that I had a bad life in any way. In fact, on the outside it was all good. I had a great family, a nice home, friends, and all the trappings of what it takes to be happy, but on the inside I was a complete mess. I felt like Dorothy following the Yellow Brick Road in search of a wizard to save me.

When I was sixteen, I found him.

He drove a silver Beetle with black lightning bolts streaking down each side. The speakers and the clutch were lit up in blue neon. No joke, blue neon. He had a golden afro and sported a white tank top with belled-out jeans. He tattooed our astrological signs side by side on his thigh. His sign, Sagittarius; mine, Scorpio. He was a second-generation Arab Muslim dating me, a Jewish girl from the 'burbs.

I'm sharing this experience with you in an effort to teach you the meaning of idols. From the *Course*'s perspective, an idol is someone you make better than yourself, your friends, and your family. You believe your idol is your source of happiness. So *he* was my first idol, and man, did I dig him. He became my *everything*. He was my lunch buddy, my social life, my dance partner, my prom date, and my best friend. He was *it*. On his end, the only thing he loved as much as me was his band. They wore silver sequined jumpsuits and played a hybrid of ska and electronica. And like any good groupie I became one with the band. I'd do anything for him.

I thought he was incredible. I remember waking up on Valentine's Day to my mother screaming from the living room of our sixth-floor apartment. "Look out the window!" she yelled. I ran to the window to see that he had spray-painted a huge red heart in the snow. Inside the heart it read, "Happy Valentine's Gabrielle." I was living in a fairy tale.

This fairy tale lasted more than two years. Then he graduated, and my first idol fell. Nothing was the same after that. He went to college and was more interested in meeting new people and being away from home. He got totally hooked into college life and broke up with me. I was like Bella in *Twilight*. My Edward left me alone and I had nothing without him. And, much like Bella, without my boyfriend I was vulnerable to vampires. But in my case the vampires were in my mind. I remember staying in bed for weeks—maybe a month. I couldn't eat, sleep, or breathe. This love was my first drug, and now I had to come down from the high.

Something Special

Man, did I think he was special. In fact, this was my biggest problem in the relationship. I put him on a pedestal and turned him into an idol. I began to view him as above everyone else in my life (including myself). So I was completely devastated when he broke up with me. This act of turning someone into a worshiped idol is one of the craftiest tricks in the ego's grab bag. This trick in particular is what really took me down.

Throughout this chapter I'll offer up an understanding of how this trick furthers your belief in separateness and deepens the fearful illusion. I'll teach you about the "special love relationship" that the ego hooks you into with romantic partners. In addition, I'll show you how the ego makes all kinds of relationships and situations "special." You'll learn that this idolizing isn't all that special when you see its nasty effects. In fact, it is one of the ego's most powerful tools for keeping us stuck in the dark by separating us from others. Let's start with the "special love relationship."

The Special Love Relationship

When your source of happiness lives in the arms of another human being, you're totally screwed. The ego convinces us that all the love we need is in one "special" person. This is what the *Course* calls a "special love relationship." This kind of relationship differs from your other relationships in that you come to believe you need this person to be complete. The special love relationship is exclusive, and it makes that one special person better than you and everyone else.

My high school romance is the perfect example of the special love relationship. I made him my idol, my happiness, and my source of security in life. My ego convinced me that in his arms I would find all the serenity and happiness I was seeking. This was my ego's tool for keeping me stuck in the dark and away from my true source of inner love.

There is no way that special love can ever work. No one person can be your source of happiness. But without knowing where to find that true source, one will keep searching for it in all kinds of people, hoping to find *the one*. This was the case for me. The breakup only reinforced my limiting beliefs that I was unsafe on my own, so I began a committed search for yet another "one special love." I believed the only possible way for me to recover from the loss of my first idol and the hole inside my heart was to fill it with another special relationship. Just as when Bella turned to Jacob to recover from Edward, I, too, found my werewolf.

For the next ten years I overlapped relationships to feel "safe." I was so afraid of being alone that I totally compromised my own needs to stay in a relationship. Remember that this pattern was based on my ego's tiny mad idea from childhood, that without male attention I wasn't good enough. The ego had convinced me that without a man I was incomplete and therefore unsafe, taking my fear from the past and projecting it onto the present. In retrospect, I can see that this fearful addiction was based on the ego's lies. The story wasn't real, but it sure as hell felt real at the time. I was convinced of it.

This fear lived deep inside my mind and took over my reality. It kept me clinging onto relationships that were totally wrong for me, for fear of being alone. In addition, the fear made me completely inauthentic and insecure. For more than a decade I lived in a delusional nightmare of codependency and a search for that "one special love."

The Romantic Illusion

Sound familiar? I bet it does. I'm confident that the concept of special love will resonate with many readers. Romantic relationships are the ego's playground, and nine times out of ten our ego will turn the chance of romantic bliss into a freakin' nightmare. The ego feeds us illusions. What often happens is that we create a completely delusional story in our mind of who this person is, and how amazing he or she is. We project all kinds of special ideas, such as "When I have that ring I'll be happy," "He is all I need," "I'm complete now that I have love." Yada yada yada.

To make matters worse, the ego has convinced us that we cannot live without a "special" partner. This need for a special partner is a primary cause of codependency. Such fear-based thinking leads us to do whatever it takes to make people happy so that they don't leave. We become inauthentic and subservient so that we don't lose our special relationship. We put the needs of others before of our own, and deny our true feelings. We do all this in the name of special love.

This ego behavior is totally manipulative and chaotic. I was a hundred percent caught up in these types of codependent patterns owing to my belief in special love. I would do whatever it took to keep a relationship alive, even when it was clearly no longer working. I'd dress a certain way, try to "be cool" all the time, and always play it off as though I were super easygoing. The worst part was that I'd put my "special love partner" before all my friends, family, and personal goals. I'd reschedule my plans, go far out of my way, and bend over backwards to make my special love partner happy. Ironically, all the behavior that I thought was keeping them was actually turning them off. My inability to be authentic, mixed with an underlying needy energy, was not very attractive. Consequently, these relationships never had a long shelf life.

When, inevitably, the relationship would end, I felt as though my life would end with it. I was so afraid to be alone that I'd do anything I could to get into another relationship. This fear lived deep inside my heart. It was so real to me at the time. I felt as though I would literally die if I were alone. My happiness, serenity, and peace relied on my relationship status.

Future-Tripping in the Illusion

The ego also uses future projections to hook us into the illusion. Often we project specialness onto someone we've just met. One wink, flirtatious text, or hint of affection will lead us down the ego's road of special future-tripping. Within minutes, in our imaginations we're walking down the aisle and decorating our home. The ego will grab any shred of attention we receive, and become addicted to it. Our ego has the capacity to convince us that someone we don't even know is super special. This is clearly a romantic illusion.

Special Doesn't Stop Here

My special projections didn't stop with romance. I made my work special, certain friends special, celebrities special, and on it went. I had certain friends I'd spend time with at the drop of a hat, whereas I couldn't be bothered to answer the phone when others called. These were all responses to how "cool" I thought other people were and how "cool" I'd be by association if I hung out with them. I placed all kinds of outward projections onto others, which fueled my ego's illusion that everyone was different and that some were more special than others.

The concept of "special" is based on anything we make an idol of—anything we perceive as better than others or ourselves. The ego has all kinds of ways of convincing us that people are special. When we perceive that someone is more special than others, we're thinking with separation. We've forgotten that we are all one, and we've hooked back into the ego's thought system of better-than and worse-than.

The nastiest special relationship is the one we have

with ourselves. To this day I have to work very hard to combat my ego's habit of talking about how damn special I think I am. Flaunting our own specialness is a sign we've been hangin' with the ego for too long. In one way or another we've all made ourselves more special than others. Possibly you see yourself as more special than the intern in your office, or the homeless person on the street, or your younger sibling. The world around us thrives on this separation of more special versus less special. It shows up everywhere.

I've also found that we can do a back-and-forth special dance. At some of my most insecure times I'd see a pretty, put-together woman on the street and think, "She's better than me because she's thin," or "She clearly has better style than I do and therefore more money because she can afford those shoes." Then I'd reverse the specialness by "protecting myself" with a nasty comeback such as, "Whatever, that's last year's handbag and she's actually not as thin as I thought. I'm prettier than she is anyway." This thinking would reverse the specialness back to me.

The Special Teacher

Another major way our culture has created specialness is through the teacher-student relationship. When I began following Marianne Williamson's work, I idolized her to the max. I saw her as this guru who knew it all. When I became friends with Marianne and forged a personal relationship with her, I carried along this thinking. In my first letter to Marianne, I admitted that I was working hard not to make an idol of her. My willingness to open up about my ego's thinking really helped me release a bit of the special projection. Outing the ego is empowering because we are reminded that it's a projection in our mind rather than our reality. I'm not gonna lie, though: I work on this daily. I adore Marianne dearly and I have a hard time not seeing her as a special idol. But when I reconnect to the work, I remember that the light I see in her is a reflection of the light I see in me.

We're All Special

The *Course* teaches that we're all special. This is hard for us to grasp at first. Because we've spent so many years perceiving others as better or worse than ourselves, we cannot possibly see ourselves as equal. We've become so accustomed to thinking with separation that we have a hard time disassociating from the concept that everyone has an equal amount of awesomeness on the inside. This type of thinking gets people really tripped up at times.

"How Do I De-special a Relationship?"

Relinquishing our special ties takes a serious commitment to change. I once received an e-mail from a client saying, "I've tried meditating, praying, and praying again, and I still cannot release this special relationship. I've made him a McSpecial with a side of fries. How do I de-special someone?" I got a kick out of this e-mail. Her desire to *de-special* that one relationship was wonderful, but I explained to her that it's not about this one person in particular. The problem is our overall belief in the concept of specialness. I told her to take the focus off releasing this *one person* and begin to commit to releasing all the people she's made special. I guided her to witness the ego in action whenever the illusion of specialness came up. Her work was to take an inventory of whom and what she'd made special, including herself. Then I asked her to commit to a moment-by-moment perceptual shift of choosing to release the illusion of specialness.

No one can be expected to release the illusion of specialness overnight; therefore I guided her to understand that this was a long-term goal that would require daily practice and dedication. The goal of the exercises in this chapter is to help you recognize how the ego's special trick has separated you from others. By looking closely at your special illusions, you'll once again expose the ego to the light. If you're ready to take another stab at releasing your ego's illusion, check out the suggested steps for releasing the special relationships.

"DE-SPECIAL" STEP 1. WHOM HAVE YOU MADE SPECIAL?

The first step to relinquishing the ego's projection of specialness is to spot-check whom you've made special. This step is dedicated to taking a daily inventory of your ego's special projections. Look closely at whom and what you've made special. Ask yourself: Whom have I made the most special, and how? Maybe you've made your boyfriend special, or your teacher, or a celebrity. You can also look at how you've idolized certain things other than people, such as a job, a career path, or an ideal weight. Use your journal and write out all the ways you've created special relationships within your life. Shine light on those special relationships and make a list of your top ten. Include yourself in the list if it applies.

"DE-SPECIAL" STEP 2. OUT IT

One of the most powerful ways to release your special projections (even temporarily) is to out them. For instance, when I admitted to Marianne that I'd been making an idol of her, I was able to release the ego's power. By merely acknowledging that I'd made her special, we were both able to laugh at the ego's mad idea and begin to release the projection.

Once you recognize where your ego has created special relationships, you can begin to call them out. Speak openly about how you've perceived others, and stay committed to seeing things differently. You may not want to tell your special relationships how special you think they are; instead, just share with your friends. By outing your ego to a friend, you weaken the ego's projection and begin to see others as equal.

"DE-SPECIAL" STEP 3. CHOOSE TO SEE IT DIFFERENTLY

Combating the ego is a choice. In all situations we have two choices: see with the ego or see with love. Each time you witness your special projections and say them out loud, you have a choice to defend them or release them. The ego will work hard to keep you in the dark by reinforcing the specialness in others and yourself. Therefore, it is important that you continue to choose to see equality in others.

You can bring this choice into your daily practice. Whenever you witness that you've made someone special, choose in that moment to see things differently. This simple mental shift will do all the work for you. The moment you choose to deny the ego, you invite in love. Say to yourself in that moment, "I choose to perceive this person as equal and know that the light in them is equal to the light in me."

In addition to practicing this mantra, you can use meditation as a tool for releasing specialness. Through mediation you can reconnect with the essence of all people rather than the projections that you've placed upon them. Follow my lead and allow yourself to release special illusions through the following meditation.

De-special Meditation

(For the audio version, visit www.gabbyb.tv/meditate.)

Sit up straight in your seat, with your palms facing upward.

Breathe gently in through your nose and out through your mouth.

Identify a person you have made special.

Imagine their body entering into the room with you.

Looking directly at them, witness a ball of golden light forming in their heart.

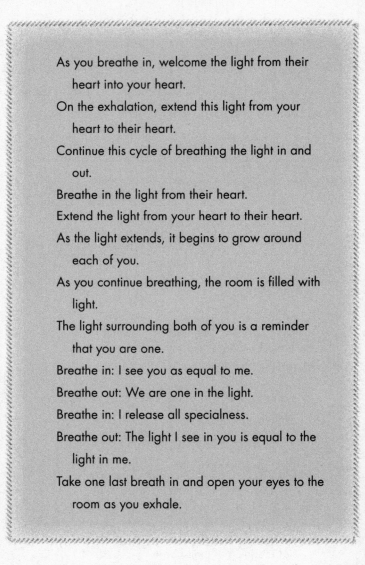

As you breathe in, welcome the light from their
heart into your heart.

On the exhalation, extend this light from your
heart to their heart.

Continue this cycle of breathing the light in and
out.

Breathe in the light from their heart.

Extend the light from your heart to their heart.

As the light extends, it begins to grow around
each of you.

As you continue breathing, the room is filled with
light.

The light surrounding both of you is a reminder
that you are one.

Breathe in: I see you as equal to me.

Breathe out: We are one in the light.

Breathe in: I release all specialness.

Breathe out: The light I see in you is equal to the
light in me.

Take one last breath in and open your eyes to the
room as you exhale.

This meditation is a powerful tool for reigniting your
inner belief in oneness. Each of us believes deep down that

we are all one. We know that specialness is just an illusion. We've just forgotten. Through meditation you can allow your inner guide to lead you to remember. Practice this meditation often to deepen your belief that we are all equally special.

Each time I call out the ego on the illusion, I weaken its strength. This is major work. Our ego has spent a lifetime convincing us of separateness and persuading us to believe in special forms of relationships. You may find yourself resisting this concept. That's cool. Just remember that whenever you make someone special you separate yourself from the opportunity to know true, connected love. You forget that we are all one.

I have to practice these tools often. I have a daily practice of releasing my special illusions, and I plan to be working on this until the illusions disappear. Who knows, it could take a lifetime. But regardless of how long it takes, I'm proud of the miraculous shifts I've already made.

As we continue on this journey together, I'll guide you to call on your ~*ing* often. Bring these three steps into all your lessons and know that your ~*ing* will lead the way. Relying on your inner guide is a major theme in the upcoming chapter as we begin to ask our ~*ing* for help. Turning to the help of your inner guide may seem difficult at first, but keep an open mind. Remember that the plan of the ego hasn't been working, and stay willing to see things in a new way. This willingness is all you need to allow spirit to help you out.

4

Ask~ing for Help

Trust not your good intentions. They are not
enough. But trust implicitly your willingness,
whatever else may enter.

—A COURSE IN MIRACLES

•—◆—•

In college I studied theater. This was the perfect major for me, because it let me escape from the world. Unable to find meaning in my own life, I chose to portray the lives of others. I didn't get it at the time, but the best actors are those who know themselves well—people who can travel deep into their own truth and bring forth their authenticity. I didn't even know what the word *authentic* meant back then: this led to a pretty difficult four years in a conservatory theater program.

During the first three years of theater school, I tried every which way to figure out how to make this degree program work for me. Finally, something got my attention. Third-year students were introduced to the Theater of the Absurd, a type of theatre developed in Paris during the 1950s. The work of the Absurdist playwrights expressed the belief that we live in a universe where human existence has no meaning, where attempts to assess our life's situation are absurd or essentially pointless. The Absurdist playwrights I studied focused on horrific or tragic images, characters caught in hopeless situations forced to carry out repetitive or meaningless actions, and plots that were cyclical or straight-up preposterous to our worldly minds. These characters resonated with me deeply. I was diggin' it. Playwrights such as Eugène Ionesco, Samuel Beckett, and Harold Pinter became my homeboys. I felt a deep connection to their work. These playwrights clearly had inner struggles going on, and their work made me feel as though I wasn't the only person wondering where we came from and why we were here.

I was still searching for meaning in my life. As I became more closely connected to Absurdist theater I realized that I'd become an actor on the stage that was my life. I was playing out archetypal roles that I thought were cool, acceptable, and worthy of acknowledgment. I now could see how my internal projector screen was showing the movie of my life. My connection to the Absurdist playwrights was another massive reminder that there was an existential way to view the world. I no longer felt alone in my inner beliefs. It was as if I'd been guided to their work.

More Denial

My college love affair with the Theater of the Absurd had a good run. Unfortunately, hiding out in the back of the theater reading Beckett had to come to an end. College graduation came and went, at which point I was tossed out into the "real world." I graduated in 2001, right after the dot-com bubble burst. Much like today, the economy had taken a turn for the worse. We were told that there were no jobs "out there" and to take whatever we could get. With a degree in theater and no desire to be an actress, I felt pretty lost. I interned, picked up odd jobs, and promoted parties to pay my bills. I continued to search for meaning in a seemingly meaningless reality.

Then, on September 11, 2001, things got way worse. I walked out of my apartment that morning to find people running north, covered in ash. I looked several blocks down Seventh Avenue and saw smoke pouring out of the World Trade Center. This was the end of the world as we knew it.

Like all New Yorkers, I have a story of where I was on 9/11. The horror of my story pales in comparison with the stories of people who were in the Twin Towers or who lost loved ones there, but it was an experience I'll never forget. Believe it or not, as much fear and terror as I saw that day, I saw an equal amount of love. The love I saw was overwhelming. Cabdrivers shepherded people uptown, neighbors acknowledged each other for the first time, strangers hugged on the street. Everyone was connected, it seemed. On that day our city released all separateness. No one was more special than anyone else. We were all one. There was so much fear around us that we had no other choice but to call on love for help. We prayed, lit candles, and prayed some more. We all turned to something greater than ourselves: we turned to love. I felt as though angels were looking down on us that day, smiling with pride as we turned to love for help.

I felt as though for a few months following 9/11 we held on to this way of being. People raised money, held hands, and took time off from their worldly priorities to be with family and friends. Then, when survival was no longer our concern, something seemed to shift. It felt as though as soon as we were slightly back on our feet, we forgot about love. At this point many of us turned to separation in a greater way than we'd known before, and ego ran riot. Politicians promoted spending, news anchors promoted fear, and racism took on a whole new form. Separation, attack, judgment, and fear were on fire.

In addition, many of us worked hard to numb our sadness. Like good New Yorkers, we drank, ate, and got back to work. Our "achieve" mentality was greater than ever. This was totally the case for me.

At this time, my ego's limiting beliefs spiked. In the wake of 9/11 I was living in the city, working odd jobs and single for the first time in years. In addition to the chaos surrounding me, I still grappled with the thought that I wasn't good enough unless I was in a romantic relationship or professionally successful. Since I was single, I felt as though I had to find another way to define myself. So I worked super hard to succeed in business. While all my friends were afraid not to have jobs, I was too afraid to have one. I needed to perceive myself as entrepreneurial in order to feel that I was doing something unique and remarkable. I needed a special identity. My drive for success was based on my ego's need to feel "special." So I jumped on the ego bandwagon and projected myself onto the world as a young entrepreneur.

I pulled together the skills I had acquired in theater school and in life. I was great with people and loved to promote things. This led me to position myself as a publicist. I'd been promoting parties at nightclubs for years, so I knew a thing or two about publicity. In addition, I could sell anything, thanks to my enthusiasm and determination to make it work. So I found a business partner, converted some nightclub owners into clients, and set up shop. With five hundred dollars in the bank, I incorporated my business, bartered for office space, and started invoicing for monthly retainers. My fear of not "making it" lit a fire under my ass to get my business off the ground—and fast.

I Was Somethin' Special

Now that I was an entrepreneur, *I had arrived.* Or so I thought. With this credential I had a new way of projecting myself onto the world: I was a twenty-one-year-old New York City entrepreneur representing the hottest nightclubs in town. My friends got off on the fact that all they had to do was say "Gabby" at the door to get access to all the hottest spots. I wore my title like a tattoo on my forehead. I thought I was pretty "special," and therefore better than most everyone.

My specialness led me to drop old friends and get totally hooked into the New York City "scene." Talk about illusion. This crowd was totally obsessed with the ego's projections. The scene was all about what we wore, what we did for a living, and who we knew. Those were the only details we cared about. No one even had a last name. It was Tommy the model, Jessica the door girl, or Mike the owner of [insert name of fancy company here]. This was all that mattered. Our egos projected our specialness onto one another to further our illusion that this world we'd created was real.

My need to feel special was not all that cool. Even though I'd found some way of perceiving myself on the outside, I still knew I was a fraud on the inside. I filled this hole with romantic relationships, binge eating, gossip, shopping, and the party scene. I stopped caring about my family and friends and instead became obsessed with the celebrity I'd brushed shoulders with the night before and being on the list at the latest new club. To make matters worse, my oh-so-special career was actually based on this crap. My business was promoting nightclubs.

Brief Encounters with Love

In the midst of this outside hustle, I could still hear my ~*ing* whisper from time to time. This whisper guided me to empower other young people with my career chutzpah. As a young entrepreneur, I'd been asked to speak at local universities on the topic of starting a business. Whenever I'd speak, I'd feel a rush of love come over me. I never needed to prepare my talks. It was as if someone were speaking through me. I flowed. After every lecture the young women in the room swarmed me. They were totally psyched to see someone their age out in the world, "making it." Little did they know I'd been out drinking till 4:00 a.m. But regardless of how hungover I may have been, something shone through me each time I lectured.

Around that time I was introduced to another young entrepreneur for business-to-business purposes. We'd meet weekly and brainstorm on how we could collaborate. Then one afternoon we started talking about all the amazing women we knew who had their own businesses. We agreed that they all needed some help promoting their ventures, and we decided to help them. In that one conversation we conceived the vision of the Women's Entrepreneurial Network (WEN), a network for women to connect and help further their endeavors. We immediately organized a networking event for all the female entrepreneurs in our Rolodexes. Three hundred women showed up.

WEN was a hit! It was too bad that the other areas of my life weren't flowing as freely as my speaking engagements and WEN events. Each day my business partnership grew more abusive, my addiction to the party scene intensified, and my need to be in a relationship amplified. I was on an endless search to feel good enough. And my ego had convinced me that everything I needed in order to feel complete was "out there." So I kept looking.

Shifting the Projector

After a few years in the New York City scene, my addiction to special romantic relationships began to dwindle as I became more obsessed with the special relationship with myself. I worked hard to convince myself that I didn't need a romantic partner to feel complete. This codependency began to look weak to my ego. I convinced myself that I was so kick-ass that I didn't need men as crutches anymore.

As soon as I made the commitment to be single, I transferred my addiction. I turned to my other love: partying. I put down the man and picked up the bash. This was an easy move for my ego. Once again I turned to something on the outside to complete me, and I found this completion in the nightlife scene. This was my home now, and the nameless faces in the club became my family.

Then I made a deal with the devil. My "casual" cocaine habit quickly morphed into a nightly routine. I didn't realize it while it was happening, but I was dying a slow death. I was hooked. The high I'd get from coke gave me everything I needed to stay out late and go home single. I lost my sex drive, my real friends, and more than twenty pounds. All the people I hung around with at this point were cokeheads. We were one and the same. I remember thinking, *Everyone does drugs.* Everyone I saw, anyway.

Hooked into the drugs as I was, there was still a whisper in the back of my mind reminding me of something better. I remember walking up to certain strangers in the nightclubs saying things like "You're good. And good knows good." I'm not sure whether this was prophetic or pathetic. I'd wax philosophical at after-parties, telling strangers about my plans to be a motivational speaker and self-help book author. I quoted the books I'd been trying to read and I proclaimed myself "super spiritual." I had no effing clue what spirituality meant, but there was something cool about perceiving myself that way.

Things spun out of control. Day turned into night and night turned into day. There was no weekend in my world. I was the girl out at the club on a Sunday wondering where the party was. I remember waking up to the clashing sounds of garbage trucks in the midst of a nasty hang-over after two hours of sleep. My addiction got dark really fast. Every morning around 5:00 or 6:00 a.m., I'd return home from hours of partying. As I was walking home, people were leaving for work. I remember walking past the subway seeing people going to their offices. I was going nowhere.

Coming down was the worst. I'd do whatever I could to come down without too much depression. I'd pop some kind of downer, like Klonopin (a prescription anti-anxiety drug) or whatever drug I could convince the doctor to give me. I'd write in my journal until I fell asleep. In each entry I'd write about how I needed to stop using drugs and clean up. But then I'd fall off the wagon later that night. My life was a nightmare and I couldn't wake up. I couldn't wake up because I was unwilling to ask for help.

Things got really bad. I had no real friends, my family was constantly disappointed in me, I weighed about ninety-eight pounds, and my voice was totally shot. My business was going under, my business partner wanted me dead, and my self-loathing was at an all-time high. I was severely de-pressed from the drugs, and I literally had lost my mind. I couldn't remember where I'd parked my car the night be-fore, or the name of the intern I'd hired a year earlier. I was a mess.

I Heard a Voice

My friends unsuccessfully attempted an intervention. It didn't work because though they weren't as bad as I was, they, too, were into drugs. I couldn't take them seriously. Then one night after a balls-out party I went home to try to come down and write in my journal. I remember writing, "I need help. God, Universe, whoever is out there . . . I surrender." Then I fell asleep. The next morning, October 2, 2005, I woke up to a loud inner voice. The whisper I'd been hearing for years was now a piercing call. The voice said, *Get clean and you'll have everything you want.* I was overwhelmed by this quick response to my cry for help. I had no other choice but to listen to the voice. It was clear that this was the answer.

Hear~*ing*

The voice I heard that morning is what the *Course* refers to as the Holy Spirit or Internal Teacher. I call it ~*ing* (inner guide or spirit). Our ~*ing*, as the *Course* defines it, is the intermediary between the fearful world of the ego and the loving mindset with which we came. The sole purpose of our ~*ing* is to guide our thoughts back to love. It is said in the *Course* that the moment we chose the tiny mad idea and separated from love, the spirit was placed inside our sleeping mind as a "call to awaken." The voice of our *~ing* dwells in what the *Course* refers to as our "right mind," and the primary function of this inner guide is to undo the ego's separation and guide our mind back to love.

Our *~ing* is always guiding us to use the world we see as a teaching device for reconditioning our fearful mind back to love. Our *~ing* is aware of all the pain, guilt, and fear we experience, yet knows none of it is real. When we turn to our *~ing* for help, we will always be guided out of the ego's illusions and into reality. Teaching us "true perception," the *~ing* guides us to replace our ego perceptions with love when we are ready to let those perceptions go. Our *~ing* does not judge our process and is patient as we're guided to learn. Our *~ing* is like a teacher who never gives up on us.

Our *~ing* is always on; we just forget to listen. As we become faithful to the ego, we deny the voice of our *~ing*.

Hitting Bottom to Hear

Often we need to hit a hard enough bottom to actually listen to the voice of our *~ing*. In my case I was so wrapped up in the ego's projections of the world that I was unable to truly hear the call for love inside me. I had to hit my knees and surrender in order to hear. This moment of surrender is what allows the voice to come through. It says in the *Course*, "*Trust not your good intentions. They are not enough. But trust implicitly your willingness, whatever else may enter.*"

It took a lot for me to surrender to my ~*ing*. I had to be a strung-out junkie to surrender and receive guidance. I'd hit rock bottom. Hitting bottom is actually a miracle because it creates a situation in which you are out of options and must ask for help. All the bottoms I've hit throughout my life collectively have been the catalyst for my greatest change. This bottom was my hardest, but in retrospect it was worth it. I had to fall apart to be willing to surrender to help and welcome in the voice of my ~*ing*.

I listened to that voice and have been sober since that day. The voice that intervened that morning was the voice of my inner guide. This was the whisper that had been with me for years, reminding me of a better way. I'd denied this distant whisper until I had no other choice. Hitting bottom and surrendering was the best thing that ever happened to me. It cracked me open and led me to hear the voice of my ~*ing* again. The willingness to hear this voice was all I needed to receive the guidance. The *Course* teaches that with the slightest willingness you will receive guidance from your inner guide. Our relationship with our ~*ing* is like having a mentor or a teacher. The ~*ing's* sole purpose is to guide our thoughts back to love. Listening to the voice of your ~*ing* is central to the teachings of *A Course in Miracles*. Asking your ~*ing* for help is crucial.

My clients often get tripped up about the concept of communicating with their ~*ing*. They've become so accustomed to letting the voice of the ego run the show that welcoming in a voice of love seems difficult and somewhat confusing. In fact it's quite the opposite. Establishing a relationship with your ~*ing* is meant to be simple. All you have to do is ask. A gentle surrender to the love that lives within you is all you need. I've laid out some key tools for opening your heart and mind to igniting your relationship with your inner guide.

Three Steps to Turning Your Will over to Your ~*ing*

STEP 1. GENTLY SURRENDER

You can't force the voice of your ~*ing* to come forth. It's important to realize that the loving guidance has always been inside you, so you don't have to fight to find it. You just need to slow down and surrender. You may have felt a connection to your ~*ing* while in savasana at the end of a yoga class, walking on the beach, or through meditation. What's happened in these situations is that you've slowed your mind down enough to hear the voice of your inner guide. Hearing your ~*ing* requires a gentle surrender.

This surrender is often thrust upon us, as in my case

when I heard the voice guide me to get sober. I had hit such a hard bottom that I had no choice but to surrender to another inner voice. As hard as that bottom was, my surrender was gentle. I released my will to the care of something greater that night when I wrote in my journal. I asked for help.

Regardless of whether you've hit a hard bottom or just want to change, I'm sure you're ready to receive loving help. Why not? All you need is to be open to the possibility of guidance and surrender.

STEP 2. ASK FOR HELP

There is a big difference between wanting help and asking for it. Your ~*ing* is always with you and always guiding you, whether you listen or not. But once you're willing to hear the guidance, the next step is to ask for it. The act of asking for help deepens your surrender and awakens the voice of your ~*ing*. Your ~*ing* loves to be called on.

There are many ways to ask. Some powerful ways to call on your ~*ing* are through prayer, journaling, and internal dialogue.

- *Prayer.* There is a prayer from the *Course* that I say each morning. It invites my ~*ing* to enter into my day and take the lead. The prayer is, *"Where would you have me go? What would you have me do? What would you have me say? And to whom?"* This is a powerful way to begin your communication with your ~*ing.* This prayer surrenders your will over to the care of your ~*ing,* allowing the guidance to come forward.

- *Journaling.* My first correspondence with my ~*ing* unconsciously came through in my journal the evening of October 1, 2005, the night before I got sober. The moment I wrote "I need help. God, Universe, whoever is out there . . . I surrender," I was speaking to my ~*ing.* Feel free to ask your ~*ing* for help through your writing. Trust me, you're being heard.

- *Internal dialogue.* When I first began to invite my ~*ing* into my life, I would connect through my internal dialogue. As I struggled with my sobriety, forgiveness, and fear, I'd internally ask my ~*ing* for help. This was like a silent prayer. Each time I'd ask for help through my mind, I'd receive a loving response of some kind. Sometimes my anxiety would lift just knowing that I'd surrendered my problem. Other times I'd literally hear my ~*ing* speak back. By simply asking for help in my mind, I would receive the guidance.

STEP 3. WAIT PATIENTLY FOR A RESPONSE

The final step in asking your *~ing* for help is to wait patiently for a response. Treat your *~ing* like a mentor you really respect. Know that the response you will receive will have a profound impact. Therefore, be willing to wait patiently—it's worth it. Most likely you'll receive a response quickly, and it can come in many different ways. Some typical ways you'll hear the guidance are outlined below.

- *Intuition.* We'll often hear our *~ing* as an intuitive feeling that comes over us. We'll feel as though we just know what direction to take. This intuition will not be based on fear; rather, it will come through as calm and peaceful. Our intuition will guide us to feel a certain way, to know something as truth, or to take certain action.

- *An inner voice.* Throughout the first few chapters I've been referring to this inner voice I kept hearing. You may think I'm a total nutbag, but I ask that you keep an open mind. When we hear the "voice" of our *~ing*, it is almost like we're reading a book. You know how when you're reading, it's almost like you're hearing the voice of the narrator come through the page? That's what our ~*ing* sounds like. It's an inner dialogue.

- *An external message.* Often our ~*ing* will bring us messages and guide us to certain circumstances to help resolve an issue. When I first began paying attention to my inner guidance system, I started to pick up on some super cool coincidences. For instance, whenever I'd ask my ~*ing* for help with an issue around my addiction recovery, I'd receive a phone call from a friend in my recovery program. It was like clockwork. It felt as though my inner guide had sent out a media alert that I needed help and my friends picked it up on the universal wire. These calls would come in almost instantaneously, and my friends would be there to help me work through whatever was coming up. My ~*ing* was working through others to help restore my thoughts back to love.

Connecting to our inner guide is very simple. All we have to do is surrender, ask, and patiently wait for a response. Begin your practice when you feel moved to surrender. Know that by simply picking up this book you've already surrendered to the guidance of your ~*ing*.

As we move into the next chapter you'll learn the most powerful tool for deepening your connection to your ~*ing*.

Chapter 5 focuses on the miracle of forgiveness. Forgiveness releases us from the ego's stronghold and reignites our faith in love. Through the tools in the upcoming chapter you'll learn new ways to let go of your ego's projections and deepen your connection to spirit's truth. The exercises thus far have led you to see your ego in action. Recognizing the illusions you've created in your own mind will help you see your part in all situations and therefore support your forgiveness practice. Forgiveness helps us transcend our ego's fear and reconnect with our inner peace.

PART 2
The Answer

5

The F Word

Do you want a quietness that cannot be
disturbed, a gentleness that never can be hurt,
a deep abiding comfort, and a rest so perfect
it can never be upset? . . . All this forgiveness
offers you, and more.

—A COURSE IN MIRACLES

inety days into my sobriety, I could see more clearly. Three months of detox, sleep, coffee, and recovery meetings really did me good. One day at a time I stayed clean and rebuilt my life. I was showing up for myself big-time.

My recovery program emphasized forgiveness. There is a collective understanding within the sober community that serenity is a must-have and forgiveness is nonnegotiable. The core belief system is based on surrender and detachment from our old ways of being. This group and these principles offered a powerful bridge back to life.

One of their primary suggestions was to get on my knees and pray. I had no idea to whom or what I was praying, and I felt totally odd getting on my knees. *But I wanted what they had, so I did what they did.* I got on my knees every morning and every night and recited their suggested prayer. At first this ritual felt awkward, but with time I grew to like it. I felt I was making a commitment while connecting to a power greater than myself. I began to feel a lot physically while praying. At times I literally felt as though someone were standing above me, gently pressing me down as I prayed. I took this as a sign that I needed to stay down and keep praying.

Praying for myself became a daily practice. I asked for guidance, serenity, and peace. I asked for another day clean. This was difficult at first because I was so angry at myself for how I'd treated my body, my family, and my friends. I had a lot of cleanup to do. The people in my recovery program guided me to take a fearless inventory of my actions and recognize my shortcomings. Then they led me to release them to a higher power, aka God. The terminology behind this recovery work was new to me, but I was open to it nonetheless. Though I had no relationship with this "God," I was open and willing to learn. My recovery program reinforced that we could create a "God of our own understanding." This theory was much easier for me to wrap my head around. I always intuitively felt that there was something out there looking after me—a greater power. For years I'd felt this presence, but had no idea how to define it or consciously connect to it. I was relieved to know that all the guidance, energy, and intuition I'd felt throughout my life wasn't crazy after all.

To create a deeper connection with this Higher Power, I was guided to strengthen my practice of self-love and forgiveness. A major step in this process was to boldly assess my negative patterns. This process was profound for me. By taking this inventory I came to understand that fear was a common cause of most of my issues. Fear of being alone, fear of not being good enough, fear of getting too fat, fear of not having enough—the list goes on. Fear sat in the director's chair, calling the shots. Once I understood that fear had been in control, it was easier for me to forgive my past. I was able to honor myself for doing the best I could with an ego that had taken over my mind like a virus. I knew now that I had a disease in my mind. By praying for the release of these defects I was able to slowly begin to let go of the anger I felt toward myself. I was able to see myself with love for the first time in a long time.

My Dark Fantasy

When you first get clean, you're likely to experience a "pink cloud" period—you're super psyched to feel healthy and clear-headed. This was the case for me. Life began to flow and things got way better. Then, out of nowhere, my pink cloud turned gray. As soon as my ego got word that I was happy, it reached into its bag of tricks and took me down fast. Just because I was clean didn't mean I'd kicked my ego's patterns. The ego had a lot to latch on to, as I still was undergoing residual backlash. I was *feeling* for the first time in years, and therefore a whole bunch of shit was dredged up—everything I'd been numbing with the drugs. Even though I was praying every day and working on forgiveness, I still felt a tremendous amount of guilt, anger, and sadness over the wreckage from my past. The guilt I felt was the perfect tool for the ego to hook me into the illusion that the world was out to get me, and that I was unworthy of love.

To make matters worse, my ego created a whole new projection of specialness. I thought I was super special for being sober. I thought I was better than all the people I'd been partying with, better than my old friends, better than my business partner, and way better than anyone who needed drugs and alcohol to have a good time. This was a new kind of special that hooked me back into the ego's illusion of separation.

The Wall

For many people in early sobriety, the act of getting out of bed is an accomplishment. In my case I had no choice but to get out of bed to keep my PR company alive. My drinking and drugging hadn't done much for my business partnership, and it sure as hell hadn't done much for our bank account. So, in the midst of my personal recovery, I was rebuilding a business. Because I'd been such a hot mess for the majority of our professional relationship, my partner didn't have much reason to believe in me—even if

I was ninety days sober. Her resentment was strong and she wasn't ready to let it go. I know in her heart she was proud of me, but she wasn't willing to forget.

This drove me crazy. I felt as though I was constantly under a microscope. Not to mention I felt terrible if I ever needed to change a plan or come in late. This was the ego's way of keeping me stuck in the past. My ego had convinced me that not showing up on time or changing plans was horrific because it was something I used to do when I was hungover. Now when I had a legitimate reason to change plans or come in late, my ego would go nuts, making me feel terribly guilty. This was the perfect example of the ego taking a past experience and replaying it in the present moment. As a result, I was always on the defensive.

I brought up this issue in my recovery meetings. Week after week I'd bitch and moan about my resentment toward my business partner. But rather than join my hate parade, my friends in recovery guided me to see my part in the problem. They helped me see how I was perpetuating the dynamic by defending my current actions and projecting my own guilt onto her. They suggested I continue to pray to fully forgive myself. This I was willing to do. Then they suggested I pray for her. This confused me. *Why should I pray for her?* I thought. *I am the victim of drug addiction and I am the special one getting sober.* They encouraged me to get over myself and take their suggestion. They asked me to pray for her to have all the peace and happiness I wanted for myself. Most important, they suggested I be willing to forgive her.

They taught me that by defending myself I was making things worse. There is a lesson in the *Course* that reinforces this concept: *"In my defenselessness my safety lies."* By defending against her anger toward me, I was reinforcing the illusion. My defense was adding fuel to the fire and reiterating that I'd done something wrong. By choosing defenselessness instead, I could stay in the present moment rather than dig up the past. This was hard at first, but I was willing.

Release

Despite my willingness, I still hadn't officially thrown down the *F* word and forgiven her. I was toying with the idea, but had trouble committing. Then that winter I took a ski trip out west with a friend. Her flight back home left before mine, and mine got canceled due to a snowstorm. I was left behind and psyched to have another day to ski. I woke up the next morning and was the first person on the chair lift. As I traveled up the lift I looked to the right and to the left, and all I could see were snow-capped mountains and a clear blue sky. I gazed down at the mountain covered in powder, thrilled that mine would be the first skis to hit the snow. I was in heaven.

Then, like clockwork, an ego thought burst my love bubble. I immediately started obsessing about having to face my partner the next day in the office. I got hooked into the idea that she'd be mad at me for coming back a day late even though I was snowed in. This ego tornado was about to rip through the peace of my snow day.

Then I experienced a divine intervention. I heard an inner voice say, *Forgive her.* These odd voices and moments of peace were becoming the norm. I was getting used to hearing this inner voice, and I was now fully willing to listen. So I took the suggestion from my inner guide and I said a prayer. I prayed for her to have all the peace and happiness that I wanted for myself. Then, in an instant, something lifted. I immediately felt lighter and more serene. I could see my surroundings more clearly and I could breathe more freely. I released my anger and forgave. Free from my resentment, I felt my skis hit the powder and I flew down the mountain, unburdened and exhilarated.

My Dark Fantasy Turns to Light

From that day forward our relationship was never the same. I was a big step closer to knowing the miracle of forgiveness. I learned that forgiveness isn't just about letting the other person off the hook—it's about releasing ourselves. When I forgave her I set myself free from the bonds of the ego. The ego had convinced me that I was separate from her and that I was the victim. This perception that I was a victim led me to attack her in order to protect myself. It also led me to defend against her illusion, thereby reinforcing it. This is a vicious cycle. The darkness I saw in her was a reflection of the darkness I believed to be true in myself. Sure, it seemed as though I'd been harmed and that I couldn't possibly forget. But holding on kept me connected to the projection of being the victim, making me feel like crap on a daily basis. I'd wake up each day to rehearse the role of victim.

The only way out for me was through forgiveness. By choosing to forgive and perceive her with love, I released myself from the ego's story. I realize now that I wasn't mad at her; I was mad at myself for believing in the projection of hatred that we'd created. I knew in my heart that only love was real, and that she was just projecting her own fear onto me. I knew deep down that she wanted to see with love, too. I set myself free by choosing love over fear.

Not only did I feel relieved, but I noticed a massive shift in her energy. The day I got back, she didn't bother me about coming in late. In fact, she was happy to see me. Our dynamic had shifted because I had shifted. The outside world reflects our internal state, and when we shift our perceptions, the world shifts accordingly. The newfound light I saw in her was reflecting back at me.

Practicing the *F* Word

Forgiveness is totally awesome. When you connect to light within others, you can see them as equal and release your resentments. If the light in you reflects the light in them, you can choose to see only their light. It is your choice to forgive and release the darkness. It is your choice to see with love.

Forgiveness tears down the ego's walls of separation and reunites us as one. The anger and fear of the ego's illusion disappear. There's no more "he said, she said." It all just lifts. It feels as though chains have been removed and you've been set free from a lifetime of terror. Why continue rehearsing the role of victim when you could be free and happy?

Now is the time when I throw down "the F word" and start teaching you the *Course*'s tools for forgiveness. I will break it down in four steps. While there are suggested steps, the process of forgiveness is unique to everyone. There is no specific time frame, and no need to rush the process.

The first step is to recognize how the ego has been attacking others. The second step is to know that the attack on others is merely an attack on you, and to become willing to release the illusion. Finally, you'll let your ~*ing* take the wheel and guide you to forgive. All you'll need for transformation is some willingness and your ~*ing*. Now let me break it down for you.

Breakin' Down the F Word

F WORD STEP 1. RECOGNIZE THE ILLUSION

"An unforgiving thought does many things. In frantic action it pursues its goal, twisting and overturning what it sees as interfering with its chosen path. Distortion is its purpose, and the means by which it would accomplish it as well. It sets about its furious attempts to smash reality, without concern for anything that would appear to pose a contradiction to its point of view."

This passage from the *Course* reinforces the destruction that occurs when we're unwilling to forgive. I spent four years letting this distorted way of thinking dominate my professional relationship. My willingness to see this differently and recognize my unforgiving thoughts launched the forgiveness process.

The first step toward forgiving my business partner was to recognize the illusion that my ego had created. I looked closely at the situation, and witnessed how I'd made myself the victim and made her wrong about everything. I'd decided to see only her anger and resentment and focus on her darkness. Upon looking more closely at the situation, I realized the darkness was not in her, but was an illusion I'd created in my mind and played on loop. I had two choices. I could choose to look at her darkness or to see her light. By choosing to look at her darkness, I was amplifying the darkness that existed in my mind.

Recognizing that this was my choice didn't mean I ignored her part in the situation. In fact, the *Course* says, *"This does not deny the darkened spots of sin in someone, but only that they are irrelevant to my perception."* I was able to acknowledge her negativity, but chose not to hook into it. Remember that you have a choice in what you see. If you choose to see a person's darkness, you strengthen your darkness within. If you choose to see their light, you shine from the inside out.

Once I genuinely understood that the darkness I chose to see in her was amplifying more darkness inside me, I was willing to release her. I saw my projection clearly and was open to release what the *Course* calls the "wall I had placed between us."

This is a challenging step. You'll realize what is taught in lesson 190 of the *Course*, which is that the gun you've been pointing at others you've actually been pointing at yourself. In other words, the guilt is not in the other person, but rather, as the *Course* says, "I *am the secret murderer.*"

Though this may not be comfortable, it is a crucial step. Simply look at the ways in which you've chosen to focus on the darkness rather than the light. Ask yourself, *How have I chosen to see darkness in this situation?*

F WORD STEP 2. RELEASE JUDGMENT

"Forgiveness, on the other hand, is still, and quietly does nothing. It offends no aspect of reality, nor seeks to twist it to appearances it likes. It merely looks, and waits, and judges not. He who would not forgive must judge, for he must justify his failure to forgive. But he who would forgive himself must learn to welcome truth exactly as it is."

This passage from the *Course* guides us to see how judgment reinforces our unwillingness to forgive. By judging my partner, I kept our unforgiving dynamic alive. Once I released my judgment against her, I was able to take a huge step toward forgiving her. Take this time to acknowledge how you've been judging those people you need to forgive. Ask yourself, *How have I been judging?*

F WORD STEP 3. BE WILLING TO FORGIVE

An awesome line from the *Course* reads, *"Do you prefer to be right or happy?"* It's far too often that the response is that we'd rather be right. Being "right" doesn't get us anywhere. We can bend over backwards to reinforce the idea that we're victims, but that doesn't make us feel good. The willingness to release the need to be right is a major step toward forgiveness. This step will guide you to the happy fact that all you need to do is be willing to release the role of victim and choose to see something different.

As soon as I became willing to stop being right and start being happy, I was able to welcome in an opportunity to forgive. Without my willingness, I wouldn't have been led to forgive my partner that day on the ski lift.

Look closely at the choice you have made, and become willing to choose differently. Say out loud, "I am willing to release the wall that I have placed between us." Then sit in meditation and let me be your guide. You can use the written meditation below or download my guided meditation from www.gabbyb.tv/meditate.

F Word Meditation

Begin your meditation with this silent prayer:
"Inner guide, please lead me to know the truth.
Lead me to release all attack, fear, judgment, and
anger. Help me forgive.

I welcome forgiveness as my safety, serenity, and
inner peace.

I welcome happiness and release.

Thank you."

Sit up straight in your seat.

Take a deep breath in through your nose and let it
out through your mouth.

Continue this cyclical breath.

In your mind, invite in the image of someone you
have been resenting, possibly even yourself.

See this person standing before you.

Look them in the eye.

Breathe in: I am willing to forgive you.

Breathe out: I see the truth and the truth is only
love.

Breathe in: I choose to see the light in you.

Breathe out: The light I see in you is a reflection of
my inner light.

Breathe in: I choose to forgive.

F WORD STEP 4. ASK YOUR ~ing FOR HELP

"Do nothing, then, and let forgiveness show you what to do."

The final step is simple. The *Course* teaches that this step is not our responsibility.

Once you look at how the ego has kept the illusion alive, you see how you've chosen its dark fantasy. The *Course* suggests that you look at the darkness without judgment, and remember to laugh at the tiny mad idea of separation. When you do this, you can release this mistake to the care of your ~ing. Know that when you turn to your ~ing for help, you can release the illusion and be led to forgive.

Once I looked closely at the darkness I'd focused on in my relationship with my partner, I was able to see that it was my choice. Then, by releasing my judgment of her and becoming willing to forgive, I was prepared to turn to my ~ing for help. The final step was the easiest. I just prayed each day to let my ~ing intervene and set me free from my resentment. I didn't know how or when I'd forgive her, but I knew guidance was on the way. I remained patient, allowing my ~ing to take the lead.

Now let your ~ing step in. Ask for help and remain patient as your inner guide transforms your thoughts back to love, releasing the illusion for good. Begin a daily prayer practice of asking for help and releasing your resentment over to the care of your inner guide. Say out loud, "I choose to see this differently; thank you for guiding me to forgive." Then be patient. You cannot control when or how forgiveness will come. Just stay willing and open to forgiveness. Your ~ing will show up in many unique ways. For instance, I had no idea I was going to forgive my partner on a ski lift! There's no way I could have planned that.

Just stay willing and open about this process, and you'll learn that "*the secret walls of defense are no longer needed, and so have disappeared. In their place is the light of forgiveness, which shines the way to the home we never left. And thus it is no secret we are healed.*" Forgiveness is the bedrock of the spiritual journey you have embarked on with me. Through forgiveness you can shine light on the darkness of the ego and find inner peace. In the next chapter the *F* word will come in handy. I will teach you how my *Course* work has taught me that all relationships are assignments. Through my dedication to forgiveness, I've been able to show up for these assignments with love and grow more spiritually connected. Take this powerful tool with you as we continue to add new layers to your journey back to love.

6

Relationships Are Assignments

No one is sent by accident to anyone.

—A COURSE IN MIRACLES

Early addiction recovery is like plugging the holes of a sinking ship: once you plug one hole, another one appears. This was the case for me. As soon as I put down the drugs and the alcohol, all my other addictions flooded back in. I turned to food, work, shopping, and relationships to avoid dealing with my ego's fear. Overeating was a great way for me to numb out at first. I'd plan each meal hours in advance for a sense of control. Then I'd binge to fill myself up. This pattern kept me focused on something other than my pain.

At first I just ate over my feelings, and then I began to date over them. When overeating no longer worked, I turned to my best avoidance tactic of all: romantic relationships. Sounds like a broken record, right? It is. The ego replays the same projections over and over to keep us from healing. Rather than focusing on inner growth, my ego convinced me to keep looking outside for serenity and peace. Though I was feeling much healthier, I was still hooked on the ego's illusion that I wasn't safe without a man. I jumped in and out of six-month relationships, with someone always waiting on the sidelines. My codependency followed me around like a sick dog. This was very shameful for me.

To make matters worse, I continued to repeat the same patterns in all my relationships. *Remember, the ego takes the fear from the past and projects it onto the present and the future.* These insecure patterns were based on my deep-rooted fear of someone leaving me alone. Therefore, I'd do whatever it took to keep the relationship going. This played out in some super-whacked-out ways. For instance, I tried to be cool by going along with whatever the guy liked—I was never my authentic self because I wanted to be what I thought they wanted. I denied my truth. Playing the role of "cool girl" never worked. Ironically, this behavior was the opposite of what men wanted. They wanted to be with a confident, authentic woman—not a girl trying to act cool.

My ego's pattern was to hold on to the relationship by manipulating someone to view me as cool so they wouldn't leave. This created a very nasty dynamic because though I was acting "cool" on the outside, I was a complete mess on the inside. My mind was in a constant frenzy, obsessing over when he'd call, when we'd get together, and what the future held for our relationship. My ego nailed me with the future-tripping. Within a week of entering a new relationship, I'd fast-forward to see myself walking down the aisle and celebrating our son's bar mitzvah. This future-tripping stemmed from my ego's belief that one "special" person would save me as soon as I had a ring on my finger. Even though I never voiced these thoughts, I know the energy behind them was apparent. No matter how cool I acted, I always gave off a vibe that I was needy, insecure, and incomplete without a man. This energy was totally vile; therefore, the relationships would always end. Worst of all, I felt terrible that I didn't have enough self-love to combat the ego's projections of special idols.

Sin and Guilt

Now that I was sober and committed to the lessons of the *Course*, I could witness the chaotic patterns I'd play out in my train-wreck romantic relationships. By this point in my recovery I was wise enough to recognize that I was caught in another ego pattern. This made me hate myself. I could see clearly how I'd turned my back on love and let the ego mindset take the wheel. Each day I spent stuck in my co-dependence disconnected me from spirituality. This decision to forget love and choose fear made me feel as though I'd done something wrong. This is what the *Course* refers to as "sin." Though I didn't realize it, deep down I felt I'd turned my back on my loving truth.

The inner belief that I had sinned drowned me in guilt, which came from the fact that my mind had joined with the wrong teacher, the ego. Each time I'd spin out in some addictive relationship pattern, I'd feel guilty about it, as though I'd killed the potential for happiness and self-love. Guilt is the feeling we experience as a response to the belief that we've sinned against love—it's a projection of the sadness we have for neglecting love. Whenever we choose the ego over ~ing, we subconsciously think we've sinned and therefore feel guilty. Think about it. If deep down we believed that only love was real, wouldn't we feel devastated if we dropped that love and picked up fear instead? Of course we would! That's why we feel so crappy when we choose the ego over love as our teacher. We think we've done something terrible, and we also think *we* are terrible. Unconsciously we believe we deserve punishment because we turned our back on love.

The involuntary feeling of having sinned against love really brought me down. Guilt arose from this sadness. This guilt was inevitable because deep down I knew that I was denying this awesome other way of being. Underneath all my codependent patterns was an inner cheerleader reminding me that I was independent and wonderful. Instead of listening to that voice of love and recognizing that the problem was in my mind, my ego instead focused on special romantic partners to keep the illusion alive.

Since we don't realize the problem is in our mind, we take that guilt and project it outward. This creates more guilt. Then we seek guilt in everyone and everything. Projecting guilt onto others is a really crafty trick. Each outward projection keeps us from recognizing that the problem is in our mind. If we don't recognize it in our mind, the ego can survive. Therefore the ego leads us to believe that we can relieve our guilt by attacking others and projecting sin onto them. For instance, whenever I felt guilty I blamed the outside world. I blamed my incompleteness on the guy who didn't like me, the client who ended the contract, or the friend who wasn't returning my calls. I did this rather than recognize that the only incomplete problem was my belief in incompleteness. The ego's "protection" of guilt actually creates more of it and we become unconsciously attracted to it.

Denial

To keep me from turning inward for help, the ego reached into its bag of tricks and pulled out denial. The ego denied love in order to keep me stuck in the darkness, convincing me that fear was my only source of safety. By denying love, the ego made fear my companion. Therefore I needed to hold on to these projections in order to function in the fearful world I'd accepted—once again the ego convinced me that all of the safety, security, and peace I was seeking was in the arms of a special partner.

To further deny the potential for love, my mind became more convinced of my inadequacy and unworthiness. I held on tightly to the stories I'd grown to believe in: "I can't be alone," "I'm not good enough for them," and so on. By digging up my inadequacy the ego hooked me back into idolizing my romantic partners and seeing myself as separate. By separating myself from these romantic partners I was denying my own greatness and perceiving them as better than I was. The ego's denial protected my belief in fear. Though things were getting better in most every area of my life, the ego held on to my fear in romantic relationships. It held on for dear life.

Feeling Like a Fraud

I lived for a while in this pseudo-recovery mode, still battling my codependency, in and out of the guilt cycle. Though the ego had cornered this one area of my life, I still grew tremendously in all others. I stayed sober and worked on my spiritual practice, prayed, forgave, and positively changed many aspects of my life. This work was so inspiring to me that I felt the desire to share it. My former lecture-circuit routine of speaking on panels and in classrooms about entrepreneurship and marketing had now shifted. At this point I was more interested in lecturing on happiness and recovery than on vocational topics. In addition, I had fully released my PR career and had begun supporting myself as a life coach and speaker.

My work was well received. I believed deeply in what I

was teaching, and my messages resonated with many young women. My lecture rooms grew from forty people to a hundred within a few months. The lecture halls looked like sample sales, only the women were searching for happiness rather than a discount on designer clothes. My coaching practice began to take off, and I was doing this work full-time.

I loved lecturing and coaching—but deep down I still felt guilty. Even though I'd made miraculous changes in my life, my ego was still in the driver's seat when it came to my romantic relationships. I was paralyzed by the fear of being alone or not being good enough for a romantic partner.

The guilt got worse when I started coaching young women on their relationship issues. I remember guiding one of my clients through a breakup. I taught her the *Course's* messages of how the ego makes romantic partners into idols and how the relationship was an assignment. In the midst of my lesson I felt overwhelmed with guilt. I knew in my gut that I was a fraud. I heard my ~ing say, *Get it together, girl! You need to teach this stuff. It's time to kick this fear once and for all!* This inner voice screamed loud enough for me to stop avoiding and surrender. I couldn't continue this cycle of replaying my ego's romantic fears only to feel guilty that I'd denied love, and I no longer felt satisfied by projecting this guilt onto others. I had to turn down the volume of my ego and release this limiting belief once and for all.

Willingness to See Relationships as Assignments

My willingness to change was all I needed. The *Course* had taught me, *"What is concealed cannot be loved, and so it must be feared."* I couldn't conceal my issues in relationships any longer. It was time to shine light on the problem and be willing to release the ego's stronghold.

With the slightest willingness I was guided. It so happened that my *Course* study at this time was focused on how relationships are assignments. *A Course in Miracles* tells us that all relationships are chosen by our ~*ing* for one purpose: to learn to see each other as love. The *Course* teaches, *"When you meet anyone, remember it is a holy encounter. As you see him, you will see yourself. As you treat him, you will treat yourself. As you think of him, you will think of yourself. Never forget this, for in him you will find yourself or lose yourself."* After reading this I could breathe again! In an instant it became clear to me that my romantic dramas were an opportunity for growth rather than a lifelong prison sentence. This part of the text taught me that I was guided to every relationship to transcend the ego's belief in separation, that if I welcomed each encounter as a holy encounter, I could learn to stop judging, fearing, attacking, and making others special, and instead see them as one. See them as myself. All I had to do was welcome the holy encounter. It was time to stop hiding from these awesome assignments and let the healing begin. So I committed to rip off the Band-Aid and let my ~ing do her thing.

I turned to the *Course* for further guidance on how I could show up for these so-called "holy encounters." I quickly learned that each relationship we enter into offers us two options: to show up as two separate people looking for completion in one another; or to show up as two whole people coming together to enjoy their wholeness. Now, I didn't know too many people I considered whole, and it became clear to me that I wasn't alone. We all had work to do! And if we waited until we were fully healed before we started a relationship, we'd put Match.com out of business. Therefore we have to recognize relationships as assignments that will bring all our neuroses to the table. When we show up for these assignments we can start dealing and begin healing. The *Course* positions relationships as one of the most significant opportunities for us to learn and grow. Through another person we can come to know ourselves.

When we're stuck in the ego's illusion, we believe that all our encounters with others are random and accidental. Before I could see my patterns I envisioned each romantic partner as someone I'd stumbled upon or met at a bar or through a friend. Now I understand that none of these relationships was accidental. The *Course* teaches the opposite: there are no chance encounters. When we perceive the relationship as an assignment, we can begin to see how our intentions have created perfect opportunities for either ego misery or transformational growth. If we're willing to grow spiritually and call on our ~*ing* for help, we'll be guided to the perfect relationship assignment that will provide us with the best possible learning opportunities. If we're unwilling to grow, then we'll continue to play out the same crazy crap in all our relationships. The form of each relationship assignment is unique, but the goal is to come together to ignite the memory of love.

Now that I understood that relationships were assignments, I agreed to show up for whatever came my way. Since I was willing to change, I knew that I'd be guided to the perfect romantic partner. I was psyched for my next relationship because it was time to get to work. However, my idea of the perfect partner was much different from what the Universe had in store for me. I thought I'd be guided to a nice guy with whom I could share and openly work through my issues. What I really needed was the exact opposite. If I were truly willing to release my pattern and show up for the assignment, then I'd be guided to the "perfect guy" who'd dig up all my shit so that I'd have to surrender to and choose love over fear. And that's what I got.

Mr. Big Assignment

Once again I called in the same type of relationship that I'd been attracting for over a decade. He was handsome, smart, artistic, cool, and totally unavailable. I feared this at first, but deep down I accepted it as my assignment. This guy was perfect because he'd bring up all my issues around not feeling worthy without male attention. Had I entered into a relationship with a guy who doted on me, I wouldn't have had a chance to grow.

Each day in this relationship was a struggle. My deep desire to feel complete on my own battled with my horrifying need to be saved. This inner turmoil went on for several months. I acted out in all the old ego ways by attacking myself, attacking him in my mind, and fueling my fear of abandonment with my ego's crazy mind games. None of the ego's stories were real, but neither was the relationship. What I wanted out of it was not what I was receiving. This brought up all of my issues. I felt inadequate and less-than. I made him super special and idolized him like crazy. I held on tightly to this relationship and did everything I could to seem cool in his eyes.

In the midst of all this old behavior, I knew there was a better way and I was still willing to accept it. I wasn't sure how I'd fully release my ego in this area, but I did the best I could to cope. It wasn't that he was a mean guy; he just wasn't that available. He was super into my professional success . . . and other than that, pretty into himself. I was crumbling on the inside, wishing he would want what I wanted and manipulating him with ass-kissing and a "cool girl" attitude. This was manipulation because it wasn't my truth. I acted like this to try to make him stay.

After a year in this unfulfilling relationship I had to find solace. I'd spent my nights crying and my days paralyzed by the fear of losing him. I was desperate for relief. I'd hit bottom, and it was time to ask for help. So, rather than continue jumping through hoops for his attention, I hit my knees and started praying.

~ingTervention

It's funny how willing I was to surrender certain issues to my ~ing, whereas I let my ego run the show with my relationships. This area of my life was the ego's stomping ground in my mind, and surrendering was an incredible challenge. But I was no longer willing to stay chained to the ego. There were no more quick solutions to this problem. No "five steps to getting a man" or "six steps to 'I do.'" None of that worked. My only option was to put down the practical and pick up the spiritual. The *Course* taught me that I couldn't recover from the ego on my own. I needed an ~ingTervention. My *Course* work had taught me that when you welcome the Holy Spirit (~ing) in for guidance, you will receive. The *Course* says, *"The Holy Spirit always sides with you and with your strength. As long as you avoid His guidance in any way, you want to be weak."* I had to side with the strength of something greater than myself. Once again, I turned to my ~ing for help.

My ~*ing* had hooked me up every time before, so I followed the *Course's* suggestion to invite in my inner guide for help. I got on my knees each morning and night. I kept asking for help. I still wasn't clear about whom I was talking to, but I pretended it was a big sister or a friend. I'd say, "Inner guide, I need a hook-up here. Once again I'm obsessing over a guy and I am ready to release this cycle. Show me what you've got!"

Though I didn't feel immediate relief, I noticed many moments of guidance. For instance, a friend invited me to a lecture that provided me with great spiritual tools for releasing romantic illusions. I also continually heard about books that were powerful for overcoming codependency and love addiction. Then I was guided to a women's group that came together to support one another's codependent patterns. Whether I knew it or not, I was being guided. I replayed Marianne Williamson's audio lecture *The Language of Letting Go* over and over like a Top 40 hit. She cited the *Course's* messages on forgiveness and release, and reminded me to welcome the assignment and remain willing to change.

Letting Spirit Take the Wheel

I began to see my ~*ing* get to work. All the guidance I was receiving was tremendously helpful. I relished my meditation, Marianne's audio, and my recovery groups. I experienced many moments of relief and began to feel taken care of. I was still acting out with my ego in romantic relationships, but I was making progress. I accepted progress rather than perfection and I stayed down on my knees in prayer.

The *Course* teaches that prayer is the medium of miracles. When we pray for our *~ing* to help, we welcome a new perception. In our prayer we release our control and stop trying to manage every detail of our lives. I felt this deeply. When I prayed I allowed a power greater than myself to take control. I welcomed in guidance, I welcomed in a shift in perception, and I created a miracle. In this case the miracle was that I began to feel better and allowed my *~ing* to lead me to heal.

Welcome Your Own *~ing*Tervention

The purpose of this chapter is to help you begin to see your relationships as assignments. Once again we'll follow the *Course* and keep it simple. Rather than try to figure out each issue and find a solution, you'll just turn to your *~ing* for help. Allow an *~ing*Tervention to occur and let spirit lead you to see what you need to learn from all relationships. My willingness to let spirit lead me is what enabled me to show up for my relationship assignments and stop denying my fear. The fact that I'd called on my *~ing* for help is what allowed me to hear it fully. Our *~ing* is guiding us all the time, but if we're not open to receiving, we'll miss the guidance. Therefore, this chapter is an opportunity to bring your ~ing into your relationships. As the *Course* teaches, "*It is only in relationships that salvation can be found.*" Allow the following steps to guide you as you begin to see your relationships as opportunities to heal. These exercises will shine light on the dark illusions the ego has created in relationships. You, too, can experience miraculous guidance as soon as you stop manipulating and start praying.

Be Willing to See the Assignments

We can apply the following steps to all relationships in our life. We begin by welcoming in the assignment. If we're unwilling to receive the assignment, we'll continue to bulldoze past it and stay stuck in the illusion. That's no fun. Remember, the ego's illusion in relationships kicks up all its nasty tricks. In all ego-driven relationships you will attack, judge, and make separate and special. The ego goes to town when other people are involved. Once we understand that each encounter is an assignment, we begin to illuminate the ego's tricks.

Look at the Problem as It Is

Witness how the ego has set up your relationships. Whenever we perceive a problem we project it outward, typically onto others. We start to tell ourselves, *The problem's not in me, it's in someone else.* This lesson will help you see that all our suffering comes from a belief in our mind—a wrong-minded choice to believe in fear. The *Course* suggests, "*No one can escape from illusions unless he looks at them. For not looking is the way they are protected.*" Rather than shrink from the illusions of the ego and avoid the problem, we can simply look at it. When we acknowledge that we created the problem in our mind, we can see how the ego interfered. This is when suffering ends. The moment we recognize that we've chosen incorrectly, we can choose the right teacher. That is the miracle. In my case, I recognized that I was stuck in the ego's guilt cycle by teaching others to be fearless when I was stuck in fear—and that moment led me to ask for a miracle. The miracle helps us recognize that we've chosen to believe in the nasty world of the ego, and that it is not real. The miracle occurs when we remember that fear is not real. We have chosen to dream the dreams of separation and guilt so that we remain asleep in the ego's nightmare.

If we truly want to end our suffering, we must recognize that *we* put it there and that we chose it in our mind. When we recognize that what we've experienced is of the ego, we can then invite spirit in. Spirit can enter into our mind to heal the ego's projections, reminding us that we are all one. Suffering and sickness come directly from the feeling of separation. The healing comes from realizing that we are not separate from anyone.

This exercise is designed to help you see that your problems are not external to you, but instead are in your mind. Most of this work is about truly realizing how we've grown to trust the ego over love. Each time we look at the ego directly, we come closer to knowing it is not real. Take your time with this exercise. Each time you witness yourself projecting fear onto others or blaming a relationship for your problems, gently remind yourself, *The problem is not in them, it's in my mind.* Acknowledging this truth will guide you to become willing to welcome an ~*ing*Tervention.

Welcome an ~*ing*Tervention

Begin your work with a practice of reviewing your relationships. Look closely at how the ego has played a role in each one. Ask yourself, *What is my assignment?* and then sit in meditation for five minutes and let your ~*ing* respond. For additional guidance you can download my "Meditation on Relationships" from www.gabbyb.tv/meditate. Allow my voice to guide you as you welcome in your *~ing* for guidance.

Meditation on Relationships

In silent meditation we welcome in guidance to
see all our relationships as holy.

Sit up straight in your chair with your feet planted
firmly on the ground.

Gently breathe in through your nose and out
through your mouth.

Identify your most challenging relationship.

Invite your inner guide to remind you of your
interconnectedness.

Breathe in: *~ing*, help me see love in this
relationship.

Breathe out: I welcome this assignment.

Breathe in: Thank you for helping me change my
mind about my wrong projections.

Breathe out: Thank you for reminding me of what
is real.

I welcome in the holy encounter where I can see this
person as my equal. Where we are both love.

~ing-Write

Immediately following your meditation, pick up your pen and ~ing-write (freewrite) for ten minutes. The topic of the ~ing-write is "How have I projected my fear onto others?" Let your pen flow and allow your ~ing to guide you to understand your assignment.

Show Up

It's one thing to recognize the assignment, but it's another thing entirely to show up for it. Remember that showing up for the assignment is one of the most powerful ways to restore your thoughts back to love. By seeing love in the face of another person you know the true meaning of oneness. Allow all your resentments to become assignments and show up for them one day at a time.

Know that you'll receive all the support you need along the way. Keep in mind that your ~ing works through people; as the *Course* says, *"No one is sent by accident to anyone."* Pay attention to those who are there to serve your growth. Listen and be guided.

In the coming chapter you'll deepen your understanding of the holy encounter. Take your work from this chapter with you as I guide you to deepen your faith in miracles. By committing to the work, you will learn to rely on your ~*ing* rather than on your ego. As you start to feel the relief of choosing love over fear, you'll come to wonder why you ever chose otherwise.

7

The Holy Instant

The holiest of all the spots on earth is where an
ancient hatred has become a present love.

—A COURSE IN MIRACLES

sking my ~*ing* for help became a daily habit. This practice of constant contact with spirit activated the guidance around me. By consciously asking my ~*ing* for help, I experienced tons of synchronicity. People I needed to connect with would call out of the blue, books I needed to read fell off the shelf, and I felt a strong overall sense of connection to the Universe. I didn't perceive any of this as coincidence or dumb luck, but rather as frequent messages from my inner guide.

Then the synchronicity became even groovier. One of my neighbors suggested I set up a business-to-business meeting with a woman named Rha Goddess, who, like me, worked to empower young women. A week later, another friend independently suggested I meet Rha Goddess. These back-to-back referrals were enough for me to accept the Universal memo and e-mail her to schedule a meeting. She responded to my e-mail by saying that she couldn't meet right away because she'd be out of the country visiting a spiritual healer in Brazil. I was shocked: I, too, was going to be visiting the same spiritual healer, the same week as

Rha. I flipped out over this synchronicity, but it didn't seem to faze her.

Though there weren't many people at the spiritual grounds in Brazil, we never did meet there. On the flight home, I connected to the woman sitting next to me on the plane. I told her what I did for work and that I lived in New York City. She replied, "You must meet this woman." She then handed me the business card of Rha Goddess. I laughed as the Universe hit me over the head yet again. One week after I got back from Brazil, I traveled to New Orleans for Eve Ensler's V-Day event (a global activist movement to stop violence against women and girls). When I got there, I looked over the line up of performers and speakers for the first day. Rosario Dawson was speaking on the main stage at noon, followed by Jane Fonda at one o'clock and then, at two, a poetry performance by guess who? Rha Goddess! Clearly I needed to meet this woman. The guidance was so apparent that I felt overwhelmed with joy. I loved this magnificent synchronicity because it reinforced my faith that I was being guided. I was able to see clearly how my ~ing was leading me to Rha for some important reason.

Finally we met. After her performance, we gave each other a big hug and laughed about how a power greater than ourselves was working hard to get us together. We agreed to set up our long-awaited meeting later that month.

We decided to meet for dinner in Brooklyn. The dark, rainy day mirrored my state of mind. As usual, I was tripped up about my romantic relationship. Even though I'd been showing up for the assignment and taking many fearless actions, I was still trapped by the ego with the fear of being alone, not being good enough, and feeling incomplete. In an effort to release some of this fear, I spent the entire day meditating.

Finally I pulled myself together and drove to Brooklyn to meet with Rha. The moment we sat down, we began talking about our personal lives rather than business. Remember, we didn't know anything about each other except for what we could glean from a few Google searches. She told me about her spiritual beliefs and her coaching practice. She also told me about her magnificent husband and how she had manifested the relationship. She explained how she got over her negative relationship patterns and became clear about what she wanted in order to free up space to call in her man. She exuded light when she spoke about her husband and their relationship. Then I heard my ~ing speak loudly: *Ask her to be your coach!* I listened to my ~ing and said, "Do you still coach people?" She responded, "In fact, I do. Each year I coach a handful of people who are already deep into their spiritual journey. My work is to take them to the next level. I coach people just like you."

From that day forward Rha was my coach. It was clear to me that my call for help was answered. Spirit works through people. When we ask our ~ing for help, often it comes in the form of another human being. Many times these people we're guided to will turn out to be our greatest teachers. In this case my ~*ing* was leading me to meet the perfect guide for releasing my romantic illusions.

Showing Up for the Assignment

When the student is ready, the teacher appears. I was ready to get to work. Rha and I agreed that releasing my romantic illusions topped my list of things to work on, and she put me on a six-month plan of facing those demands. She helped me become even clearer about how I was limited by my belief that I was incomplete without a man. She helped me feel past wounds and honor all of my feelings as equally important. Then she guided me to become honest and unapologetic about what I wanted in a romantic partner. Finally she helped me realize how my current relationship had taught me everything I could learn at that time, and that it was no longer serving me. All this work, combined with my *Course* studies, led me to create some miraculous shifts.

Patiently Receiving Guidance

Within six months of working with Rha, I had more clarity than ever before. For the first time in my life I was unapologetic about what I wanted in a romantic relationship.

It was clear that my desires did not match up to my current relationship. At first this revelation really kicked my ego into high gear. I judged my boyfriend for not being able to give me what I wanted, and my mind went into attack mode. However, this type of ego thinking no longer resonated with me. I had shone a lot of light on this dark area of my life, and through my *Course* work and Rha's coaching I was able to choose not to judge and attack. Rather than go all psycho on him, I decided to throw down a forgiveness F-bomb and let him go. I welcomed in the idea of releasing this relationship once and for all. I had been using the relationship as a crutch, and it was time for me to walk on my own.

My intuition guided me to take my time with this departure. Had I rushed through the breakup, I'd have been screwed. My ego would have nailed me with fear, self-attack, and second-guessing. Therefore I took my time to release him properly in my mind before I released the form of the relationship.

Once again I turned to the *Course* for help. The *Course* teaches that when we forgive, we're recognizing that whatever we think someone has done to us actually has not occurred. It's not about pardoning someone's wrongs; it's about seeing them as *not wrong* in the first place. I didn't fully comprehend this at first. Rather than let my logical mind figure it out, I brought it to my prayer and meditation. I prayed out loud, "*~ing,* help me forgive him and release him. Help me see him as innocent." Then I sat in a meditation in which I allowed my ~ing to create new thoughts and intervene with my ego. I visualized him entering into my meditation as I saw myself sending light from my heart to his heart. After a few minutes I began to see great rays of light pouring from the top of his head down to his toes. These same great rays of light were pouring from my head to my toes. I felt overwhelmed with a feeling of love. Eventually my image of our bodies was no longer visible, and all I could see was light. I felt at peace. All that was left was love.

Coming out of the meditation, I reflected on the experience through an ~ing-write. In my writing I came to realize that I didn't need to forgive my boyfriend for something he'd done. I was guided to do quite the opposite. My ~ing led me to see how false my attack and judgment had been. For instance, all my anger toward him was based on what I'd projected internally and perceived externally. My mind projected thoughts like "All men leave," "I'm not good enough," and "He's not giving me what I want." I was projecting my fear onto him, thereby perceiving him as a total asshole.

By realizing that I'd perceived this about him based on my own internal projector, I was able to begin to let him off the hook. This in turn led me to become even clearer about how my thoughts had created my reality. I came to realize that he was doing the best he could to manage his own ego's projections. I could now see how I'd forced my need to be saved onto a guy *who didn't want to save me*. Rather than realize this, I'd made him wrong for not meeting my ego's needs. This revelation offered me tremendous relief. As soon as I shifted my perception I began to see him with love. I saw him as innocent, accepted him, forgave him, and released him. I let great rays of light shine over the darkness.

The Holy Instant

My experience of releasing my boyfriend through the guidance of my ~ing is what the Course refers to as the "Holy Instant." The Holy Instant is the release of the illusion by way of forgiving the illusion itself. Once I recognized his innocence and saw my fear as the only problem, I was able to forgive the illusions my ego had created. The Holy Instant is the moment when we choose our ~ing instead of the ego as the teacher. By turning to my ~ing for guidance, I let love intervene through my mind. I called on spirit to help me see my boyfriend differently and to deepen my understanding of forgiveness.

This experience didn't just lead me to a deeper understanding of forgiveness—it showed me the true meaning of a miracle. The Course teaches that the shift in perception is a miracle. The moment I chose to perceive my boyfriend as innocent, I was able to love and accept him. In an instant, all my attack thoughts, judgment, separateness, hatred, and fear lifted. I experienced the Holy Instant. As the *Course* says, *"The holiest of all the spots on earth is where an ancient hatred has become a present love."* This present love was all I needed to release the illusion once and for all.

Letting Go

The Holy Instant prepared me to step up to the plate and face my biggest fear. After a morning spent in prayer and meditation, I headed to my boyfriend's apartment. With full confidence and love I told him how much I appreciated our time together and that I accepted that he wasn't able to give me what I wanted. I owned my part and apologized for controlling or manipulating the relationship in any way. My final words were, "I accept you, I forgive you, and I release you." He was somewhat disappointed but proud of me. He said, "That's the most mature breakup I've ever experienced." We hugged good-bye and agreed to remain good friends. I released him.

Slowing Down to Receive Guidance

This was the first time that I fearlessly walked away from a relationship without having another guy waiting in the wings. Most important, it was another step I'd taken toward truly understanding the meaning of forgiveness. I was proud of the work I'd done with Rha and my commitment to the *Course*.

In retrospect I can see how spirit was always guiding me. I was guided to the perfect assignment: the unavailable guy. Then my willingness to ask for help guided me to Rha, who would help me work through my limiting beliefs. Finally, I was guided through my meditation to choose my *~ing* over my ego, forgive my boyfriend, and release him. The guidance was working through me the whole time. I was led to the Holy Instant.

We are always being guided, even though we often block it. The *Course* work opens us up to witness the guidance and co-create our lives with spirit. Each time we surrender and ask our *~ing* for help, we will receive a loving response. Then we have to be present enough to receive it. The receiving step is crucial. The moment I stilled my mind through meditation, I was led to see my boyfriend as love and light. Had I chosen not to meditate, but instead to try to figure it all out on my own, I wouldn't have allowed the Holy Instant to occur. Receiving the Holy Instant happened in the midst of my stillness. Through prayer we surrender, and through meditation we receive guidance. I had to slow down in order to receive the miracle.

Practicing the Holy Instant

The *Course* teaches that you cannot bring the Holy Instant into your awareness if you don't want it: "*Your practice must therefore rest upon your willingness to let all littleness go.*" Littleness is the plan of the ego. Our ego believes that there is a way to control the outcome of all situations through an outward action. Our *~ing* does the opposite by taking care of fearful thoughts internally. By turning inward for the miracle, we accept that spirit has a much better plan than we do, and we allow the guidance to flow.

All we need is to want the Holy Instant and fully release this desire to the care of our inner guide. The *Course* asks that we surrender *our* plans for happiness and let our *~ing* take over. By releasing our plan, we release the ego. The goal is to value no plan of the ego before the plan of our *~ing*. In the matter of ending my relationship, I prayed, meditated, and received. My willingness to release my ego's plan for happiness allowed my *~ing* to intervene. Choosing my *~ing* over my ego created the miracle of a loving breakup.

Daily Practice

The *Course* teaches: *"You can claim the holy instant anytime and anywhere you want it. In your practice, try to give over every plan you have accepted, for finding magnitude in littleness. It is not there. Use the holy instant only to recognize that you alone cannot know where it is, and can only deceive yourself."*

Each time we turn all conflict over to the care of our ~*ing* we experience an internal shift. We open the door for spirit to intervene and offer creative possibilities. These creative possibilities come through our mind in the form of thoughts like "Maybe I should see it his way," or "I have a part in this, too." These ~*ing*-driven thoughts allow us to see the situation with love and therefore bring in forgiveness as our primary tool for release. Through forgiveness we experience the Holy Instant, where *"an ancient hatred becomes a holy love."*

Accepting our ~*ing*'s plan on a daily basis will guide us to a feeling of inner peace. This is a simple practice. When you turn your thoughts over to your ~*ing*, you don't have to figure anything out. There is nothing complex about this. The only complexity is in your mind. Recognizing the simplicity of this practice supports our commitment to the Holy Instant.

The *Course* says: "*You could live forever in the Holy Instant, beginning now and reaching to eternity, but for a very simple reason. Do not obscure the simplicity of this reason, for, if you do, it will be only because you prefer not to recognize it, and not to let it go. The simple reason, stated simply as what it is: The Holy Instant is a time in which you receive and give perfect communication.*"

By giving over our desires to the care of our inner guide, we will receive everything we need. The simplicity lies in the fact that our *~ing* is always right because spirit thoughts are based on love. With love there is an answer and a miraculous outcome for everything. Our job is to get into the practice of choosing love all the time. Since I'd been practicing thinking with my *~ing*, the step of choosing love began to be involuntary. This is the goal: to turn to love more often than to fear, so that one day, love is all that's left.

A Timeless Practice

This practice does not require time; it requires willingness. Once again, you don't have to *do* anything but be willing to receive guidance. Your willingness opens up your mind to communicate with the love of your *~ing.* When you're trying to make something happen, you're communicating with your ego. Your *~ing* won't ask you to change anything on the outside. Instead it will guide you to change your mind. Surrender your thoughts to your ~ing for help. By choosing to let spirit intervene, in a short time I was able to release an illusion that had been plaguing me for twenty-eight years. Choosing spirit is the path of least resistance—and the solution.

Our next step is to begin practicing the Holy Instant. By now you've become clear about your ego's patterns, surrendered them to your ~ing, asked for help, and turned your will over to the care of your inner guide. But as demonstrated by my story, the work doesn't end there. You need to stick around for the miracle! It's time to start practicing the Holy Instant in all our affairs. The more frequently we choose our ~ing, the more faith we'll have in the guidance we receive. The miraculous shift requires our faith because the shift is in our mind. Welcome in the Holy Instant and start to truly shift your perceptions and create miracles.

Communicating with Your ~ing

The *Course* teaches, *"Every thought you would keep hidden shuts communication off, because you would have it so."* When you stop asking your ~ing for help you temporarily put the communication on hold. This was true for me for nearly three decades. I was stuck in my fearful relationship patterns because I wasn't allowing my ~*ing* to intervene. There was no potential for loving internal dialogue because I was letting my ego run this part of my life. But as soon as I seriously invited in my ~*ing* for help I was able to receive the guidance and open up the lines of communication.

In order to practice the Holy Instant, we need to communicate our desire for help. Begin communicating with your ~*ing* through prayer. Say out loud or in your mind, "Inner Guide, thank you for helping me see this with forgiveness, acceptance, and release."

The purpose of this prayer is to surrender your issue to the care of your ~*ing*. By truly giving it away, you receive guidance. The reason I suggest your prayer include the words "thank you" is that they imply that the prayer has already been taken care of. The words "thank you" reinforce our faith in spirit. Just be willing to ask for help and say the prayer out loud or in your mind. You can even write it on a piece of paper. Just put it out there and know that it's being heard.

Meditat~*ing*

Immediately after your prayer, sit in a meditation. I will guide you in this step through the written meditation below or through the meditation you can download from www .gabbyb.tv/meditate is titled "Great Rays Meditation." It is imperative that we calm our mind and allow our ~ing to come through. Otherwise our ego will think over the guidance. After asking your ~ing for help, continue the communication through meditation. The meditation step was powerful for me in creating the Holy Instant. In my meditation I was able to still my mind and clearly receive guidance.

Great Rays Meditation

To activate the Holy Instant, pray out loud or in your mind.

Then sit up straight in a seat or on the floor, with your palms facing upward.

Take a deep breath in through your nose and let it out through your mouth.

Continue this breathing throughout the meditation.

Hold in your mind the relationship that you need help with.

Identify the area in your body where you may be feeling discomfort around this situation.

Breathe deeply into that area of your body.

On the exhale, release.

Say in your mind, "I turn this fear over to my
  inner guide for transformation. I welcome the
  guidance."
Breathe in: I welcome guidance. I see you with
  light.
Breathe out: I release fear.
Breathe in: I choose love and light.
Breathe out: I accept this.
Breathe in: I welcome in great rays of healing
  light.
Breathe out: I choose to see only love and light.
Continue these mantras and allow your ~ing to
  guide your thoughts.

~ing-write

Right after your meditation, pick up your pen and begin
~ing-writing. Write at the top of the page, "How can I see
this with love?" Then begin freewriting.

Let your ~ing do her thing . . .

Where Is the Love?

Next, pay attention to where there is love in your ~ing-write. There may be some residual fear, but most likely the words coming through were compassionate and forgiving. Highlight the lines that resemble your willingness to forgive. Look closely at the love that you've offered up onto the page. This was the most enlightening step for me. When I chose to see love, I was able to see my boyfriend's innocence—he was doing the best he could. In addition, I was able to see how he'd become the victim of my illusion. By honestly witnessing your part in the situation, you'll come to see the innocence in others. Become clear about how your ego has created this illusion, and choose love over fear.

Let Your ~ing Host the Party in Your Mind

The *Course* says, *"In your practice, then, try only to be vigilant against deception, and seek not to protect the thoughts you would keep unto yourself. Let the Holy Spirit's purity shine them away, and bring all your awareness to the readiness for purity he offers you."*

Now that you have the tools for creating the Holy Instant, it's up to you to invite it in. This thinking began to sink in for me because of my willingness to invite spirit in for help. The more I conversed with spirit through prayer and meditation, the more I allowed loving guidance to enter in. Allow your ~ing to host the party in your mind, and politely remind your ego that it's not on the guest list. Practicing the Holy Instant makes us host to love rather than hostage to fear.

Practicing the Holy Instant will prepare you to grow your relationship with spirit. In the coming chapter I'll share my experience of how I truly embraced spirit as my guide. As we continue on, stay connected to your prayer and meditation practice. Through this work you will receive more and more guidance to help you welcome a new way of perceiving the world. As you'll see in the coming chapter, choosing love over fear makes for awesome experiences.

8
Accepting My Invitation

Seek to change nothing, but merely to accept everything.

—A COURSE IN MIRACLES

◆

For more than fifteen years my mother has been living with a health condition. She spent a decade relying solely on holistic healing methods. Acupuncture, homeopathy, Reiki, juice cleansing, and a good old meditation practice did the trick for quite some time. Her willingness to receive alternative methods guided her to all kinds of unique health-care approaches. Most significantly, she was guided to a spiritual healer referred to as "John of God." This man is known throughout the world for performing miraculous healings, which can cure all types of life-threatening conditions and deepen one's spiritual connection.

Soon after she learned of this John of God, it turned out he was visiting the States and healing at The Omega Institute (a spiritual center) fifteen minutes from her home. She signed up immediately to visit him and receive a healing.

At first I balked at her plans to seek help from John of God. I chalked it up to one of my mom's hippie retreats. My ego judged her for not following the western approach to healing. Though I perceived myself as "open and spiritual," my ego clung to science and familiar healing methods as the primary treatments for diseases. Therefore I remained uncertain about her visit to see John of God from Brazil.

Despite my skepticism, she held fast to her belief. She visited John of God and came home beaming. Reflecting on the day, she spoke of the thousands of people dressed in white, powerful energy, and many miraculous healings. She'd watched John of God say a prayer over a woman in a wheelchair—within seconds the woman stood up and walked for the first time in years. His healing was shared through the exchange of energy and through powerful loving intention. People shared stories with my mother about how they recovered from cancer, depression, and many other life-threatening conditions. These stories empowered her and strengthened her faith in his work.

She went on to tell us about her personal experience with the healer. "He asked me to come to Brazil," she said. She explained that he invited certain people to visit him at his spiritual hospital in Brazil to receive further healing. My mother then exclaimed, "I know he can help me, and I'm going to Brazil."

"I'm going with you," I said. The words flooded out of my mouth. I had no idea why I was so quick to respond— it was as if someone were speaking through me. Everyone (including me) was confused by my instantaneous pledge. Only an hour earlier I was skeptical of John of God, and now I was signing myself up to travel across the world to see him?

Immediately I realized what I'd committed to, and felt a bit freaked out. I was not one to make impulsive decisions. But there was no turning back; my mother was already on the phone with the travel agent, booking our flights. She was thrilled to have a companion on her healing quest. I took her happiness as a sign that I was to accompany her and support her healing. Little did I know I was in for some major healing of my own.

Synchronicity

In the short time leading up to our trip, I received many signs of guidance. When I'd gotten in touch with Rha Goddess, she told me she'd be visiting John of God at the same time. In addition, several people mentioned his name in the months leading up to my trip, which was odd because I'd never heard of him prior to my mother's discovery. It didn't stop there: every part of the planning process was fully guided. The moment I decided to pick up the phone to coordinate some travel details, the travel guide contacted me out of the blue—at the exact moment I was calling her. Each time one of these synchronistic occurrences took place, I felt less and less skeptical. I saw them as signs of guidance.

Accepting My Invitation

We arrived in Brazil on March 15, 2008. The trip had awakened a lot of dormant feelings. I was reminded of my adolescent experience at the ashram; once again I was in a supercharged spiritual environment, surrounded by people seeking healing. At the ashram, however, I'd been largely unaware of my own energy and the energy of others. I'd also been in a much funkier place in my life, which led me to attract funky energy. I remembered what my mother told me about how I had the capacity to pick up other people's energy. Remembering this made all the difference: I was prepared. Not to mention I actually felt blessed with positive energy rather than weighed down by negative energy.

I was twenty-eight at the time of my visit to Brazil. At this point in my career, I was a full-time life coach and lecturer. I was teaching spirituality to the best of my ability, though in many ways I felt disconnected. I was teaching from my head rather than from my heart, which made me uncomfortable. I knew spirituality wasn't just about theology. It wasn't enough to understand the concepts on a detached, intellectual level. I wanted to *know* my own experience of spirit and teach from an authentic place.

The first night in Brazil, I spent hours journaling. At

one point I wrote, "I want to know what spirit really means to me." In that moment I signed another sacred contract with the Universe. I'd set a new intention through this written prayer, and man, oh man, was my prayer answered. By making this commitment I was accepting the invitation to know a deep spiritual connection.

Each day in Brazil brought new learning and miraculous occurrences. In the morning we'd visit the spiritual hospital where John of God performed his healings. I was drawn to this space like a magnet. Each time I approached the building I felt a rush of love come over me, as if energy was passing through my body. As the week went on, I felt more and more subtle yet astonishing physical sensations. My left hand started to feel numb, and my palm would heat up. This feeling of energy passing through my hand grew stronger each day. I brought this to the attention of the shaman who served as our guide. She replied, "That is beautiful, my dear. You're receiving the energy." She explained that I was feeling this energy in my left hand because it was my receiving hand. I didn't quite know what to make of this, but I accepted it and enjoyed the cool, unusual experience with an open mind.

I witnessed many auspicious occurrences. One morning I woke up inspired to paint. I painted a picture of my mother under a waterfall that flowed pink and red. This image represented the waterfall cleansing her. Her health condition was related to her blood; therefore I painted the water pink and red to represent a cleansing of the blood. Later that day we went on a guided hike. At the end of the path was a sacred spot they called the "holy waterfall." Each of us was to walk under the waterfall and ask for a blessing. I was behind my mother. I watched her stand exhilarated under the waterfall as the water washed over her—she was receiving a natural healing from the earth. I was overcome with joy when I realized the image I'd painted was right in front of me in physical form.

This waterfall was just one of many miraculous sights. I saw double rainbows, I saw water boil without being heated, and I witnessed incredible healing moments. But none of what I saw with my eyes compared with what I saw in my meditation. While in Brazil we spent many hours in deep meditation. We'd sit in large groups and meditate while John of God performed his healing. He would heal and bless hundreds of people a day. He explained to us that the group's collective meditation supported his work. Our intention and energy helped sustain him as he healed others.

Though we were serving John of God through our meditation, we were also receiving our own healing. I was taught that many past wounds are healed through meditation. For instance, I experienced a mind-blowing meditation in which I was walking on the beach in Martha's Vineyard with my father. We were holding hands, smiling and laughing. This image represented release and forgiveness. In that short meditation I was gifted with the Holy

Instant of seeing my father as only love, and releasing all my past resentments. I came out of the meditation and said to my mother, "I've forgiven Dad. I've released my past resentments. It's over." From that day forward my relationship with my father has been beautifully transformed. In one meditation I was able to release twenty-eight years of ego projections. I was guided to forgive.

My Request

When you visit John of God for healing, you're asked to bring a clear intention of what you'd like healed. You can request anything from a physical healing to the release of an old thought system. My request was clear: *I want to deepen my spiritual connection. I want to know spirit.* I wrote this message on a piece of paper, held the intention in my mind, and went before him to offer up my request. He smiled as my request was translated from English to Portuguese. He responded, "You're being guided to know spirit." I immediately began to receive clear signs of guidance. The response to my request came in many forms.

I spent the last week in Brazil filled with love and with my newfound connection to spirit. The feeling of energy entering into my left hand became constant. I began to feel as though someone were holding my hand almost all the time. As totally wacky as this seemed on the surface, I was surprised by how comfortable I felt. The feeling of this presence grew stronger when I sat in meditation. Whenever I sat, I felt an unmistakable rush of love through my whole body. My anxiety would lift immediately, and my body felt as if it were wrapped in a warm blanket. While in Brazil I found myself sitting in three- to four-hour meditations. Time flew by.

I also began to feel this presence of spirit come to me through my thoughts. While in Brazil I'd hear my inner voice speak loudly and more clearly than ever. The thoughts I heard no longer sounded like mine; for instance, I kept hearing an inner voice say, *Stay connected to the light. Keep inviting in the light and love of spirit.*

This voice connected to me through my writing, as well. On the last night of our trip I stayed up late writing. As I wrote I began to notice that the words coming through me were no longer mine. Then my hand started to move involuntarily. The writing became rapid and the diction seemed foreign. At first this freaked me out, but I went with it. As my hand scribbled quickly across the page, clear guidance came through. I wrote: "Stay connected to spirit at all times. Everything you're seeking is in the light of spirit. Your work is to be one with spirit so you can heal others." The writing became illegible as it spilled onto the page. I underlined this passage and made another commitment to keep this spirit connection alive.

The people in Brazil suggested that in order to feel this

connection to spirit when I returned home, all I needed to do was to invite spirit in. This message reinforced the *Course's* Holy Instant. I understood the Holy Instant on a deeper level now. It became clear that the more I called on spirit, the greater my awareness to the loving guidance around me became. This spiritual connection was the beginning of a serious relationship with my inner guide.

My deep desire to know spirit led me to truly believe in a power greater than myself. This power was no longer a concept from a book, a suggestion from a friend, or a cute gerund I referred to as *~ing*. It became a presence that I could no longer deny.

Hanging Out in the Light

Upon arriving back in New York, I feared that I'd lose this connection. So I took the Brazilians' advice and invited spirit into every area of my life. Spirit, aka *~ing*, became my closest companion. Whenever I felt uncertain, fearful, physically ill, or stuck in ego, I'd turn to spirit for help. I talked to spirit upon waking and before going to sleep. I'd connect to spirit before a date, a business meeting, a hard workout, or a night out with friends. I found that by inviting spirit into my life I enhanced all my experiences. Relying on my inner guide became instinctive and natural. The more I called on spirit, the more love I felt around me. My continued willingness to welcome this presence deepened my spiritual connection daily.

As my spiritual connection strengthened, my meditations became super trippy. I started to feel guidance more physically, hear my ~ing more clearly, and see the world in an entirely different way. I'd see sparks of light with my eyes closed. These sparks resembled the supportive presence I knew was always with me. Then I began noticing these same sparks when my eyes were open. They were like laser beams of light. I'd reactivated the spiritual connection I felt through my high school meditations. The important difference was that this time I wasn't afraid of it. I could now work with this powerful energy to enrich my life.

Knowing Spirit Has My Back

It became clear to me that this inner guidance system was like a GPS for life. Each time I'd come up against some kind of issue, I'd turn inward for help. My ~ing guided my romantic relationships, business deals, and daily interactions. I was also guided to take care of my health in a new way. My addictive patterns began to subside. The years I spent tormented by issues around food—overeating and obsessing about calories—were over. Within a few short years those issues seemed to disappear. I no longer needed food or a relationship or a credential to fill me up. I was finally full.

This feeling of guidance also supported my self-confidence. Now that I understood that all the love and safety I needed was inside me, I could stop searching for it. I no longer felt the desperate need to be accepted, to seem cool, and to prove myself to the world. That's not to say that I was totally released from those patterns, but they did change dramatically. I no longer needed anything on the outside to complete me. This inner connection was all I needed. My daily practice of connecting to spirit helped me maintain positive energy. Because my energy vibrated at a positive frequency, I was attracting more positivity. Knowing how to access this state was all I needed. I felt clear-minded, calm, and powerful. Whenever I lost track of this feeling, I'd bring myself back to equilibrium through meditation and prayer. Having this connection was all I needed.

Physical Healing

Deepening my spiritual connection greatly enhanced my physical body, too. I felt more energized, stronger. In addition, for years I'd lived with a hernia. By this point in my spiritual growth I wanted to patch up this area of my body. Metaphorically, it felt leaky. John of God reinforced the message that spirit was always working through our western doctors and never to shy away from traditional medicine.

Therefore I scheduled a surgery for December of 2009 (one month before the launch of *Add More ~ing to Your Life*). A week before the scheduled surgery, I woke up to a loud inner voice saying, *Postpone the surgery until after the book tour.* Spirit's communication was clear and to the point. I had full faith in this message, and I called my mother to tell her about my ~ingTervention. My mother replied, "I've been expecting this call." She went on to tell me that one day earlier she, too, had heard an inner voice. Her ~ing said, "Gabrielle won't be having her surgery at this time." This brilliant synchronicity sealed the deal. I called my doctor immediately and postponed the surgery. In retrospect I can see clearly why spirit intervened. Had I undergone the surgery at that time, I'd have been totally screwed because my book shipped early and I was called in to do several speaking engagements and TV appearances. Remember, spirit has a much better plan for us than we do. Now that I had a clear connection with spirit, I could allow these ~ingTerventions to occur and receive valuable guidance in all areas of my life.

Being a Messenger

It soon became clear that I couldn't hoard this connection for myself. I had to honor the message I received in my writing and *work with spirit to help heal others.* I did just that.

As I became more confident in my connection to spirit, I invited my coaching clients to sit with me in meditation and share in this experience. Some clients loved this so much that we'd meditate for hours over our scheduled time together. Each woman I coached had been guided to me much as I'd been guided to my coach, Rha. It was clear that we all had work to do together. My clients approached my spiritual guidance with open minds and hearts. Rather than freak out in reaction to my "out there" suggestions, they paid attention and got excited. Their faithful response to my teaching was a beautiful mirror for my own faith in my spiritual connection. And as the *Course* says, *"To teach is to learn."* Therefore, each woman I taught strengthened my own faith and practice.

Seeing Sparks

The sparks I saw in my meditation began to show up in my outward vision all the time. Whenever I was around certain people or in certain spiritual communities, I'd see these sparks of light. At times I felt as though I were witnessing the world from afar, standing across the street and watching myself experience life. The world looked brighter and life began to flow. These sacred experiences reinforced my faith in spirit on a daily basis.

Building Your Own Relationship with Spirit

The *Course* teaches, *"Let your self be one with something beyond it."* I posted this quote on my desk as a daily reminder to turn inward and embrace my spiritual connection. This was my experience. You will have your own. As much as I want to be a spiritual cheerleader, I will refrain from pushing you in any specific direction. We all have a spiritual connection of our own understanding. My connection to spirit may be similar to yours—or completely different. Know that there is no right or wrong way to connect. Some people may feel spirit when they get the chills. Others may feel an intuitive knowing that reminds them of a greater connection. There are all kinds of ways to experience spirit, and there is no right or wrong connection.

Keep in mind that your ego will resist these moments of connection. When I began feeling the energy pass through my left hand, my ego tried to convince me that there was something physically wrong with me. I intuitively knew that this was not a physical condition, but rather a spiritual connection, and I chose to listen to let my *~ing* intervene. The brighter my light began to shine, the harder my ego had to work to keep the darkness alive. Therefore I continued to rev up my connection to spirit and release my ego one thought at a time.

173

One thing to remember when opening up to spirit is that we can often experience some pain in our chakras. A chakra is an energy center, and we have seven of them, each one in a different area of our body. When these chakras are open, it means there is positive energy flow; when they are closed, it means we are emotionally stuck in some way. In our bodies we carry old pain from the past and hold it deep within our muscles and in every cell. Holding this negativity leads to disease and illness. When we invite spirit into our life, these pockets of negativity begin to break open. Sometimes we can literally feel the chakras open up as the stuck energy passes through us. Be conscious of these experiences and embrace them, knowing that this feeling is part of the process.

Remember that as you open your mind to a spiritual connection, your body will reap the benefits. In my case I began to have more energy, released pain in my joints, and saw several health conditions disappear. I no longer need certain prescription drugs that I once relied on. As my mind healed, my body followed. When we release fear and negativity from our minds, they are no longer projected onto our bodies. In my case, I became more conscious of my physical body and how my mind was affecting it. The *Course* says, *"Do not ask Spirit to heal the body. Ask rather that Spirit teach you the right perception of the body."*

This concept was key to my mother's healing. After

visiting John of God her physical condition actually got worse. Often things get worse before they get better, so that the underlying issues can come to the surface and be acknowledged. The severity of her condition helped her to connect more deeply to her spirit. As a result, my mother was led to the right doctor who would be her guide throughout her healing process. (Remember that spirit works through people.) But this was only part of the guidance. The primary guidance she received was through her mind. As she embarked on a year's worth of serious medication, she continuously called on spirit for guidance. This call was answered through many miraculous internal shifts. For instance, my mother had spent the majority of her life caring for others, and for the first time she allowed herself to be cared for. This experience was part of spirit's intervention, as it was a necessary step in the healing of her mind. Her year spent undergoing the medication was one of the most peaceful times in her life. Many of her past emotional hangups shifted and she regained faith in spirit. Since then, regardless of the status of her condition, she lives fearlessly. Her right perception of her physical condition is her healing. Today she coexists with it peacefully. Though she still lives with this condition, she knows why. She understands the ways in which this condition has been an assignment in her life, and honors this experience as her qualifier to knowing the true meaning of a spiritual connection. What's cooler than that?

Accept Your Invitation

Now it's time to open up to your own experience of spirit. By this point in your journey you may or may not have felt your ~*ing*'s guidance. Maybe your ego's been too strong for you to notice, or maybe it felt unnatural to think in this way. Though you may have resisted your ~*ing*, you still may have noticed unique synchronicities or guidance of some kind. Pay attention to the ways you've experienced this Universal guidance in your own life. For example, maybe there is a story behind how you found this book. After publishing my first book I received several e-mails from people saying things like "The book literally fell off the shelf," or "My mother bought the book for me right when I needed it." My response to these e-mails was, "You read it when you need it." As soon as you're willing to receive guidance, the help will come in a form that resonates with you. These types of scenarios reinforce our recognition of the presence of guidance around us. Remember that we're always being guided.

Regardless of your spiritual or religious background, you're entitled to welcome more guidance into your life. The suggested exercises throughout the book thus far have warmed you up to accept your own invitation from spirit. Your inner guide has been beckoning you for years, and now it's time to listen. In the coming steps I'll guide you to pay attention to your ~ing and witness the guidance. I'll offer you tools for unblocking any resistance to this presence, and I'll guide you to listen to the messages you receive. Whatever issue you may be struggling with, whatever problem you may be suffering from, there is a spiritual solution. When you welcome spirit into your life and accept your invitation, you'll know a new way of being and a life beyond your wildest dreams. Fear will lift; anxiety, resentment, and attachment will slip away. You'll feel a presence greater than yourself leading you on a path toward true serenity and peace. You'll know that all your obstacles are opportunities, and you'll learn to lean on a power greater than yourself. Most important, you'll no longer feel the need to figure life out. You'll just *be*.

STEP 1. SAY YES TO SPIRIT

The *Course* teaches, *"Love will immediately enter into any mind that truly wants it."* This was the case for me. All it took for me to deepen my connection to my spirit was the desire to know more. My request to John of God was a statement to the Universe that I was ready to accept an authentic connection to spirit. My call for spirit allowed me to receive. Each of us has an infinite capacity to receive spiritual guidance; we just need to be open to letting it in.

If you feel ready to accept your own spiritual invitation, it's time to sign a sacred contract. All that is required is a commitment to receive. Don't be afraid of this invitation. You will have your own unique experience with spirit. We all have an inner guide connecting in a way that we are capable of receiving. My connection happened to come through meditation and writing, and primarily by physically receiving energy. For others it may be as simple as a strong intuition or receiving guidance through other people. This step isn't going to dictate how you receive, but it will blast open consciousness of the guidance that is around you. You will receive in whatever way your inner guide feels is appropriate for you.

If you're ready to accept your spiritual invitation, let's create a sacred contract with the Universe. Write a letter to your inner guide. In your own words, invite your ~*ing* to become more present in your life. Clearly acknowledge that you're ready to know more and you're willing to receive guidance. Then sign the contract and close it with a thank-you. Thank your ~*ing* for the guidance and support.

STEP 2. UNBLOCK

The more you believe in this contract, the more you will receive. Keep in mind that your ego will want to judge this experience. Ego will lead you to believe that the guidance you're receiving is all coincidental happenstance. In other cases your ego will convince you that your desire to connect with your spirit is unwarranted and impossible. It is important to pay attention to your ego at this time. Do your best to forgive yourself for getting hooked into the ego's fear, and continue to release all blocks.

The most powerful way to unblock yourself from receiving guidance is through daily prayer and meditation. Remember: prayer is the time to ask, and meditation is the time to listen. The reason I have kept my connection to spirit alive is that I invite spirit into my life every day and listen for the guidance. Remove your ego's blocks daily with a dedicated prayer and meditation practice. This practice is simple. Begin each day by turning your will and your life over to the care of your ~ing. This is a great time to use the prayer I referenced from the *Course* in chapter 4: "*Where would you have me go? What you would have me do? What would you have me say? And to whom?*" Then simply sit in a five-minute meditation and listen to the voice of your inner guide. Begin your meditation by breathing in *I welcome guidance*, and breathing out *I will receive*.

STEP 3. LISTEN

Once again it's time to meditate. You've signed your sacred contract and now you will receive more guidance. I was able to hear the guidance because I made a daily commitment to still my mind through meditation. If you've been struggling with the meditations, give yourself a break and keep it simple. This chapter's meditation assignment is easy. You don't need to turn on an audio recording or follow a written guide. All you need do is nothing. Just sit in stillness. Your desire to listen to the guidance is all you need. Offer yourself a minimum of five minutes in the morning and five minutes at night to sit in complete stillness. Listen to what comes through. Listen without judgment.

Getting into the practice of welcoming, unblocking, and listening to spirit will help you strengthen your relationship with your ~*ing*. There is no need to define this relationship: just allow it to occur. Stay open for signs of guidance and enjoy the love.

The more you welcome spirit into your life, the more fulfilled you will feel. Becoming spiritually full is the focus of the upcoming chapter. Know that each lesson is guiding you farther along the path of filling your ego's emptiness with the everlasting love of spirit.

PART 3
The Miracle

9

Spirit Became My Boyfriend

To heal is to make happy.

—A COURSE IN MIRACLES

◆

My meditation pillow became my favorite place to hang. I spent hours sitting with ambient music playing in the background, or sometimes in complete silence. In addition to my awesome meditation practice, I amped up my *Course* study, thereby strengthening my relationship with my *~ing*. Each time I called on the spirit of my *~ing*, I'd release the ego. The *Course* says, *"This Call is so strong that the ego always dissolves at its sound. This is why you must choose to hear one of two voices within you."* The *Course* teaches that the mind cannot serve two masters. Realizing I could no longer function with a split mind, I was able to commit fully to spirit's guidance. Therefore I continuously chose my *~ing*, and I became more and more happy.

Right Mind

I came to understand that restoring my thoughts back to love wasn't a one-time gig. It had to become a moment-to-moment practice of turning my fears over to my ~ing. The Course says, "Our task is but to continue, as fast as possible, the necessary process of looking straight at all the interference and seeing it exactly as it is." Therefore, each time fear crept in, my ~ing would intervene to help me see it wasn't real. Practicing the Course work daily made this way of perceiving the world almost involuntary. This way of thinking is what the Course refers to as "right-mindedness," which occurs when we perceive fear as an opportunity to forgive and restore our thoughts back to love. Each time I witnessed an attack thought, a judgment, or a sense of lacking, I saw it as a call for love and asked my ~ing for help. My inner guide led me to forgive these thoughts and recognize them as illusions, thereby relinquishing the separation and reconnecting my mind with love.

Thinking this way showed me how much power I had over my own personal experience and how my thoughts greatly affected the rest of the world. For instance, when I felt disconnected from someone, I would send him or her loving intentions and immediately feel connected again. Or when I felt powerless over a situation, I'd turn to my ~ing for help and feel empowered the moment my thoughts returned to love. Each time I turned inward for help, I received guidance and strengthened my right-mindedness. The "right mind" or miracle-mindedness is when our mind is faithful to love. When we think this way we believe in love, so we instinctively choose it when faced with conflict. This way of thinking is based on a belief system far beyond the ego—it's based on love.

My New Relationship

Each day spent in prayer and meditation deepened my relationship with my spirit. This relationship was fulfilling, nurturing, inspiring, loving, honest, and faithful. This was the relationship I'd been searching for all my life. I soon realized that all the love and support I'd been lusting after in a man was inside me all along. The classic line "all the love you need is inside you" was true! For years I secretly wanted to believe in that philosophy, but I couldn't fully comprehend it until I lived it. My dedication to spirit led me inward to a true source of love and safety. I was no longer looking for love—*I was living in love.*

Comfort

I felt an overarching sense of comfort when I connected to my ~*ing.* As soon as I centered into my meditation I'd feel as though I were wrapped in a warm blanket. I felt the presence of spirit through my thoughts, experiences, and even physical senses.

Whenever I felt fearful or anxious, I'd turn to my meditation pillow or say a prayer and connect to the spirit of my inner guide. Within seconds, spirit would blast through the fear and help me reconnect with the feeling of love. I felt this presence rush through my limbs and fill me with serenity and peace. It was like I had a built-in Xanax without ever popping a pill. What's most lifting and satisfying is that this sense of peace is always available. I now had a relationship with spirit that filled me with love. There was an infinite amount of love to call on at any given moment: all I had to do was ask. This connection provided me with security and a sense that I was always being taken care of.

Security

I had lived most of my life in fear. Now, for the first time ever, I was at peace. It actually felt odd. My ego resisted this sense of security by trying to convince me that it was too good to be true and that the awesomeness would disappear as soon as I faced a major challenge. But my connection to spirit was too strong for the ego. Whenever my *~ing* sensed ego doubt, spirit would intervene and save me from my old fearful way of being. The presence of spirit was protecting me from fear.

I finally felt safe. The security I was seeking in a romantic partner was now available to me through my connection to spirit. All my codependent analysis showed me that I was desperately seeking someone to save me. At last my need to be saved dissolved and I finally felt secure. This sense of security came from within, and I knew it would never leave me. I no longer had to search for safety on the outside because I was totally taken care of from within.

Loving Experiences

The presence of spirit came through not only on my meditation pillow, but in every area of my life. I experienced many moments of love that I had been unable to access before. Many of these experiences came through some kind of physical activity or while spending time in nature. In the middle of a long run I'd feel love rush through me. I'd feel it while hiking in the woods, swimming in the ocean, or walking in the park. In the midst of these physical activities I'd be taken over by a sense of joy and peace. Outdoor physical activity became a beautiful catalyst for igniting my inner spirit. Moving in nature really turned my ~ing on.

As I listened to my intuition, I was guided to many other loving experiences. One afternoon I was overwhelmed with work. In the midst of a potential breakdown I heard my ~ing say, *Stop working and go to the coffee shop.* I followed this inspired thought and walked over to the café on my corner. I ordered a soy-milk latte, as usual. As soon as I paid my bill I turned around to find one of my childhood friends sitting in the corner. She was visiting from out of town and staying for less than forty-eight hours. We were thrilled to reunite, and we spent the next three hours sitting together in the coffee shop, catching up. Within minutes of seeing her, my work anxiety disappeared and I restored my right-mindedness. When I returned to work, my ~*ing* was back on and my inner peace was restored. Spirit had led me to this loving experience and taken me out of my own way.

Witnessing these loving experiences showed me how divinely guided I'd become. These kinds of moments always had been available in the past, but I'd been too blocked to notice them. My old way of living would have let my ego trample over my intuition and I'd have shrugged off the guidance to go to the coffee shop. Or, more likely, I wouldn't have heard the message in the first place. My relationship with spirit had become so strong I was able to receive the guidance and experience many loving, miraculous occurrences.

Inspiration

The relationship I created with my ~*ing* was full of inspiration. Each time I sat in meditation or called on my ~*ing* through prayer, I received an inspired response. It's often said that when you're inspired, you're "inspirit."

Through my spiritual practice I'd cleared space to receive inspiration daily. My connection with spirit rocketed inspiration through me.

This inspiration came in handy while writing my first book, *Add More ~ing to Your Life*. At the onset of the writing process I invited spirit to intervene. I asked for inspiration throughout the writing process. I'd never written a book, and therefore a lot of ego crap crowded my mind. Rather than freak out, I turned the fear over to my *~ing* and let the guidance move through me. I began a daily prayer practice of releasing my writing fears over to the care of my inner guide. As a result of turning my fears over, I was fully taken care of. Each time I sat down to write, I asked my *~ing* to enter in. This invitation ignited my connection with spirit, at which point inspiration began to flow. Some nights I'd stay up very late writing. My fingers moved fast across the keyboard as my thoughts poured onto the page. I could feel an inner voice working through me. Thanks to my constant contact with my spirit, the writing process was fluid and actually fun. Calling on my spirit eliminated all doubt and never failed to provide me with the inspiration I was seeking.

Once again my *~ing* had filled me with something I'd been chasing on the outside. I no longer needed to rely on a romantic partner to feel inspired. All I had to do was stay connected to my *~ing* and let the inspiration flow.

Support and Guidance

With spirit I could do anything. I felt supported unconditionally by my inner voice of love. Whenever I got caught in an ego tornado, spirit always had my back. If I ever veered off track, something would happen to knock some sense into me or I'd be hit over the head with clear direction back to love. Whenever my work or personal situations were held up for any reason, my ego would get frustrated and nasty. But when I reflected on the outcomes, I'd immediately see how spirit intervened in the holdup.

This type of guidance came when I was trying to get a signature on an important contract. For some reason the lawyers were delayed and the deal points were difficult to negotiate. It was taking many more weeks than I'd expected. My ego was freaking out, trying to convince me that I'd lose the deal or that something would go wrong. When we finally agreed to terms and were about to sign the agreement, another opportunity came in. It was divine timing because I needed to include a clause in the original agreement that would allow me to participate in both projects. Had I signed a day earlier, I would have been locked out of the other deal. It became clear to me that spirit was playing a role in this holdup. Guidance comes in many forms, even when things seem not to be moving the way we want. The *Course* reminds us that spirit has a much better plan for us than we do. This type of guidance began to happen all the time—so often that I came to accept and embrace any holdups or setbacks.

Loneliness Disappeared

I now felt as though I had an internal companion with me at all times. Turning to my ~*ing* regularly meant I never felt alone. I'd longed for this feeling since adolescence. Now that I was united with love on the inside, I always felt connected to something and my loneliness lifted. I truly enjoyed just being with spirit. I'd crave that time spent alone in my apartment in meditation, listening to music, writing, or drawing. I'd leave parties early to go home and meditate. I valued this time spent in silence with spirit.

Spirit Showed Up for Me

All my life I'd ached desperately to be heard. My new relationship with spirit solved that problem. Each time I asked my ~*ing* for guidance, I received an inspired response. Once again these responses came in the forms of an inner voice, stream-of-consciousness writing, inspired intuition, and brilliant synchronicities. It felt good to be heard at last. As long as I was patient I'd receive the response. I learned that when I'd get impatient and try to control the response in any way, I'd block it. Instead I asked for help and patiently waited for my ~ing to respond. Rather than push and scream to be heard by the world, I now simply turned inward, and I always received a response.

I Found "It"

I had fallen in love with spirit. This was a love I'd never known before. I'd become full with inner peace. Since I was no longer searching for love and fulfillment in a romantic partner, I was able to let men off the hook. And because I no longer expected my parents or friends to save me, I could let them off the hook, too. I could now enjoy my relationships for exactly what they were at any given time. I was able to release my major expectations and allow people to be the best they could. I was full of spirit and complete. For the first time in my life I understood the meaning of true love. I now knew that love was not a onetime feeling I could access from a boyfriend. Love is in everything. I felt the presence of love in nature, in the company of a new friend, reading a book, or riding a bike. Love was not something to be acquired; it was something I always had. I learned that love is unselfish and abundant. The love supply is infinite; it can't ever run out. You can either be aware of it or not. All I had to do was sit in meditation, smile at a stranger, perform a random act of kindness, or think with my ~ing, and I'd reactivate my awareness of love. My relationship with spirit guided me to *"release the blocks to the awareness of love's presence."*

The Bridge

In this stage of my spiritual development I was in a place referred to by the *Course* as the "bridge." The bridge is *"the distance between illusion and truth, perception and knowledge."* This bridge is described as spirit's vision of peace and forgiveness. It is a transition in our perspective on reality—this transition is from the fear of the ego back to heaven: the inner state of knowing love. At this time I felt as though I really was walking over a bridge from my old life into a new world—and I wasn't walking alone. I was literally surrounded by the presence of spirit escorting me over the bridge. The *Course* says, *"Truth has rushed to meet you since you called upon it. If you knew who walks beside you on the way that you have chosen, fear would be impossible."* I now knew I had a companion, a guide, a teacher, and a friend. Through the guidance of spirit I exchanged my dark fears for miracles and continued to walk over the bridge.

Healing

My faith in spirit was the answer to all my life's problems. From codependent addictions to physical conditions, I was healing. The *Course* has a magnificent line that inspired me throughout this healing process: *"Can you imagine what it means to have no cares, no worries, no anxieties, but merely to be perfectly calm and quiet all the time?"* A year ago this would have sounded like a pipe dream. Now it was my reality. My worries and anxieties had evaporated. I was calm.

Spreading the Love

My mind was being restored to what the *Course* calls "true perception." The *Course* describes this as the experience of true communication in our right minds, allowing spirit to be shared through us. It became clear that I had to use this spirit connection to strengthen my commitment to serve others. I had cleared space within my own mind to receive love, and now it was time to share it.

My connection to the love of spirit was reflected back to me in many ways. One in particular was the response to my work. My coaching groups grew larger, and my lecture halls were packed. While teaching and lecturing, I found it incredibly easy to speak extemporaneously. I'd write an outline for a lecture and bag it at the door. I could riff for hours on the topic of love and spirit. I could answer every question that came at me. This was easy. The answers were always the same. It all came down to love.

The women in my community were continually reaching out for help. There came a point at which I was no longer able to mentor and guide each of them individually. I had a hard time saying no to their calls for help. So I turned inward for advice. I asked my ~ing how I could share this love with the masses and not totally burn out. My ~ing replied, Get online! This was the solution! Right away spirit guided me to create a social networking website called Her-Future.com for women to find mentors and be mentors.

Through the Internet I was able to hold space for a community of women connecting, serving, and loving one another. The site was a hit from the get-go. Thousands of women became members and began to carry the conversation. Each time I'd log on to the site I'd feel a rush of love come over me. Women created groups (Power Posses) based on topics ranging from health and wellness to shared prayer. Love was bleeding through the computer screen. This website reinforced my newfound knowledge of the fact that love is in everything. I learned that the energy and intention behind this site traveled through the Internet. Whoever needed to find the site would find it and use it as a guide back to love. I received thousands of e-mails from women saying things like "I found this site right when I needed it." Little did they know, spirit got them there. Spirit was working through the site to guide us to heal one another.

The powerful connections I now had with the women in my life filled me up even more. I felt a fiery spark within my community. These relationships illustrated a lesson from the *Course* based on the special love relationship. The *Course* teaches us to make our brotherly relationships (friendships) more romantic and our romantic relationships more brotherly. That was what was going on for me. Because I now found romance and sparks within my companionable relationships, I was able to take even more pressure off men. This was another way spirit worked through me to overcome my codependent patterns. I now understood the true meaning of having romantic brotherly relationships.

Had I told anyone that I was in a relationship with spirit, they'd have freaked. When I tried to explain this connection to my friends, they resisted it. That didn't matter. I honored their processes and recognized that their egos couldn't comprehend what was going on for me. I understood this because I, too, never would have been able to grasp this awesomeness without firsthand experience. Odd as these experiences sounded to others, they felt more right to me than anything I'd ever known. My spiritual connection helped me trust myself, enabling me to release all those who resisted my newfound ways of being. I trusted my inner guidance and didn't allow skepticism to influence my flow. I welcomed the feeling of peace and unconditional love.

Your Relationship with Spirit

It is important to acknowledge once again that everyone has a spirit connection of his or her own understanding. Even those people who have full faith in the ego connect to spirit without even realizing it—possibly through their love of a musical instrument or playing sports with friends. Think about those moments when you feel chills pass through your body or you experience wild synchronicity. This chapter's work will be dedicated to becoming conscious of our own personal relationship with spirit. Throughout the book we've been strengthening our relationship with spirit, and now it's time to witness how that relationship has grown. I'll encourage you to look closely at the ways spirit has intervened in your life—how you've been guided and when you're most connected. By paying attention to these moments you'll become more mindful of participating rather than rushing past. I can think back to many moments in my life when spirit was trying to intervene, but I just wouldn't slow down enough to listen. The goal of this chapter is learning to pay attention. Become the witness of spirit in your own life in order to become more conscious of this connection and do your part to enhance the relationship. Growing this relationship will provide you with the entire fulfillment you desire so you can live with ease.

Watering the Plant

The exercises thus far have been like seeds planted for you to grow your relationship with spirit. Now it's time to water the plant you have created. Each time you honor spirit, your relationship grows stronger. Think about it with regard to interpersonal relationships. If you're ignoring all the love you receive from someone, you may lose track of the connection. Spirit is available to all of us, all the time, and it's our job to pay attention to the connection and allow it to grow.

STEP 1. PAY ATTENTION

To become more conscious of how spirit connects to you, let's begin with a list. Make a list of all the ways you experience spirit. If you are unsure, use these examples as guidelines. Possibly you feel spirit as chills running through your body, a strong intuition, synchronicity, or an inner voice. You may experience spirit as a rush of love coming over you when you're with certain people or in certain situations.

Often people feel spirit through physical activity, such as after a long run or while dancing. Pay attention to the times when you feel a connection to a power greater than yourself. Make this list and become consciously aware of when spirit pats you on the back.

STEP 2. BE MINDFUL

Now that you have your list, it is important to be mindful of these moments. Instead of rushing past them, take them in. Allow yourself to swim in the feeling of love. There was nothing cooler than my time spent soaking up the love of spirit through meditation or exercise. Become still, and welcome the presence into your mind and body. Allow spirit to pass through you, and enjoy the connection.

STEP 3. ADD WATER

Now it's time to add water by activating spiritual encounters. For instance, if you know that you can access a spirit connection through ~ing-writing, then ~ing-write. If you know you can access spirit through yoga, unroll your mat. Take time out of your day to choose to spend time with spirit. This commitment to connect to spirit is like taking care of a plant—you must add water for it to grow.

As you strengthen your relationship to spirit, you will begin to feel more complete from the inside out. This is when you start to release attachments and extend a confident energy of inner peace. In my case, exuding this wholeness magnetized people and situations that were equally healthy. As my relationship to spirit grew greater and greater, my relationships with other people followed suit. In the coming chapter you will see how in our completeness we call in healthy relationships that reflect our inner light. This is what the *Course* calls the "holy relationship."

10
Love Wins

The holiness of your relationship forgives you
both, undoing the effects of what you both
believed and saw.

—A COURSE IN MIRACLES

◆

The comfort, security, inspiration, support, and love I received from spirit was everything I'd been searching for in a man. Now that I had access to this spirit connection, I was truly fulfilled. I shone from the inside out. My friends and family regularly remarked on how chilled out and relaxed I'd become—they referred to me as "calm" and "centered," which was totally new. This was amazing because for most of my life I'd been a complete head case. Now that I'd connected to spirit, the people who surrounded me reflected back my calm internal state. Oddly, this transition felt natural. I was able to gracefully shed my old frantic way of being and embrace my new chilled-out approach to life. I welcomed this new perception.

As a result of my inner shift, the Universe began sending me many gifts. My career was moving forward fast. My friendships deepened, and new romantic opportunities fell in my lap. I was vibrating at such a high frequency that my energy was magnetizing greatness. I was now attracting amazing, available men who really wanted to be with me. The fact that I was calling in this type of man showed me how much I had transformed. I was no longer putting out a needy vibe or desperately seeking safety in someone else. I was now complete, inspired, and whole. Therefore, I was meeting awesome men who dug me as much as I dug myself. My inner light was shining outward and everyone felt it.

Spirit Had a Better Plan

Though I was super happy being single, spirit guided me back into a relationship. It gradually became clear that I had things to learn by being in a relationship. There are times in our lives when the finest learning and healing occur while we're on our own, whereas at other times spirit directs us to the perfect romantic partner for the best growth opportunity. In this case I was guided to revisit an old relationship—the guy who I'd peacefully broken up with a year earlier. I never could have expected this; I thought it was over for good. I knew from my *Course* study that the relationship had never ended on a spiritual level, but that the form of the relationship had just changed. Even though we'd been physically apart for more than a year, we'd been spiritually connected: the energetic connection between us never died.

I often felt his energy while sitting in meditation. My ~*ing* would guide me to loving thoughts about him, which would bring up loving feelings, and hours later he'd e-mail me, saying, "Thinking about you." The entire time we spent physically apart, we remained energetically connected. As soon as we both released the relationship fully, spirit could intervene and lead us to what was truly right. And as the Universe would have it, we were brought back together. I welcomed the assignment, knowing that spirit would do for me what I couldn't do for myself. I knew for sure I couldn't have planned this!

I was guided back to him to experience what the *Course* calls the "holy relationship." The holy relationship happens when we undo the unholy or special relationship by shifting the goal of guilt to the goal of forgiveness. In the holy relationship we are guided together to transcend the ego. After having separated for a year and done our own work, we felt more complete and ready for a fulfilling romantic relationship. The *Course* teaches that in the holy relationship, *"Each one has looked within, and seen no lack. Accepting his completion, he would extend it by joining with another, whole as himself."* Though neither of us was fully healed, we were much more whole than ever before. In the relationship's first incarnation, we were two incomplete people coming together in an attempt to become whole. That clearly didn't work. This time around we were guided back together to further transcend the separateness of the ego and step into our holy relationship.

The *Course* teaches: *"The holy relationship, a major step toward the perception of the real world, is learned. It is the old, unholy relationship, transformed and seen anew. The holy relationship is a phenomenal teaching accomplishment. In all its aspects, as it begins, develops and becomes accomplished, it represents the reversal of the unholy relationship. Be comforted in this; the only difficult phase is the beginning. For here, the goal of the relationship is abruptly shifted to the exact opposite of what it was."*

This new incarnation of the relationship offered me the opportunity to let go of past resentments, enjoy each moment, and welcome all the new learning that comes with holy love.

Invisible Force

Spirit is the ultimate matchmaker. Whether we realize it or not, we're always being guided in and out of relationships in order to experience the good, the bad, and sometimes the super ugly. When we follow this guidance and allow our *~ing* to take the lead, we can heal and grow so that we're ready to experience holy love. As soon as my former boyfriend and I came back together through forgiveness, I felt spirit intervene like an invisible driving force. Now our relationship was based on acceptance and forgiveness, and therefore it was holding space for spirit to be present.

Don't get me wrong. Every day wasn't rainbows and butterflies. The fact that our relationship carried old baggage made it the perfect assignment at the time. It was exactly what I needed in order to put my *Course* tools to work and get closer to knowing holy love. I spent plenty of hours ruminating on fearful thoughts. But the miracle was that I was only a head case for a few hours rather than several months. Now I had the necessary tools to combat fear, release the separation, and return to love. This relationship offered me the ideal opportunity to strengthen my spiritual practice even more.

I was ready, willing, and able to show up for this new assignment. But I knew I faced a challenge: because things were going so well, my ego amped up its game, reaching for thoughts of infidelity and lingering bitterness. My ego literally took fears that did not exist before and tried to pummel me with them. For instance, I couldn't shake the ego thought that my boyfriend was going to find a woman whom he liked more than me. This fear was based on our relationship's old form. My ego was dragging my past neuroses into the present. None of it was real. I had two choices: I could choose fear and sabotage my relationship, or I could laugh. The *Course* teaches us not to take the ego and its world seriously, for this makes fear real in our minds. Instead we are urged to laugh gently at the ego's "tiny mad idea" and all its seeming terror. By laughing gently at these mad ideas, I was able to release them one by one. Each time I released an ego thought, I developed a stronger tie to the holiness of the relationship.

While I laughed at the ego, I bolstered my practice by calling on forgiveness as the primary tool for maintaining my holy love and releasing the ego's fear. I prayed daily to let go of the past and forgive the ego's illusions. Through forgiveness I reminded myself of the ego's falseness. I also enlisted the help of a visual reminder by keeping a photo of the two of us on my desk with a Post-it that read, "I release all fear and I know we're being guided." I recited a daily mantra: "I forgive you and release you." And I blessed him each morning before I began my day. I'd say a silent prayer asking spirit to surround him with love and help me release any ego thoughts about our relationship. This daily surrender kept me connected to love and protected the relationship from ego backlash.

Whenever my ego would attack him with fear-based illusions from the past, or flip out about the future, I'd call on forgiveness, release the thought, and start over. Rather than attack, I forgave him, forgave myself, and forgave the thought. Forgiveness became my automatic reset button, which kept me in a state of equilibrium. Because I was so conscious of maintaining the flow of love, spirit continued to be very present within the relationship. Plenty of assignments came my way, but they always led to positive outcomes. For instance, I'd often find myself digging up past fears, such as "I'm not good enough," and "He's going to leave me." In the past, I would've taken out those fears on him or let my mind concoct dark scenarios. This time I turned to my *Course* work for guidance. I'd witness the ego's "tiny mad idea" and recognize it as a fear from the past. Then I'd shine light on how I'd made him special and better than me by seeking completion in the relationship. Finally, I would forgive him and myself. This practice of forgiveness released the illusion that he was separate and immediately restored my connection to spirit and the belief that he and I were one. I worked hard, but I was fully supported by my spirit connection.

Practicing forgiveness was not the only method I used to maintain loving flow: my meditation practice was instrumental as well. I often practiced the "Great Rays Meditation" that had brought me solace in the past. This was the meditation in which I held an image of him and me together and created a vision of light extending from his heart to mine. Through my breath this light expanded until it took over our bodies, transforming us into great rays of light. Practicing this meditation was a powerful reminder that when spirit intervenes, fear can melt away. Love is all that's left.

Releasing Symbols and Specialness

The new incarnation of this relationship offered me optimal opportunities for serious *Course* work. I was challenged to truly release all specialness that I'd placed on the relationship. The *Course* teaches us that the ego's primary focus is on form and symbols. Projections take a range of forms: "He doesn't make enough money," or "Why hasn't he proposed?" or "She doesn't share my religion." The *Course* teaches, *"When you decide on the form of what you want, you lose the understanding of its purpose."* The work in this case is to shift our focus from the form of the relationship to the purpose, which is love. When our primary focus is love, we can release our outside symbols and reconnect with truth. We let go of all the baggage our ego has placed upon it. In my case the practice of forgiveness was guiding me to release all attempts at specialness and attachment to form. When we detach from the form of the ego, we remember that everyone is one. There is no separation and there is no "special love."

The *Course* teaches, *"When we put form, symbols and specialness before purpose we lose our truth."* Another powerful way to release these symbols is to welcome love and inspiration from all areas of life rather than from just one special partner.

I had the opportunity to experience a tremendous amount of love and release of specialness when I went on my book tour. I left town for more than a month. This time away from my relationship could have really set off my ego, getting me into a super needy zone by rousing my fears of losing him. But I did just the opposite. I focused on the love of my life rather than the form. I released the need to perceive my relationship as my only source of love and inspiration. In doing so, I opened the floodgates to receive inspiration and love from every person I came into contact with. While on the road, I spent time with hundreds of women. Women throughout the country were showing up to hear me speak. In each new city I bunked with friends. It was like I was on a month-long slumber party. The love I experienced while on the road filled me up. The ego couldn't thrive, couldn't even survive, in my completeness. Therefore I never felt needy or skittish while away from my boyfriend. We missed each other, but never felt any lack. I was inspired, taken care of, and complete, no matter where I was or who I was with.

I also had the opportunity to enjoy the fiery sparks within my friendships. I spent hours laughing and celebrating life with incredibly inspired women. I felt a sisterhood I'd never known before. By letting go of my grip on the romantic relationship, I was able to truly experience others.

Holy Encounters

The *Course* compares our ego's separation to the idea of sunbeams being separate from the sun, or waves being separate from the ocean. Just as a sunbeam can't separate itself from the sun, and a wave can't separate itself from the ocean, we can't separate ourselves from one another. We are all composed of the same beams of love and are part of the sea of truth. The way to begin to understand this truth is to understand that all encounters are holy encounters. Each person we come in contact with offers us a divine assignment to see love or fear. When we make it our commitment to see love in all relationships, we begin to release the separation and find holiness in all. By choosing to see love in all people I came in contact with, I was able to truly release my ego's separate thoughts. Witnessing these holy encounters of love guided me to release my boyfriend one loving encounter at a time. When I could see love in everyone, I no longer needed it from one special person. There was no separate love.

Mirror

This relationship was also the perfect mirror for me to continue to spot-check my lingering shortcomings. One particular ego thought I still battled was the need to make myself seem special. This issue came up a lot in my relationship. Whenever I'd talk about myself too much or change the conversation to focus on me, my boyfriend would call me out. At first I reacted defensively—but then I turned to my ~ing for help. I used the tool of the universal mirror. The *Course* teaches, *"Perception is a mirror, not a fact. And what I look on is my state of mind, reflected outward."* I learned through this message that the outside world was reflecting my internal state. My discomfort around his response to my perceived specialness reflected my own disgust with my behavior. He mirrored back to me what I needed to work on. This mirror image was a guide to stop defending and start changing my patterns. I took his mirror as a cue to get to work on releasing my special self. Each time I'd have the urge to make myself special, I would say a silent prayer and ask for it to be released. This was really tough at first. It's hard not to get defensive when someone calls you out on your shit, but I worked with the *Course* lesson not to defend against the illusion. If I defended myself, I was strengthening the ego. Instead I looked directly at the ego's behavior, forgave myself, and asked spirit to guide my change. Difficult as it was for me to change this pattern, doing so greatly enhanced my spiritual connection and all my relationships. In this way, my relationship guided me to become more complete.

Gratitude

As I connected with spirit to forgive, embrace holy encounters, and release symbols and specialness, I also practiced gratitude and appreciation. Focusing on gratitude unleashes the love that lives within us and blasts light on the ego. When my ego would try to take me down with fear talk, I'd shine light by concentrating on everything I was grateful for in my relationship. I was pulled up with gratitude rather than dragged down to wallow in feelings of lack. And I didn't limit my gratitude to my romantic relationship; I focused on why I was grateful for all my relationships. This really helped me "de-special" my romantic relationship. I made it a point to reach out to my family and friends and acknowledge how much I loved them. When I looked at my friends and family with gratitude and appreciation, I was able to see my romantic partner as equal to them. This strengthened the wholeness of the relationship and dismantled any residual special form. Furthermore, appreciating him created more abundance within the relationship. Love breeds more love.

Truth

We had each kept our own side of the street clean. We made a commitment to each other to bring all our dark illusions into the light by outing our egos whenever necessary. Therefore, our holy relationship continued to maintain its flow. We spoke up when things were off, and we forgave when necessary. This daily dance of love was everything I could ask for in a relationship. Most important, my fears were truly separate from me now. When old fearful thoughts came up, I immediately saw them as false. They no longer had a hold on me. I could witness the thought, forgive it, and let it go within seconds. This was a miracle. I was now connected to a truthful faith in love.

Spreading the Love

Now that I was serene in my relationship, I was able to revel in the good stuff. I no longer wasted hours and days mired in codependent fear and attack thoughts. This holy love invigorated me. I had abundant time and energy and could share it with the world around me. One amazing effect of being so chilled-out in my holy relationship was that I could show up for my coaching sessions and lectures in a powerful way. Had I been in a tripped-out mindset about my relationship, I never could have served with this type of truth. I would have been focused on my own ego crap and disconnected from the service of spreading the ~ing. Instead I was able to show up fully, with a clear head and an open connection to everyone around me.

What's more, I was truly able to witness my brotherly relationships become more romantic and my romantic relationship more brotherly. This *Course* lesson, which I introduced in chapter 9, was apparent and tangible. Once again, I was filled with ladylove and all the awesomeness that goes with it. My female friendships became so awesome that I stopped *needing* all my fiery sparks to come from my romantic partner—*all* my relationships fired me up. I was feeling equality in my relationships for the first time. I had released much of the "specialness" I'd created, and therefore was able to spread the love. I now savored the time with my girlfriends equally with the time I spent with my boyfriend.

Becoming Whole

Holy love is available to all of us. However, the goal is *not* to search for the holy relationship. Rather, the goal is to release the blocks to our own wholeness. As the *Course* teaches, "*Your task is not to seek for love, but merely to seek and find all the barriers within yourself that you have built against it.*" When we find those barriers and release the blocks, we become whole. By becoming whole, we will attract our likeness. When we no longer need someone else to complete us, we are ready for holy love. Therefore the work in this chapter is designed to further deepen your connection to spirit and guide you to become more whole. Spirit will take care of the rest.

Even though this work is dedicated to your own personal wholeness, we will welcome all relationships into the practice, remembering that relationships are spirit's primary teaching mechanism. Therefore, begin by looking closely at all the relationships in your life, and identify the ways in which they have been your guides.

STEP 1. HOW HAVE YOU INVESTED IN THE ILLUSION?

Remember that the *Course* teaches, *"Insistence means investment."* Therefore, what we insist on focusing on, we're actually investing in. I encourage you in this step to witness what you've been investing in. In what relationships are you reactivating the illusion? The goal of this step is to witness where you're activating more fear by insisting on focusing on it. When we recognize these patterns, we can insist on investing in love instead. For instance, had I insisted on investing in my old illusion that I wasn't good enough for my relationship, I'd have destroyed my opportunity for holy love. By focusing on the good stuff, I chose to insist on love—and therefore invest in love.

STEP 2. WHO ARE YOUR MIRRORS?

The *Course* teaches, *"The world is only in the mind of its maker. Do not believe it is outside of yourself."* Take in this concept. The work in this step will help you further recognize how you've projected your own fear onto others. To get you closer to your own wholeness, it's time to stop pointing the finger at others and turn inward for guidance. Whenever someone rouses you, don't get angry and attack. If you attack, you only reinforce the fear. Instead, ask yourself, *What is coming up for me?* Then invite spirit in to guide you to understand your own ego block. This step is crucial to deepening our wholeness. We must use the mirror to look within for what we cannot find outside ourselves.

STEP 3. CHOOSE TO SEE NO LACK

Remember that the lack you see in others creates more lack in you. The *Course* teaches, "*Sin is a strictly individual perception, seen in the other yet believed by each to be within himself.*" Take this step to understand that the sin you see in others reinforces the darkness you see in yourself. Through forgiveness you can weaken this darkness. Once again, strengthen your forgiveness practice by choosing to perceive love rather than darkness. Step by step, choose to perceive joy and love in the darkest spaces. We're not beholden to a mindset or a fear. No matter how big or stubborn it is, we can choose to see it differently. You can use your prayer practice to help guide you, and turn to the forgiveness meditation for further release. Through this work we actually can choose to perceive ourselves differently. We're not beholden to a mindset or a fear, no matter how big or stubborn it is.

Releasing Meditation

(Follow my lead. You can also download this
audio meditation from www.gabbyb.tv/meditate.)

Sit up straight in your chair, with your feet planted
firmly on the ground.

Breathe in through your nose and out through
your mouth. Hold an image in your mind of the
person or people you need to forgive.

Breathe in: I choose to see you without lack.

Breathe out: I choose to see you as love.

Breathe in: I release all fearful projections.

Breathe out: I remember that only love is real.

Breathe in: I call on forgiveness to heal.

Breathe out: I ask for release.

Breathe in: I see you as love.

Breathe out: I see me as love.

Take one last deep breath in and release. When
you're ready, open your eyes to the room.

STEP 4. LET SPIRIT INTERVENE

The *Course* reminds us that the holy relationship, "*a light far brighter than the sun that lights the sky,*" is chosen by spirit as a plan for our reconnection with love. We can now rest easy knowing that we don't need to push, manipulate, or control the outcome. All we have to do is forgive and choose to see love. Through our forgiveness practice we will continue to invite spirit in to take the lead. The *Course* reminds us, "*Every mistake you and your brother make, the other will gently have corrected for you.*" Spirit ("the other") will never fail to guide the relationship to holy bliss. You need not do anything. Just let spirit do her thing.

Inviting spirit into your relationships will give you a sense of empowerment. You will no longer feel as though you need to know the how, why, and when. Instead you can relax, knowing that spirit has a rockin' plan. The more we turn over our relationships and desires to the care of our inner guide, the more peaceful our lives become. You'll learn in the coming chapter just how powerful this shift can be.

11

Expect Miracles

Miracles are natural. When they do not occur,

something has gone wrong.

—A COURSE IN MIRACLES

•—◆—•

For nearly a year I was on spiritual cruise control. Everything was jamming. I experienced many miracles and grew to expect them—my commitment to love and spirit had me totally hooked up. I knew the Universe had my back; as my inner life expanded, my ego became tame and my outer life began to mirror the abundance I felt inside. Life was great: my boyfriend and I manifested the home of our dreams; I was working on many new professional projects, lecturing throughout the country; and I'd become respected in my field. There was absolutely nothing wrong. Then, dependably, the ego crept back in. My ego decided to second-guess all the greatness, convincing me it was too good to be true. As a result, I started judging others and attacking myself. Specialness was at an all-time high. My old controlling fears even began to sabotage my miracle-mindedness. In short, my ego freaked out.

Everything was all fine and good when my accomplishments were within the realm of what my ego found reasonable. But the moment my internal and external states hit a higher plane, my ego karate-chopped my spiritual flow.

Hooking into these fear-based thoughts lowered my energy and weakened my connection to spirit. I'd moved into a funky space and disconnected from the loving presence of my inner guide. I was now dealing with thoughts like "You can't have it this easy. Something is bound to go wrong." These thoughts could take me down, lower my energy, and disturb my flow.

My thoughts informed my energy, and my energy informed my experiences. I saw how my low-level thoughts of disbelief weakened my connection to spirit, thereby attracting old chaotic patterns and negative outcomes. Each time I'd get hooked into the thought that "this is too good to be true," I'd start second-guessing situations and feel fearful and unconfident. These feelings of inadequacy and unworthiness created more negativity. In this negative state I struggled to do good work, flailed about in my relationships, and felt my overall sense of peace slam out of balance. Considering that this pattern stemmed from my own mind, there seemed to be a simple solution: *Just keep my thoughts positive and life will flow again.* But it wasn't all that easy. I'd rev up my *Course* work and get connected back to my ~ing. This would work for a while, but my ego was determined to take me down. Ego had rocked out the nastiest trick of all: fear of greatness.

But I had an advantage over my ego and was able to resist its backlash. I turned inward for help and asked for guidance, knowing spirit would have a solution. In a meditation

I waited for a response. Coming out of my meditation I felt the intuition to walk over to my bookshelf. My hand passed over the shelf and landed on Marianne Williamson's book *A Return to Love*. I smiled and welcomed the guidance. I opened the book to a page that had been dog-eared. Then I laughed upon realizing what I'd been guided to read. The page I turned to featured Marianne's most famous quote:

> *Our deepest fear is not that we are inadequate. Our deepest fear is that we are powerful beyond measure. It is our light, not our darkness, that most frightens us. We ask ourselves, Who am I to be brilliant, gorgeous, talented, fabulous? Actually, who are you not to be? You are a child of God. Your playing small does not serve the world. There is nothing enlightened about shrinking so that other people won't feel insecure around you. We are all meant to shine, as children do. We were born to make manifest the glory of God that is within us. It's not just in some of us; it's in everyone. And as we let our own light shine, we unconsciously give other people permission to do the same. As we are liberated from our own fear, our presence automatically liberates others.*

That said it all. I could not deny this spirit ~*ing*Tervention. In that moment spirit worked through the text to bring me back to equilibrium. Marianne's words reminded me that accepting my greatness was not something to shy away from. Greatness is our birthright and our truth. Rather than hide from miracles, it was my duty to embrace them. By shining brightly on the world, I could ignite light in others. Her words inspired me to keep it simple and, once again, surrender to my inner guide.

Back to Basics

In order to reclaim my spirit mojo, I had to get back to basics. I revisited my early *Course* work, checking back in with the ego's nasty tricks. Yet again I became the witness to the ego's fear in order to disconnect from the negativity. In the midst of this ego flare-up, I experienced many Holy Instants. I now had the strength of my spirit connection to help me immediately recognize those feelings and thoughts as the ego's tricks.

Rather than freak out and let my ego rain on my awesome life parade, I chose to pray. I prayed, *Inner guide, please enter into my mind and take the steering wheel. I am committed to love and miracles. Keep me in the flow.*

The loving response I heard time and time again was this: *You're right where you need to be. Accept all this greatness. Embrace it!* These ~*ing* reminders would tranquilize the ego and guide me back to love. Some days I'd call on my ~*ing* several times for these gentle reminders. These spirit ~*ing*Terventions also came in other forms. I often heard the voice of my coach, Rha Goddess, in the back of my mind. Her mantra was, "Let the world show up for the party that is you." I also wore a reminder around my neck in the form of a necklace I'd received from Marianne Williamson. It was a scroll pendant on a chain. Inside the scroll was her famous quote, the one that had reignited my ~ing.

The Universe Wants Us to Be Happy

Our ego works overtime to convince us that happiness comes with a price tag. Western cultures in particular have an overarching ego belief system that we have to struggle to "get there." The ego convinces us that pain has a purpose. Suffering, struggle, and pain are necessary to keep the ego alive and separate us from love. That's why my ego flipped out when things got good. When miracles began to flow naturally, my ego reminded me of pain, convincing me to think things were too good to be true. Even in the midst of my commitment to *Course* work, ego trapped me in the belief of pain to keep me small. This was what led me to second-guess the effortless flow of miracles.

Once I recognized this pattern, I committed to saying no to the ego's playing small. I had to weaken the false idea that pain has a purpose or that we have to struggle to be happy. I remembered that as long as I had faith in spirit, miracles would occur naturally. It's not that I sat on a meditation pillow all day long, expecting miracles to occur spontaneously. Rather, I stayed connected to my ~*ing* and took spiritually aligned action instead of succumbing to the ego's pushy and controlling approach to life. Since my primary goal was to stay connected to spirit, everything else flowed. Each outward action I took was backed by strong intuition and inspiration. All I needed to do was commit to the belief that with spirit as my guide, anything was possible.

Turning It Over

By this point in my *Course* study, I was practicing the third section of the book, which is the *Manual for Teachers*. The work in this section prepares the *Course* student to become a spiritual teacher. The lessons are powerful and consistently lead us to turn to our inner guides for complete healing. We are urged to invite spirit in to continue guiding us to become teachers in our own right.

There is a section in the *Manual for Teachers* titled "How Is Correction Made?" This section was profound for me. What resonated with me most was the guidance that in order to heal, it would be essential for me to let all my own mistakes be corrected by my ~*ing*. The *Course* teaches: *"If he senses even the faintest hint of irritation in himself as he responds to anyone, let him instantly realize that he has made an interpretation that is not true. Then let him turn within to his eternal Guide, and let Him judge what the response should be."*

This lesson led me to realize that even as I became the teacher, I still had to remain humble to my eternal guide. I would always be watched over as I continued to practice the principles of love. Even once I fully stepped into the role of teacher, I'd still be a student.

As I transitioned into the role of teacher, I also accepted that all my obstacles were opportunities. I welcomed each attack thought or difficult situation as an opportunity to grow spiritually. This helped me accept the great things that were happening around me because I was no longer fearful of something going wrong. I wholly accepted that a changed plan or altered course meant that something better was on the way. I was capable of living in each moment, accepting greatness and change as equally valuable components of my spiritual journey. In honoring this truth I reactivated my spiritual mojo and began flowing with life once again.

Already "There"

For most of my life I lived with the belief that I was working toward some special place or trying to attain some elite status. This theory was based on a way of thinking that is familiar to many people: that a certain level of success, a certain type of boyfriend, or a hefty bank balance will magically confer happiness upon us. I came to understand that true happiness comes from the exact opposite place. The *Course* taught me that regardless of my outside experience, happiness was my only function. Finally I understood that there was no special status or perfect relationship or amount of money that could complete me. I had "it" all along. Even though I didn't realize it at the time, peace of mind was all I was seeking. Learning to access my inner state of peace is by far my greatest accomplishment.

Accepting Right-Mindedness

Accepting happiness as my only function was a major step in fully committing to the *Course*'s true perception. Upon recognizing this, I reflected on all the ways in which spirit had worked through me to guide me back to inner peace and joy. I thought back to my most desperate moments of drug addiction and most torturous romantic struggles, and considered how all those experiences were necessary tools for my spiritual growth. My ~ing had been working tirelessly all this time. I could now look fondly on my past with gratitude for all the learning and healing I'd undergone. The *Course* says, "*What could you not accept, if you but knew that everything that happens, all events, past, present, and to come, are gently planned by One Whose only purpose is your good?*" It was now clear that all my life's experiences were gently guided by spirit. All I needed to do was stay willing, perceive happiness as my only function, and allow spirit to intervene.

By fully turning my belief system over to the care of my ~ing, I now perceived miracles as natural. This faith in miracles raised my levels of happiness and peace, thereby raising my awareness of the miracle. I felt the presence of spirit in each new encounter, knowing I'd been guided to that specific person for an opportunity to learn and spread love. I had faith in miracles and expected them.

Maintaining the Vibration

Having faith in miracles was a belief system I needed to consciously maintain. It's easy to get taken out by the ego— even when you're a miracle-minded lady. Anything from a rude person to PMS could knock me out of spiritual alignment. Knowing this, I made it my goal to stay connected to spirit no matter what. I used daily reinforcement to stay focused on the good stuff. I made reminders for myself in my phone and computer calendars. These reminders would pop up throughout the day in the form of messages such as "*I accept happiness now*," or "*I expect miracles*." These simple notes guided me back to spirit and helped me choose happiness time and time again.

Furthermore, my spiritual consciousness allowed me to

witness the Universe reminding me to stay in flow. Often these reminders would show up in seemingly unlikely places. I found loving quotes written on bathroom stalls, read inspiring messages posted on blogs or Internet boards, and heard beautiful music from inside windows as I passed by on the sidewalk. Each of these reminders reignited spirit's love and gently reminded me that spirit had my back.

Another way of maintaining my spiritual flow was to keep an eye on the ego at all times. Through my own experience and the experiences of others, I had seen time and again how crafty the ego could be. For instance, a client of mine came to me full of fear. She explained how great her life had become as a result of her spiritual practice. Her relationships, career, and overall sense of peace were flowing naturally. However, she felt a tremendous sense of fear that she just couldn't shake. She kept repeating, "Will I survive this?" I laughed when I realized what was going on. I responded, "You will survive, but your ego won't." This is a powerful example of how the ego will try to take us down when things get good. The ego cannot survive in our peaceful state. Therefore we will feel as though we cannot survive, because we've functioned for so long believing that we *are* the ego. Knowing that *you are not your ego* will help you stay connected to love. To keep my spiritual flow going, I make a daily practice of reminding myself that I am not my ego and that it's okay if my ego doesn't survive.

In order to fully maintain my faith in spirit, I had to

give up some lingering habits. One in particular was gossip. This was a tough one: my ego had ingrained this pattern in me for more than twenty years. But by this point I was way too into love and miracles to lower my inner vibration through gossip. Anytime I found myself tempted to talk about someone, I'd immediately shift the conversation. Gossip no longer served me—it felt funky. Spirit guided me to become conscious of the pattern so I could maintain my commitment to happiness and miracles. Listening to my inner guide kept my vibration high.

Thoughts Merging with Love

Over time my thoughts merged with love. I instinctively chose love on a moment-to-moment basis, thereby becoming one with my internal guide. This connection helped me focus on love in every corner of my life. I found love in a hot cup of coffee and a miracle in a smile from a stranger. My love radar was on high. It was as if the voice of my ~ing had become my voice. I was no longer leaning on my ~ing as a mentor. I'd become my own mentor. The Course says that our internal guide is always with us, even when we no longer rely on its guidance. Our ~ing is referred to as a friend who lives inside and is one with us.

I felt this oneness and fully embraced it. With each breath I felt spirit come through and heighten my loving perception. I had turned inward to connect with the wise and thoughtful part of my soul, the part of me that remembered why I was here in this world at this time—the part of me that remembered where I came from and where I was going. I looked on my past fondly, honoring my journey. Through my prayer and meditation I connected to the little girl inside me who had fearlessly faced her inner demons and transcended the darkness. This little girl represented the voice of all those who'd disconnected from their spirit at one point in time. I had rejoined with my spirit self. I had reconnected with my past, present, and future. This connection allowed spirit to fully move through me so that I could serve at my highest capacity. It was time for me to help others retrieve their connections, too.

Extending Healing to Others

Accepting my own healing and right-mindedness led me to directly and automatically extend healing to others. I had to accept my own healing before I could fully extend it. As the *Course* says, *"For you must have before you can give."* This acceptance is the sole responsibility of what the *Course* refers to as the "miracle worker." The *Course* teaches: *"By denying your mind any destructive potential and reinstating its purely constructive powers, you place yourself in a position to undo the level of confusion of others."*

Now that my constructive powers were restored and I was at peace, I could extend that peace to others. For instance, upon entering a room I could feel the energy shift when I was connected to spirit. I could intend to share light with the room, and the overall presence of the people in the space would shift accordingly.

This type of energy exchange became very powerful in all of life's circumstances, from the small (getting into a cab with an impatient driver) to the potentially unnerving (standing in front of an audience of strangers). Bringing my healing presence in all scenarios greatly boosted the energetic state of those around me. It was incredible to watch the energy shift as I intended it to. By simply saying a silent prayer and choosing always to be of service with my thoughts and energy, I was able to transform those around me. Therefore, other people's issues no longer tripped me up. I stopped feeling responsible for saving people; I understood that I could best help them by maintaining my own miracle-minded way of being. Accepting my own peace was the greatest gift I could offer the world.

Becoming a Miracle Worker

The *Course* teaches that miracles are expressions of love. When we become miracle-minded (or right-minded) we express love naturally and, as a consequence, perform miracles. Our mind creates our reality, so miracle-minded thoughts create miraculous outcomes. My commitment to love and miracles was preparing me to be a miracle worker. The *Course* teaches, "*Before miracle workers are ready to undertake their function in this world, it is essential that they fully understand the fear of release.*"

The fear of release was what I had struggled with before I was able to accept miracles. When I doubted the miracles of my life, I hooked back into the ego's thinking that I was a separate body that could be harmed and that all the awesomeness was *too good to be true*. In retrospect I understand why this freak-out occurred. My ego was trying a final, desperate tactic to hold me back from becoming a miracle worker. The ego was afraid of releasing my perception of littleness and embracing the magnitude of a miracle worker. But spirit was committed to teaching me the truth and guiding me back to love and miracles. I was reminded that my fear was a construct of my ego and not part of the truthful spiritual mindset that I'd grown to believe in. By accepting this miracle-minded way of being, I was now prepared to become a miracle worker.

Accepting Happiness as Your Only Function

To fully understand the function of a miracle worker, it is imperative that we embrace happiness as our only function.

This is a difficult step for most, owing to the ego's belief in pain and purpose. Believing in our limited capacity is what keeps us small. Regardless of how far we've come down the spiritual path, fear still lurks in the shadows, in one form or another.

At this point in your journey it's time for you to accept your greatness and welcome miracles. Becoming a miracle worker requires your full trust in the miracle-minded belief system of love. The exercises in this chapter are dedicated to accepting happiness as your only function. I'll guide you to witness when you're resisting love and miracles. Then I'll lead you to immediately invite your ~ing to intervene. Finally, I'll lead you to deepen and solidify the reconditioning process by reinforcing the daily belief that happiness is your only function. This step in the process is crucial to becoming a teacher of love. We must have faith in miracles if we're to become miracle workers.

STEP 1. HOW DO YOU DENY LOVE AND MIRACLES?

I'll preface this step by acknowledging that it's very likely that your ego resists miracles at all costs. Many of my coaching clients will get deeply into the miracle mindset, only to begin denying it as time passes. They'll stop meditating, praying, and forgiving, and cave in to the ego's faith in fear. This is totally natural if you're not fully committed to happiness and peace. We have to remember that no matter how committed we are to love, the ego is equally, if not more, committed to fear. Therefore we must be honest about how our ego plays tricks, convincing us to deny miracles. Ask yourself, "How does my ego deny miracles?" ~ing-write for ten minutes on this topic and let your truth come to the page.

STEP 2. LET GO OF LITTLENESS

Think about how often you find yourself lowering your expectations in an attempt to insulate yourself against disappointment. This is typical in our society. We are often warned against getting our hopes up for fear of failure. This is the opposite of miracle-minded thinking. In these cases the ego is once again protecting itself by playing small and hiding from great potential. The best way out of this ego trick is to reconnect with spirit by reminding yourself that whatever you desire is on its way—that, or something better. If you find yourself lowering your expectations, begin a prayer practice of inviting spirit to remind you that you're supported. Say out loud, "I know spirit has my back. I know I'm being guided to this or something better. Show me what you've got." Through this prayer you'll reconnect with the truth that the Universe is fully supporting you at all times. Fear of failure is unnecessary.

STEP 3. ASK YOUR ~*ing* TO GUIDE YOU BACK TO LOVE

As you know by now, the solution to any fear-based problem lives in the spiritual perception of your inner guide. Upon looking at this inventory of ego sabotage, once again invite your ~*ing* in for healing. Whenever you witness your ego denying miracles, ask your ~*ing* to intervene and remind you of your true perception: faith in love. To further aid in the process, you may want to leave yourself gentle reminders to choose love over fear. For instance, I have a framed print in my office that says *Only Love Is Real*. I look at it often and remember my truth. I am catapulted back into my miracle-mindedness. Leave yourself notes, Black-Berry or iPhone reminders, and calendar updates that say "I expect miracles." Work with your inner guide to commit fully to your right mind.

STEP 4. REINFORCE HAPPINESS AS YOUR ONLY FUNCTION

This happy reinforcement comes in many forms. For example, when I chose to stop gossiping, I ignited more happiness in my life. By making the conscious decision to end an old ego pattern and choose love instead, I poured light onto the ego and became more miracle-minded. I encourage you to find ways to further strengthen your love practice. Make forgiveness your primary goal in all relationships. Welcome miracles into your life and pay attention to them. See love in all people, objects, and situations. You can see love in an orange-leafed October tree, an acquaintance you bump into on the street, or a cup of steaming black tea. *Choose* to see love. *Expect* miracles.

Continue to remind yourself daily that happiness is your only function. Know that the ego will combat this each waking moment, and know that it is our job as miracle workers to bleed love. Be gentle with yourself. This isn't a new opportunity to beat yourself up every time you deny a miracle. Just stay committed and let your ~*ing* continue to guide you back to happiness.

STEP 5. PRACTICE DEFENSELESSNESS

As my inner light grew brighter, certain resisters appeared, attempting to snuff out that light. One person in particular really hooked into my energy field. This person was very stuck in her ego, which led her to attack me tirelessly for no good reason. At first my ego's response was to defend against her wrongful attacks. That didn't work. By this point in my spiritual journey, that type of ego-driven response made me feel worse. Attacking against someone else's attack created more negativity. So, rather than defensively attack back, my inner guide reminded me of a *Course* lesson: "*In my defenselessness my safety lies.*" In order to maintain my miracle-mindedness I had to stick to the *Course's* plan and practice true defenselessness. This was not easy at first, but I took it one day at a time. To help guide me along my path I thought about enlightened masters such as Jesus and Gandhi. In the midst of an attack I'd ask spirit, *What would Gandhi do?* Each attack became a new opportunity to channel my inner Gandhi and focus on defenselessness. Spirit guided me through prayer to see this person as an equal, and through meditation I cut the energetic cords between us. These exercises required daily commitment and became powerful tools that strengthened my spiritual growth.

Defensiveness will lower your miracle-mindedness and spiritual power. Practicing defenselessness is imperative to a powerful spiritual practice because it keeps you connected to love. When you defend, you fuel more attack and anger into your life and out onto the world. Begin your practice of defenselessness by recognizing whom you are defending against. Then say a prayer: *In my defenselessness my safety lies.* Finally, choose to cut the energetic cord between you and your attacker. The following meditation will be your guide.

Cord-Cutting Meditation

(For the audio version, visit www.gabbyb.tv/
meditate.)

Sit up straight in your chair.

Take a deep breath in through your nose and out
through your mouth.

Think of the person who has attacked you.

Identify the area in your body where you're
energetically affected by this attack.

Breathe deeply into that space in your body.

On the exhale, release.

In your mind's eye, invite this person's image into
your meditation.

The person is standing before you.

Envision a thick black cord connecting you both.

This cord represents the negative energetic
connection that is keeping you connected to
your ego's fear.

Commit in this moment to cut the cord.

Breathe in: I surrender my will and attack. I
welcome the cord to be cut.

Envision Gandhi, Jesus, or any enlightened master
with a large sword.

Welcome them to cut the cord.

See the cord fall to the ground.

Breathe out release.

Know that the energetic cord has been cut.

Welcome a feeling of release to pass over you.

Say a prayer for the other person: "May you be
happy, healthy, and free. May you live with
ease."

STEP 6. FORGIVE YOUR EGO

The ego will do everything in its power to block us from miracles. Now that you're in the practice of consciously choosing miracles and turning to love for help, the ego will rev up its game. As the *Course* says, *"The ego is likely to attack when you react lovingly, because it has evaluated you as unloving and you are going against its judgment. The ego will attack your motives as soon as they become clearly out of accord with its perception. It is surely pointless to attack in return."* As you become more miracle-minded, the ego will work harder. Therefore it is important to stay highly conscious of the ego's nasty tricks. Combating this ego backlash is quite simple: just forgive the ego and forgive yourself. Through forgiveness you will remember the ego's falseness and be catapulted back to love.

The upcoming chapter will help you reinforce your miracle mindset even more. The true purpose of the miracle is to be love and share love. Therefore it is your job at this time to focus on welcoming love and happiness as your primary function so that you, too, can become a miracle worker.

12

Spirit Junkie

Spirit is in a state of grace forever. Your reality
is only spirit. Therefore you are in a state of
grace forever.

—A COURSE IN MIRACLES

◦◆◦

It's pretty trippy to write your own story in chronological order. At some point you're bound to wind up in the now. And here we are, my friends, in the present moment. I've looked forward to this. The now is super cool, and I'm psyched to share the miracle of where my *Course* work has guided me.

So where has my spiritual journey brought me? I've been led to a life beyond my wildest dreams. I went far "out there" into a world I projected, only to turn inward and accept happiness as the only true perception. Through my journey I've been guided back home. Spirit reminded me of who I truly am: a spirit among spirits with the mission to be love and share love. I'm now in a place that the *Course* refers to as the "Happy Dream": a time when miracles become natural and our mind is aligned with love. The Happy Dream is a mindset—a way of experiencing the world through eyes of joy. Today I live in the world, but think with the thoughts of heaven. Having broken through my ego's chains, happiness resurfaced and love is all I choose to see. Living in the Happy Dream doesn't mean I'm an enlightened master detached from the world. I still love bright high heels, soy-milk lattes, and tight jeans that make my butt look good. Today I can love these worldly things, but I don't *need* them to be happy. Happiness is a choice I make, not a hot new purchase, a romantic partner, or a title on a business card. I choose happiness everywhere: on a sunlit sidewalk, on a crowded train, in a hip downtown boutique. But it's not the outward surroundings that make me happy. Happiness is in my mind.

In the Happy Dream I no longer think, *I want it this way.* Instead I pray, *Spirit, show me what you've got.* Offering up my desires to my inner guide detaches me from the outcome and brings me back into the present moment. When I surrender to the fact that there is a plan so much better than mine, I don't have to *go out and get and do, do, do, do.* I can relax, knowing that there is a force inside guiding me to everything I need. Then my work is effortless, my relationships are holy, and I feel complete. Welcoming this way of perceiving life is what the Happy Dream is all about. It's a full-blown surrender, allowing spirit to guide the way. Surrendering allows us to stay present in the moment and release all future expectations. Instead of analyzing our worries, we can relinquish them to the care of spirit for transformation. The *Course* teaches, *"What can frighten me when I let all things be exactly as they are?"* Living in the Happy Dream lets your attachments off the hook, accepting everything as it is. Ego's separation melts away and we feel as though we always have a friend by our side, leading us to miracles. Today in the Happy Dream I'm not yet in heaven, but I am far from hell. Happiness is what I choose. I ask for help and my thoughts turn back to love. This is not an accident and it's not luck: it is the result of my conscientious effort to change the way I think, coupled with a deep desire to believe in miracles.

The Happy Dream is available to us all. We just have to choose for it—which is to say, each of our choices must lead us to it. Choosing the Holy Instant and asking for a miracle is what will bring you back to a happy state of mind. Just keep asking. Early in my *Course* study I read a passage: *"You have little trust in me yet, but it will increase as you turn more and more often to me instead of to your ego for guidance. The result will convince you increasingly that this choice is the only sane one you can make."* I listened to this passage and continually turned to spirit for help. The more I ask for guidance, the more I believe that it is the only sane choice to make. By adding up all your requests, you, too, will eventually think to ask all the time. Asking will become instinctual. You'll truly understand that all misery is associated with the ego and all joy is associated with spirit. The *Course* teaches that our faith, joined with spirit's understanding, is all we need. And with this relationship to spirit we will *"build a ladder planted in the solid rock of faith, and rising even to heaven."* Continue to choose joy and climb the ladder back to heaven with spirit by your side.

Today I'm a spirit junkie. I feel spirit inform my mind each moment, guiding me to extend love to the world. Lesson 267 from the *Course* describes this feeling perfectly: *"Peace fills my heart, and floods my body with the purpose of forgiveness. Now my mind is healed, and all I need to save the world is given me. Each heartbeat brings me peace; each breath infuses me with strength."* I've learned through my dedication to the *Course* that love is where "it's" at. My focus on love makes anything possible. Combining my fierce desire for love with a full surrender, I live a life beyond my wildest dreams. I never could have imagined this life. In fact, there was a time when I couldn't dream of a day without anxiety and inner terror. But that's all changed. One day at a time I transformed my thoughts, and today I know true peace. Welcoming spirit into each moment allows me to live this truth. My only goal today is peace of mind. When spirit's in the driver's seat, I'm hooked up. As a messenger of miracles I offer my own spiritual connection as a healing mechanism for the world.

For me, the Happy Dream still has plenty of assignments and ego moments. But they're fleeting and come to me for a purpose: to strengthen my faith in miracles. One of the ways I remain in the Happy Dream is to remember that the purpose of living this groovy life is to share the goods. My work now is to extend my faith in miracles to everyone around me. I can share love with my doorman, my Twitter followers, and a stranger on the street. Each encounter is a holy encounter, one that offers me an opportunity to extend peace and love.

Authentic Service

It's one thing to be connected to spirit for your own happiness and inner peace, but accessing spirit to serve the world takes you to a whole new level. As a true spirit junkie I follow the *Course's* guided path to be a miracle worker. The purpose of a miracle worker is to help others shift their perceptions from fear back to love. My faith in the *Course* enables me to work with authentic power to serve at my highest capacity. The woman I am today serves much differently from the woman I once was. Looking back, I can see how much I've grown. My connection to spirit made my service mentality not about *me*, but about *we*. Reflecting on this, I turned inward and asked my *~ing, How has my service mentality grown?* Spirit answered loud and clear, *Your own healing is healing the world. Now you're an extension of love. You're no longer hiding behind service—instead you're truly serving. You are a miracle worker.* This conversation with my *~ing* was short, clear, and inarguable.

In becoming spiritually inclined, I've learned that my purpose is to heal the world and that our true job is to be miracle workers, not stockbrokers, publicists, fashion designers, and so on. I now understand that I'm here in this world at this time to heal the perceptions of those around me, thereby healing the world. I realized that in the past I'd hidden behind my outward service actions to avoid confronting my own internal issues. Instead of dealing, I was doing. My actions, though seemingly altruistic, actually had been quite selfish. They were a fabulous way for me to perceive myself as accomplished and selfless while avoiding having to deal with the terror in my mind. I was hiding from my fears by focusing on my "fight" for the rights of others. I focused on my fight for reproductive rights, my fight against violence, and other causes that, though worthy and important, served as personal cover-ups. The fight was my way of justifying the fact that I was running away from the war in my mind.

Ironically, I couldn't support any altruistic mission with the energy it deserved, because I had a spiritual disconnect. At that time, service was a way for me to avoid healing. Ego convinced me that fighting for others made me special, when in reality it furthered the separation and my own healing. Now I can look at my past "fight" and gently laugh. I can smile knowing how far I've come and honor myself for everything I did to survive—even if survival meant hiding behind a fight. Today I no longer need to change the world around me. I just need to change the way I see it.

Today I can show up for the rights of others because I've shown up for me. Now that I've chosen love over fear, I can share miracles and move forward fearlessly. My miracle-mindedness can bleed through every action, every thought. My service to others and to myself are one and the same. I understand that if I'm vibrating at a frequency of love, I am of service. My only function is to be happy. My happiness is contagious.

As a miracle worker I am not immune to anger or attack thoughts, and I cannot hide from them; rather, I turn to spirit for miracles. By choosing the miracle, I feel empowered and therefore can strengthen the energy and thoughts of those around me. I know that if my energy is aligned with faith in miracles, I am supporting more miracles.

I now have direction. I no longer need to figure it all out or know some specific outcome. I can simply invite spirit in to be my guide. As the *Course* says, *"Don't try to purify yourself before coming to me. I am the purifier."* That's what this book is about: letting spirit intervene to heal us in order to become miracle workers who help heal the world. It is our duty to clear the space in our own minds and hearts so that we can take spiritually aligned action. Only then will our actions truly have massive effects.

The Function of the Miracle Worker

The *Course* teaches, *"Miracles are natural. When they do not occur, something has gone wrong."* To become miracle workers, we must believe this statement wholeheartedly and embrace the belief system of miracles. The *Course* teaches that there is no order of difficulty in miracles; therefore, no miracle is more important than another. We cannot control the miracle. I used to ask for *the exact* miracle I wanted: for the guy to call back, the contract to be signed, or the debt to disappear. I've learned that I cannot control the outcome of the miracle; all I can do is allow it to occur. I now know that spirit's plan is much better than mine, and therefore maybe the guy isn't supposed to call back or the contract isn't supposed to be signed. When and how a miracle occurs is not up to us. Our job is simply to maintain our belief in love. As such, anytime we feel out of alignment with love, we must invite spirit to intervene and arrange the miracle. Then we expect it to occur. Our expectation supports the miracle.

As miracle workers we must always respond to wrong-minded thinking with a desire to heal it. The miracle is the denial of the ego and an affirmation of love. By inviting spirit to clean up our ego's thoughts, we shift our perception and choose love over fear. *This is the miracle.* Through our practice of forgiveness and commitment to right-minded thoughts, we support miracles.

Accepting Our Own Healing Is What Heals

The *Course* teaches, *"The miracle worker is generous out of self-interest."* My choice to heal my perceptions has been the catalyst for my own healing. Each time I choose to forgive someone, the relationship is healed and I'm closer to the true miracle-minded perception. If one person is less connected to the miracle, the miracle worker can help deepen that connection merely through her belief system. There is no convincing others of miracles: just believe in them. All I need to do today is believe in miracles and everything works out. I believe that there is a plan greater than mine, and that I am part of the function of a colossal source of love that lives inside each of us. There is nothing separate about my internal love and the love of others, and there is nothing separate from my thoughts. My thoughts are felt and heard by those who don't even know my name. My thoughts affect everything around me. Clearing space for miracles is all I have to do today. Practicing these principles in all my affairs has healed others and me simultaneously. As soon as we invite spirit to change our mind, everyone involved receives a healing. When all we want to see is love, all we see is love.

The Miracle Worker: A Teacher of Love

The *Course* teaches that we all can be miracle workers if we want it. Spirit calls on all of us, but few will answer. The message of this chapter is to inspire you to answer spirit's call—to open your heart to become a miracle worker who shares love through personal healing and growth. If you choose to be a teacher of love, there are several functions you must live by. I love this part of the gig because it's all laid out for us in the *Course's* *Manual for Teachers*. Following these suggested guidelines I remain humble and connected to my true purpose: love.

Trust

Learning to trust in the power that is in but not of me is crucial to being a miracle worker. I now understand that I'm not a separate self who makes things happen. Instead I am part of an infinite energy source that everyone can access. Choosing to access this source of spiritual power gives me the trust in spirit, not my ego, as my guide. My favorite message from the *Course* is *"Who would attempt to fly with the tiny wings of a sparrow when the mighty power of an eagle has been given him?"* I have faith in my eagle wings and I allow them to guide my direction as a student and as a teacher.

Honesty

Trust in spirit is what guides me to stay honest. My faith in miracles keeps me away from the ego's deceptive thoughts, and I remain connected to love. Honesty keeps my perceptions clean and my actions fueled by love.

Tolerance

The principle of tolerance is all about not judging others. Today I have a daily practice of releasing all judgment. When an attack thought enters into my mind, I pray for it to be transformed. Judgment implies lack of trust and honesty. Judgment lowers my spiritual connection. By committing to release all judgment, I stay connected to the service of being a miracle worker.

Gentleness

As a teacher of love, I know I cannot harm anyone. Harm comes from an inner judgment of others and reflects my own judgment of myself. Harmfulness wipes out my true function of inner peace. Today judgment and harm no longer serve me. In fact, they make me confused, fearful, and angry. Therefore, as a miracle worker I choose against judgment and in turn allow the gentleness of spirit to pass through me. This gentleness is an extension of my inner peace. Living this way makes me feel great. As the *Course* teaches, *"Who chooses hell when he perceives a way to*

Heaven? And who would choose the weakness that must come from harm in place of the unfailing, all-encompassing and limitless strength of gentleness?"

Joy

Joy is inevitable when you're aligned with spirit. Since I've chosen to follow spirit as my guide, I am led to release attack and be gentle. This gentleness always results in joy. When an attack thought comes in, I turn inward for help and immediately reconnect with joy. Why wouldn't I be joyous when love is what I choose?

Defenselessness

When my miracle-mindedness grew stronger, my defenses weakened. I no longer felt like defending myself against the attacks of others. I recognized this as investing in their illusion. When you think with love, you have nothing to defend against. Each day I practice defenselessness to the best of my ability. When I maintain a defenseless attitude and choose to see love in my attacker, I am catapulted into a state of peace. It is imperative that the teacher of love be defenseless. This attribute is a sure sign that your faith lies in miracles rather than in the ego's illusion.

Generosity

The term *generosity* has an awesome meaning to the teacher of love. In this case generosity is based on trust. The miracle worker trusts that giving things away is not a loss but a gain. In the ego's world, the concept of generosity means to give something up. In spirit's perception, it means giving away in order to keep. This is the opposite of what we've been taught by our ego minds. When we as teachers of love are generous out of self-interest, we generously give that which supports our own inner peace.

Patience

When I became certain about my spiritual connection and inner love, I knew the Universe had my back. Therefore I no longer feared the future. This released my ego's need to future-trip and hold on to the past. I forgave the past and accepted that love was guiding me forward. Embracing miracles provided me with certainty and a sense of peace. The *Course* says, *"Those who are certain of the outcome can afford to wait, and wait without anxiety."* Patience is imperative for the teacher of love, for it confirms faith.

Faithfulness

Though I've accepted love as my only function, I still waver from time to time. There are plenty of moments when the ego creeps in, but my faith in spirit always guides me back to love. The more I turn to my faith in spirit, the more faith I have that *only love is real*. The *Course* teaches: *"To give up all problems to one Answer is to reverse the thinking of the world entirely. And that alone is faithfulness. Nothing but that really deserves the name. Yet each degree, however small, is worth achieving. Readiness, as the text notes, is not mastery."*

This concept is awesome. The teacher doesn't need to be a master to teach. All you need is to choose faith in love, and your readiness will lead the way.

Open-Mindedness

Open-mindedness comes with lack of judgment. Just as judgment shuts love down, open-mindedness invites love in. The open-minded can see light where there is darkness and peace where there is pain. Through forgiveness the open-minded are set free from the ego's illusion and catapulted into a state of love.

You Are a Miracle Worker

If you've applied even a fraction of the principles in this book to your own life, you've reactivated your own inner spirit. By applying even one of the tools in this book, you've participated in a miracle. Your simple choice to perceive the world with love produced a miraculous shift. One Holy Instant is all you need to remember where you came from and reconnect with your true purpose, even if only for a moment. My intention for this book is to reignite your spirit, who will guide you back to love. If enough of us get our ~*ing* on we can change the world. My hope is that you carry these tools into your life and stay inspired to know true love. My deep desire was all I needed to restore my faith in love and miracles. If you desire this same faith, you, too, will be guided.

Each moment offers a new opportunity to strengthen our spiritual connection. Below are gentle reminders of ways to keep growing your own relationship with spirit.

STEP 1. REMEMBER "IT" IS IN YOU

In my lectures and workshops I often feel a sense of urgency from the audience. There is an underlying desperation in the room, which is based on the need to find an outside so-lution to an inside problem. There is a need to "get there." I understand this deeply. The biggest gift I've received is my faith that we're already "there." I hope this book has led you to know that everything you're seeking is already in you and there's no place "out there" to find it. Turn inward and ask for guidance. Undergoing this transformation and restoration often can feel far out of reach. Don't get dis-couraged. Continue to remind yourself that it isn't far at all. It's in you right now. Remain willing to take the necessary steps to continue turning inward and dealing with the past to clear all blocks to love. The *Course* has taught me that we take care of the future by living in the present.

STEP 2. ALWAYS CHOOSE LOVE

The key to maintaining a loving mindset is to remember that forgiveness is your primary tool. Whenever you're in doubt, throw down the *F* word, knowing that forgiveness will set you free. Love is experienced to the extent that we believe in love. In order to enjoy our own loving expe-rience, we must commit to keeping our thoughts aligned with love. Therefore, stay connected to love through your forgiveness practice. Remember what the *Course* asks: *"Would you rather be right or happy?"* When happiness is our primary function, we turn to forgiveness as the bridge back to peace. Maintain your loving connection by releasing others. Each time you feel resentment, ask spirit to intervene and transform the thought through forgiveness. By forgiving others I was healed. My own healing is now a blessing bestowed upon others and myself. Make holiness the function of all your relationships, and joy is what you'll receive.

STEP 3. PRAY AND MEDITATE

Through prayer we turn to spirit for help, and in meditation we receive spirit's guidance. These two tools are the basis of a spiritual practice. I encourage you to turn inward daily through prayer and meditation, practicing the lessons you have learned in this book. Remember to keep it simple. You don't have to figure anything out or push your prayers to be a certain way. Simply be willing to pray by turning your thoughts over to spirit. Then sit in meditation and listen. You'll be guided to everything you need in that moment. You will receive the Holy Instant. With prayer and meditation in your back pocket, you can release the ego, stop running, and enjoy stillness.

Remember that there is no need to pray for an outcome. Simply pray for inner peace. Anything you get won't solve your problem. The problem is always in our mind. The major shifts don't occur externally, they occur internally.

In addition, don't be afraid to pray with groups. There is a beautiful Power Posse (group) on HerFuture.com called Shared Prayer. Join me in this posse when you want a collective consciousness of women to pray for you or someone you love. If you're a man, join me in shared prayer on my Facebook fan page.

Finally, when it comes to prayer and meditation, let go of the rope. You don't need to manipulate your practice. Remember that your time spent in prayer and meditation is the time to relax and let your *~ing* do her thing. As the *Course* says, *"You need not do anything."* Just invite spirit in, sit still, and receive guidance.

STEP 4. SERVE

I often found that when I'd think about all the problems in the world and all the opportunities to serve, I'd become overwhelmed. I felt as though the problems outweighed my power to serve—that's when apathy would set in. This was my ego's way of keeping me small and limiting my faith in miracles. As I've grown to be miracle-minded, I know that I don't serve alone. Spirit is my guide whenever my intentions are aligned with love. Rather than become overwhelmed with all the world's problems, I'd focus on solutions. Welcoming solutions and miracles allowed me to show up fully. I then got connected to particular causes I was inspired to serve, ranging from organizations that invite recovered addicts to speak at clinics, to women's rights organizations like Women for Women International and Girl Up. When I opened my heart to be of service to the world, I also attracted new opportunities to serve. My awareness of service guided me to serve more. My sense of inspiration strengthened my spiritual connection to the work, which opened my creative mind to execute innovative fund-raising ideas, powerful Internet awareness campaigns, and grassroots events. When you're passionate about the cause, spirit energy moves through you and empowers your service.

It is also important to remember that each moment and every thought is an opportunity to serve. Spirit-guided thoughts are of service to the world because they raise the energetic vibration within you and outside of you. Thinking with loving-kindness is a service. Open your heart to be of service to the world, and you'll be led to the perfect opportunities to share love.

STEP 5. TRUST THAT SPIRIT HAS YOUR BACK

Faith is everything. When you believe in love, you can relax knowing that *it's all good*. Remember that your willingness to invite spirit into your mind will strengthen your faith. The more we call on love, the stronger our love muscle will be.

◆ ◆ ◆

I hope you use this book as a guide back to love. Remember that your work is never done. Each moment offers you an opportunity to deepen your spiritual connection and strengthen your miracle-mindedness. Keep it up, my friend. Keep it up.

Constant contact with spirit got me here. When it came time to conclude this book, I found myself putting it off. I wanted to savor the last chapter—take my time and allow the words to pour through me. And I did just that. I waited. I revisited all the chapters leading up to this point. Reflecting on the pages of this book, I was astounded to find that I didn't even realize what I'd created. There were stories and sentences that seemed as though they'd come from a higher source. I kept thinking, *I don't remember writing this.* This experience was a sure sign that I'd done good. I truly allowed spirit to enter into the process and guide me. Clearly I hadn't overthought the contents of the book, but rather allowed the work to flow creatively from my inside out. This book is an extension of my spirit and all the inner guidance that I choose to work with. By listening to this guidance, I've enjoyed every second of the writing process. I've healed more, learned more, and loved more. I've deepened my relationship with spirit throughout the collaborative effort to create this book for you.

Throughout my process of creating this work I've felt

a presence by my side. Often a rush of energy would pour through my hands, inspired ideas would come to me in the middle of the night, human guidance was always present, and new assignments led to authentic content. Each moment of this process has been guided, and I hope you've felt the presence of a power greater than me pour off each page. Each word, thought, and sentence is infused with spirit's love. Together let's say *Thank you*. We thank the infinite loving Universe and the beautiful spirit that flows through each of us. We thank spirit for your guidance, your inspiration, your lessons, and your support. We thank you for reminding us to have faith in love.

With endless love and gratitude, I send you off with a spiritual connection of your own understanding—a connection that will be yours to grow and share with the world, an everlasting companion on your miraculous journey inward. May you release your fear, have faith in spirit, expect miracles, and always listen to your inner guide.

Acknowledgments

There are many human angels who participated in the creation of this book. It is with tremendous gratitude that I acknowledge my literary agent, Michele Martin. I look forward to a lifetime of collaborations. A huge shout-out goes to Katie Karlson for your edits and divine spark. I thank Sam Bassett for your photos, Jenny Sansouci for your PA love, Haleh Nematzadeh for styling the shoot, and 5Pointz Graffiti Park for providing an awesome backdrop for our cover. Thank you to the Crown Publishing team at Random House: Tina Constable, Penny Simon, Jennifer Robbins, Meredith McGinnis, Annie Chagnot, and Tammy Blake for your enthusiasm and faith in *Spirit Junkie*. Trace Murphy, I thank you for being my editor and sharing my passion for *A Course in Miracles*.

Acknowledgments

I thank all the beautiful people who have offered me the most life-changing spiritual assignments. Thanks to my mom, dad, Mike, Harriet, Max, and all my grandparents for being my family unit this time around. We signed a sacred contract, and our love for one another is everlasting. I thank my beautiful holy love, Zach Rocklin: you are my greatest teacher and my dearest friend.

To my spiritual soul sisters who supported this book: Eliza Dushku, Latham Thomas, Elisa Hallerman, and all the women on HerFuture.com! I thank my teacher and friend Marianne Williamson. Your work inspired me to be the woman and teacher I am today. Thank you for setting me on my path. Finally, I thank John of God and all of the mediums at the Casa de Dom Inacio for teaching me to be an authentic Spirit Junkie.

ALSO BY GABRIELLE BERNSTEIN

In *Add More ~ing to Your Life*, motivational speaker and author Gabrielle Bernstein delivers a thirty-day equation to self-transformation, full of positive affirmations, physical activities, and visualization meditations. Lean how to access your *~ing* (your inner guide), bulldoze negative thoughts, and make happiness a way of life!

New from Gabrielle Bernstein, a practical and fun guide to transforming fear into love and discovering true and lasting happiness. *May Cause Miracles* offers a six-week plan for spiritual growth and a transformational mind cleanse that can weaken fear and strengthen your faith in love. Get ready for a life of abundance, acceptance, appreciation, and enlightenment!

**Add More ~ing
to Your Life
A Hip Guide to Happiness**
978-0-307-95155-7
$14.99 PAPER (CANADA: $16.99)

**May Cause Miracles
A Guidebook of Subtle Shifts
for Radical Change and
Unlimited Happiness**
978-0-307-98693-1
$23.00 HARDCOVER (CANADA: $26.95)

AVAILABLE WHEREVER BOOKS ARE SOLD